Praise for *Can American M[...]*

Michele Nash-Hoff's perspective on, and analysis of, the advances and challenges of American manufacturing can only be attained by someone who has seen it from the trenches and not from an ivory tower. Readers will come to realize the importance of "Made in the U.S.A."

> **– Steve Cozzetto,** President, Century Rubber Company

What a great history lesson on American manufacturing! We as Americans need to stop the loss of manufacturing jobs, and this book is the best way to start the turnaround. A must read for anyone who cares about our country.

> **– Donald Schlotfelt,** President, Pacific Metal Stampings

From Chapter One, a brilliant mini-history of American manufacturing, to the closing prescription for recovery and ensuing pep talk, this book will keep you riveted to your chair. The U.S. has been the world's preeminent economic force for more than a century. Will it be so at the close of this one? The author says "no," unless we wake up and reclaim our failing destiny.

> **– Dave Nuffer,** Chairman, Nuffer, Tucker & Smith

This book is rich with history and detailed research, providing a comprehensive look at the contribution manufacturing makes to the U.S. economy. It considers the effects of U.S. trade policies, offshoring, the threat to our national security, and what can be done to save American manufacturing by government, industry and individuals.

> **– Kate Hand,** *Products Finishing* magazine

To say this book provides a thorough backdrop to understanding the history of American manufacturing is an understatement... Anyone interested in manufacturing and/or the middle class will find riveting reading in this well written and thoroughly researched book. – *EMS007* e-newsletter

Even if you haven't particularly paid attention to the importance of American manufacturing to our future well-being as a nation, you'll realize its importance after reading this book. And if you have regarded American manufacturing as an important part of our survival as a nation, you'll likely come away with the opinion that it is even more important.

–**Roger Simmermaker,** author, *How Americans Can Buy American,* NewsMax.com

The author of *Can American Manufacturing Be Saved* is a measured voice of industrial experience and pragmatism – and one that believes manufacturing is absolutely the mortar than can help bind together the different elements of our fragile economy...Nash-Hoff should be required reading for U.S. industrial companies today – not to mention politicians and others who represent our interests in government and trade.

–**Jason Busch and Lisa Reisman,** *Surplus Record*

Michelle Nash-Hoff's book is a must read for any citizen who is worried about the future of their country, their children and grandchildren and the kind of world we want for them, since only a strong America can produce a world of increasing liberty, prosperity and peace. And America can only be strong if it still makes some things.

–**Dr. Sheila R. Ronis**, Dir., MBA/MM Programs, Walsh College

Michele Nash-Hoff's book is a wake-up call to all Americans to the importance of restoring American manufacturing if we are to maintain our national sovereignty and the capability to defend our country. The accelerating loss of manufacturing jobs has led directly to higher unemployment and decaying public services through declining tax revenues. This book provides a much needed road map to save and expand American manufacturing and restore the high quality of American life.

–**Roger Hedgecock,** national talk-radio host

The Reshoring Initiative's mission is to strengthen U.S. manufacturing by helping companies see that they will be more profitable by bringing their manufacturing back to the U.S. Michele has always spoken knowledgeably on this subject and was the right choice to carry our message to industry on the west coast. I appreciate Michele's personal commitment to U.S. manufacturing and to reshoring.

–**Harry Moser**, Founder and President,
the Reshoring Initiative.

Highly recommended reading for all start-up entrepreneurs. *Understand your manufacturing decisions to the fullest extent.* The dire effects outsourcing has had on our entire nation can be reversed with the right leadership decisions at the top and conscientious consumers at home leading the trend back. Jobs, the economy, and literally the entire fate of our nation as a world leader is at stake. Read this book and then tell your neighbor. Buy American! Save American manufacturing and save our country.

–**Adrian Pelkus**, President, San Diego Inventors Forum

Can American Manufacturing Be Saved?

Why We Should and How We Can

2012 Edition

Michele Nash-Hoff

COALITION FOR A
PROSPEROUS AMERICA 2012

Second Edition
Published by the Coalition for a Prosperous America
700 12th St. NW, Suite 700
Washington, DC 20005

ISBN-13: 978-1-468-17369-7

Library of Congress Cataloging-in-Publication Data

Nash-Hoff, Michele.
    Can American Manufacturing Be Saved? / Michele Nash-Hoff;
    p.cm
Includes bibliographical references and index.
ISBN-13: 978-1-468-17369-7
1. International economic integration. 2. Foreign trade regulation.
3. Economics—U.S. economy—Manufacturing 4. Globalization—
Economic Aspects—Developed Countries. 5. United States—
Commercial policy. 6. Free trade—United States. I. Title

Cover design by Joel Judal & Martin Cabral

Printed in the United States of America

10 9 8 7 6 5 4 3 2 1

To my aunt, Connie O'Kelley, with all my love,
for being my role model, mentor, and writing coach

Acknowledgments

I want to thank my friends Judy Winkler, Darity Wesley, and Sheila Washington for encouraging me to write this book, and my husband, Michael Hoff, for providing the love, patience, and encouragement to keep me going when I thought I was never going to finish it. I want to express my gratitude to all the people who provided me with data, stories, and permission to use material they had written previously: Pamela J. Gordon, Richard McCormack, Dr. William Raynor, Raymond L. Richmond, Don Rodocker, Dr. Sheila Ronis, Roger Simmermaker, Rick Sunamoto, Don Vaniman, and Jerry Wright. I also want to thank Kim Niles for his contributions to this book and Michael Collins for sharing the knowledge and experience he gained from writing his own book. I especially want to thank my test readers, who provided me with good feedback and editorial critiques as I completed each chapter: Steve Cozzetto, Paul Neuenswander, Dave Nuffer, Don Schlotfelt, Bonnie Ziesler, and my aunt, Connie O'Kelley. Last but not least, I want to thank my editors, Helen Chang and Ian Fletcher, for their quality editing, and my writing mentor, Anne Wayman. Without the help and guidance of my "team," it would not have been possible to finish writing this book and get it published.

Contents

Preface

One of my ancestors was Paul Revere, who became famous for his midnight ride to warn that the British were coming. Since my first edition was published in 2009, I've started calling myself "Paulette Revere" because I felt I was on a modern-day ride to warn people that we will lose our freedom if we don't save American manufacturing.

I am the president of ElectroFab Sales, a manufacturers' sales representative agency for job-shop companies that perform custom fabrication. After working for another rep firm for three years, I founded ElectroFab in 1985 to specialize in representing such companies, which I saw as an unfilled niche in San Diego County. ElectroFab's primary market is OEMs (Original Equipment Manufacturers) in San Diego, Imperial, and southern Orange and Riverside Counties that utilize contract manufacturing services.

The United States had just recovered from the recession of 1981-1982 when I started ElectroFab, and our sales doubled every year between 1985 and 1990. During this period, I served on the board of the San Diego Electronics Network, a professional organization for women in electronics, becoming its president in 1988. I also served on the board of the San Diego Chapter of the Electronics Representatives Association (ERA) and became its first woman president from 1989 to 1991.

Then the recession of 1991-1993 hit and our bookings dropped by half. About 80 percent of our business derived from San Diego's defense industry, so, like many other firms around the country, we had to make the painful transition from defense to commercial. We were successful in making this transition by acquiring companies to represent that could competitively perform fabrication services for the commercial industries of our region.

During this recession, the San Diego region lost more than 30,000 manufacturing jobs, 17,000 of them as a result of two divisions of General Dynamics being sold and moved to another state. This was such a shock to the economy that it captured the attention of business leaders and elected representatives at all levels of government in the region.

While serving as past president and board chair of the San Diego ERA from 1991 to 1993, I became president of the High Technology Foundation, a non-profit organization our ERA chapter had founded to promote high technology in San Diego. I recruited industry, government and media members for a High Technology Advisory Council and spoke publicly about the importance of high-tech manufacturing to the regional economy. In 1992, we sponsored a forum on "What's Being Done to Save Manufacturing in San Diego?" We lobbied elected officials at the local, state, and federal levels to improve the business climate by reducing the local business tax, eliminating state regulations that overlapped federal regulations, reducing the capital gains tax, and increasing the R&D tax credit.

In 1993, the foundation formed a coalition of 18 organizations, called the High Technology Council, to plan and produce the first High Technology Summit at the San Diego Convention Center. The purpose of this summit, held in March 1993, was to ensure that elected officials and business leaders were aware of the importance of high technology to the economy of San Diego and address ways to improve the business climate at the state and local levels. The council produced a white paper on the issues affecting San Diego's tech industries, which included recommended actions to be taken at the local, state, and federal levels.

I participated in several civic committees, a San Diego County economic strategy task force to address the future of San Diego's economy, and a team of 25 business leaders creating a vision for San Diego to achieve by the year 2003. The resulting vision was: "San Diego and northern Baja California form a major hub of international trade, commerce, and tourism for Latin America, the Pacific Rim, and other trading areas. The San Diego region's economy, environment, and infrastructure are balanced to achieve a high quality of life for our multicultural population."

However, as the San Diego economy began to prosper in the boom years of 1995-2000, most of these volunteer civic efforts stalled or ceased to exist. So, in 1996, I ran for San Diego City Council, against a three-term incumbent, in an attempt to spread my message about the importance of high technology manufacturing to the economy of San Diego to a greater audience. My low budget, grassroots campaign was unsuccessful, but as a result of that experience, I was recruited to run for the California State Assembly in 2000. I easily won the primary for this open seat, but after a hard-fought, 14-month campaign, I lost the general election. The campaign did give me a great opportunity to talk about the importance of high technology to the economy of San Diego, the need to save manufacturing jobs, and ways to improve the business climate of California.

Then came the dotcom bust of late 2000 and 9/11 in 2001, leading to a recession. The 2001-2003 recession saw an unprecedented pruning of prospects, customers, and competitors in the region. This cut across all sectors of manufacturing. It witnessed key Original Equipment Manufacturers cutting back to a fraction of what they once were, going out of business entirely, moving out of the area, or sourcing their manufacturing out of the area and even out of the country. In my more than 20 years of sales and marketing in San Diego, I had never seen it this bad.

The loss of companies didn't make local headlines, as the departure of General Dynamics had in the early 1990s, because these were mostly smaller companies, with fewer than 100 employees. Buck Knives' announcement about their intent to move finally made the headlines in 2003, and they moved to Post Falls, Idaho in December 2004. The loss of Tyco Puritan Bennett in 2002 should have made the news, as they had more than 1,000 employees in 2000, but didn't.

I started keeping a record of the companies that had moved out of state or gone out of business since January 2001. In the spring of 2003, several legislators with whom I had campaigned for State Assembly in 2000 asked me to provide them with the list. I turned the list into a report in an effort to make these legislators, and other key policymakers, aware of the seriousness of the situation. I disseminated this first report in March 2003 to legislators, local elected officials, industry leaders, and local news media. The report got attention from a local radio talk show host, Roger Hedgecock, who invited me as guest on his show. I prepared two more reports later that year and was invited on his show after each was released.

I published on the Internet two to three reports every year from 2003 to 2008, and was a featured guest on other radio shows, like the Hugh Hewitt and Kevin Fulton shows. Because I kept data that other organizations were not tracking, I became a "go to" expert on the state of San Diego's manufacturing industry and have been frequently quoted in the San *Diego Union-Tribune* and *San Diego Business Journal*.

Some of my reports were republished by other media and organizations, such as VoiceOfSanDiego.com and the e-newsletters of the American Society of Quality and the American Purchasing and Inventory Control Society.

In 2006-2007, my reports expanded from a focus on what was happening in San Diego manufacturing to issues affecting manufacturing in the nation as a whole. As I read about the downslide of manufacturing, it became my passion to do what I could to save it. I firmly believe that if we don't save manufacturing in this country, we will lose our middle class, because manufacturing jobs are one of its key foundations.

After e-publishing a report in May 2007 subtitled "Can U.S. Manufacturing be Saved?" I decided it was time to write a book on the topic. I started doing my research in July 2007. I naively thought it would be like writing 10 to 11 of my industry reports. However, it took me twice as long as I thought and was four to five times as much work as expected. (This is actually the second book I have written, but the first, *For-Profit Business Incubators,* took only six months to research and write and was edited and published by the National Business Incubator Association in 1998.)

Since the release of my first edition in May 2009 with my keynote speech at the Del Mar Electronics & Design Show, I have spoken to trade organizations; business and professional groups; service clubs like the Kiwanis, Rotary, Lions, Optimist, and Soroptimist clubs; several regional trade shows; and one national conference. I started submitting articles to a local e-newsline, San Diego News Network (SDNN.com) in August 2009. In April 2010, I started writing weekly blog articles, which I sent out to a database of several hundred (now about 1,000) people, posting on my website, SavingUSManufacturing.com, and submitting to San Diego

News Network. When the latter went out of business in July 2010, I switched to San Diego Newsroom (SanDiegoNewsroom.com). Now my articles appear on *Industry Week* magazine's blog, the *Huffington Post*, and the Coalition for a Prosperous America's Trade Reform Blog, among others.

In 2012, I became the chair of the Coalition for a Prosperous America's California chapter. I am also a strong advocate and speaker for the Reshoring Initiative founded by Harry Moser, on the steering committee for the San Diego Inventors Forum, and currently a director on the national board of the American Jobs Alliance. Because of my book and the presentations I've given, the San Diego Inventors Forum changed its focus from helping companies source the manufacturing of their products in China to helping them source in the U.S.

Introduction:
What Do I Mean by "Manufacturing"?

When most people think of manufacturing, they think of the assembly lines of large companies like General Motors, Ford, Boeing, Hewlett Packard, and General Electric. But the reality is that small and medium-sized manufacturers (SMMs) comprise about 98 percent of all manufacturing firms and employ about half of all manufacturing employees in the U.S. They provide about three-fourths of net new jobs in manufacturing every year. (Small manufacturers have 500 or fewer employees, while medium-sized ones employ between 500 and 2,000 employees.) As of 2009, the most recent census available, there were about 266,000 manufacturers in the United States, employing roughly 11.6 million workers. Of these, 260,000 were small or medium-sized manufacturers, employing 5.2 million workers. SMMs accounted for about 40 percent of the 11 percent that manufacturing represented of our Gross Domestic Product.[1]

To understand better what I mean by manufacturing, let's consider the meaning of the words "manufacture" and "manufacturing." "Manufacture" is defined by the dictionary as "to make or process a raw material into a finished product; to make or process a product especially with the use of industrial machines." "Manufacturing" is defined as "the process of making wares by hand or by machinery especially when carried on systematically with division of labor."[2]

Many articles, websites, and other books have been written about who or what an American manufacturer is. Information on the ownership of companies would be out of date before this book was published because of the global mergers and acquisitions taking place on nearly a daily basis. Therefore, I will use a very simple definition: *a company, or division of a company, that is engaged in producing a product and that has a manufacturing plant physically located within the United States.*

1

How Did Manufacturing Develop in America?

To better understand what manufacturing is today, and how integral it has been to the growth and development of the United States, it is helpful to consider a brief history of its development as a result of the Industrial Revolution.[1] The Industrial Revolution was a major shift in technological, socioeconomic, and cultural conditions that occurred in the late 18th and early 19th centuries. It began in Britain, spread to America, and gradually spread to the rest of the world in a process called industrialization. During this time, an economy based on manual labor was replaced by one dominated by industry, the manufacture of machinery, and the products made by these machines. It began with the mechanization of the textile industry, the development of iron-making techniques, and the increased use of coal. Trade expansion was enabled by the introduction of canals, improved roads, and railroads.

The Colonial Period

When Europeans began arriving on the shores of the Americas, they found a land rich in natural resources. As news reached Europe, it sparked a wave of exploration and colonization. Most early settlers came to the New England colonies seeking religious freedom, while others came to the Chesapeake Bay colonies seeking economic opportunity. There was a severe lack of economic opportunity in the Old World, where remnants of a feudal system still existed. But America offered the opportunity to own land and start a business.

Most of the New England colonists came as nuclear families in the 1600s and early 1700s. Typically, towns became collections of related families. Most New Englanders were farmers at first, but as towns were established, economic opportunities grew, in the form of apprenticeships to craftsmen and tradesmen. Teenage children were often recruited as apprentices. New Englanders lived long lives, compared to the other colonies, increasing their population. They established an education system, so most men, and slightly fewer women, knew how to read and write.

Many New Englanders turned away from farming, at least as a full-time occupation, by the 1750s. Some became fishermen, which led to a shipbuilding industry. Others turned to foreign trade, taking American goods abroad and trading them for foreign goods or slaves, who were sold mostly to Southerners. As the New England colonies grew, more immigrants came from Europe with specialized craft skills. Many had been part of artisan guilds in Europe and they formed the same in America. The guilds in colonial America involved:

- **Provisions**– Items that were edible or potable and also soap, wax, et cetera.

- **The Arts** – Music, drama, literature and other culture.

- **Smiths** – Different metals, worked in various ways.

- **Textiles** – Fabric and natural fibers; also leather, clay, et cetera.

- **Trades** – Selling or brokering goods.

- **Wrights** –Work with wood, stone, brick, glass, et cetera.

The Middle Colonies (New York, New Jersey, Pennsylvania, and Delaware) had a great deal of good farmland and became known as the breadbasket region for their wheat and barley crops. New York City and Philadelphia became the leading colonial commercial centers. Iron making began in these cities in the 1700s, and their artisans also produced shoes, glass, pottery, leather, and wooden goods.

In contrast, the Southern colonies offered indentured servitude on farms and plantations. Many colonists arrived under some version of bound labor as indentured servants. Most were male and many died soon after arrival due to disease. These indentured servants were sold to craftsmen, gentlemen, or farmers, according to their abilities. They would work for five to seven years, which would repay their passage costs, and then they were free to seek employment elsewhere.

Slaves replaced indentured workers in the South as tobacco, rice, indigo, and later cotton became the predominant crops. Only wealthy landowners could afford to maintain large tobacco or cotton plantations. Much labor was needed to operate these plantations, so the slave trade grew. Westward expansion from the coast provided the opportunity for indentured servants who completed their servitude to become property owners as farmers, shopkeepers, or craftsmen in the towns that sprang up along the frontier, which forms the states of Ohio, Kentucky, Tennessee, and West Virginia today. Strict Sabbath laws in the Northern colonies provided one day a week off for laborers, but many indentured servants, and nearly all slaves, worked seven days a week from dawn to dusk in the Southern colonies.

In colonial America, goods were mainly produced by cottage industries, in which individual artisans or craftsmen, working at home or in small shops, made a unique product, mostly for personal or household use or for a specific use within a trade. Some of the products made in this manner were home furnishings; brass, copper and silver dishes and utensils; farm implements; and buggies and wagons.

In the late 1700s, American artisans followed the English system of manufacturing, and merchants sold these goods in small shops in towns and cities. In this system, skilled mechanics were required to produce parts from a design, but the parts were never identical, and each had to be manufactured separately to fit its counterpart, almost always by one person who produced each completed item from start to finish.

As free men, independent craftsmen had the opportunity to actively participate in the representative governments of the

Northern and Middle colonies. The political organizations that arose through this gave the common man a voice. Unlike in England, where the monarchy ruled, craftsmen in America participated actively in politics, particularly in the years leading up to the Revolution in 1776.

The Industrial Revolution

In 1769, two new inventions – James Watt's steam engine and Richard Arkwright's water frame – heralded the start of the Industrial Revolution. The Watt steam engine could run rotary machinery, meaning it could power mill machinery. (Mills previously had to be located along rivers so they could be powered by water wheels.) A water frame is a spinning machine powered by water that produces a cotton yarn suitable for textile manufacturing. After the steam engine and water frame were invented, England passed laws forbidding the export of textile machinery and the emigration of those who could operate the machines, so the Industrial Revolution did not hit America's shores until 1793, when the technology was brought to the U.S.

At the same time that England was trying to protect its fledgling manufacturing with laws forbidding the export of technology, our first treasury secretary, Alexander Hamilton, formulated his plan to foster American manufacturing with tariffs to end our dependence on Europe. In his *Report on Manufactures*, delivered in 1791, he wrote, "Not only the wealth, but the independence and security of a country, appear to be materially connected with the prosperity of manufactures. Every nation... ought to endeavor to possess within itself all the essentials of a national supply. These comprise the means of subsistence, habitation, clothing, and defence." Under the Constitution he helped write, a nationwide free-trade zone was created. And in 1790, Congress enacted a series of comprehensive Patent Statutes, which made patents affordable and easy to obtain in America. (Previously, patents had required a good deal of money and influence to obtain in England.)

Hamilton wrote that tariffs would raise revenue to fund the national government and encourage manufacturing by applying the funds raised in part toward subsidies (called bounties in his time) for manufacturers. Tariffs would also protect America's infant industries until they could compete. Subsidies would be used for a number of things. First, to encourage a spirit of enterprise, innovation, and invention. Second, to support the building of roads and canals to encourage internal trade. And third, to grow the infant United States into a manufacturing power independent of control by foreign powers.

As a result of the policies Hamilton helped establish, America as a nation appeared to immigrants to be a land of opportunity, even more than it had been as a colony.

America's First Manufacturing

In 1790, an English immigrant, Samuel Slater, passed himself off as a farmer to English emigration officials and came to America with the details of the Arkwright water frame committed to memory. Working with mill owner Moses Brown, he started the first American cotton-spinning mill, at

Pawtucket, Rhode Island, for Ezekiel Carpenter. All the workers – seven boys and two girls – were under age 12.

Three years later, in 1793, Slater opened his own mill in Pawtucket, using carding, drawing, and roving machines he had designed and featuring 72 spindles in two frames. Slater and his partners built two more spinning mills by 1806, but men who had worked for him solely to learn his machines left to set up mills for themselves. By 1809, there were 62 such mills in the country, with Rhode Island and Philadelphia as the main centers. For two decades, the Rhode Island system of small, rural spinning mills set the tone for early industrialization.

In 1793, another invention catapulted the Industrial Revolution: Eli Whitney's cotton gin. This provided an abundant supply of raw material, while spinning mills produced an abundant supply of yarn.

The next thing needed was a power loom to convert the yarn into cloth. Francis Cabot Lowell, son of a leading Boston merchant family, designed a loom with the help of Paul Moody, an expert machinist, after spending time in Manchester, England learning from the English textile industry. He formed the Boston Manufacturing Company with two fellow Bostonians, Patrick Tracy Jackson and Nathan Appleton, as partners. They raised $400,000 ($22,000,000 in today's dollars) and set up New England's first textile mill, in Waltham, Massachusetts, in 1814. This was America's first integrated textile factory, in which all textile production steps took place under one roof.

The profits from the Waltham factory were so great that the partners, later called the Boston Associates, looked for new sites in the area, first at East Chelmsford (later renamed Lowell), Massachusetts and then Chicopee, Massachusetts; Manchester, New Hampshire; and Lawrence, Massachusetts. The "Waltham-Lowell system" of integrated textile manufacturing was so successful that by 1850, Boston Associates controlled one-fifth of America's cotton production.

A key characteristic of the Waltham-Lowell system was that the company recruited young, single women from the surrounding countryside for its mill hands instead of relying on traditional family labor (fathers, mothers, and children). As a direct response to the poor working conditions in Britain, from which the partners had emigrated, they voted to spend money not only on factory buildings and machinery, but also on comfortable boarding houses for these girls. They even funded a church, a library, and a hospital. Charles Dickens visited in the winter of 1842 and toured several of the factories. He recorded his impressions of what he saw in the fourth chapter of his *American Notes*, saying that "the rooms in which they worked were as well ordered as themselves... there was as much fresh air, cleanliness, and comfort as the nature of the occupation would possibly admit."

However, by 1850, following the Irish potato famine, poor immigrant laborers soon replaced young, single women workers in the factories. As owners cut expenses, factory working conditions deteriorated to the point that they became comparable to Britain.

An important profit center of the Boston Manufacturing Company was its machine shop in Lowell. In 1825, the shop was taken over by The Proprietors of Locks and Canals, a local transportation company, and in 1845 it was incorporated as an independent company as the Lowell Machine Shop. George Washington Whistler directed the building of the shop's first locomotive in 1835 by taking apart a locomotive imported from Newcastle, England to learn how it was constructed. By 1838, the shop had turned out 32 locomotives for the Boston and Lowell Railroad and other lines financed by the Boston Associates.

James Francis, who took charge of the machine shop in 1837 and fine tuned the city of Lowell's canal system, engineered the Northern Canal and oversaw Lowell's transition from locomotives to turbines. Under his direction, the Lowell Machine Shop became a leader in the fabrication of hydraulic turbines for the growing steamboat industry.

Lowell Machine Shop

The Industrial Revolution could not have developed without machine tools, for these enabled manufacturing machines to be made. The makers of clocks, watches, and scientific instruments, who had expertise in batch-producing small mechanisms, contributed to manufacturing machines in the 18th century. The mechanical parts of early textile machines were sometimes called "clockwork" because of the metal spindles and gears they incorporated. Carpenters made wooden framings, while blacksmiths and men called "turners" made the metal parts.

The development of machining skills in the early textile industry's machine shops was a crucial step in the American Industrial Revolution. Previously, Americans had relied heavily upon English expertise and machines. It took fine tools to make other tools and precise machines to make other machines. The process was slow and required much trial and error. Much of this learning took place in the Waltham and Lowell shops where Paul Moody helped train the first generation of master mechanics. These mechanics, in turn, created the machine tools that gave birth to entire new American industries.

The American System of Manufacturing

One key element of America's Industrial Revolution was the development of the American system of manufacturing. This involved semi-skilled labor using machine tools and templates or jigs to make standardized, identical, interchangeable parts, each manufactured to specific, precise measurements.

The idea for the American System actually originated in France. The French General Jean Baptiste Vaquette de Gribeauval suggested in the late 18th century that muskets could be manufactured faster and more economically if they were made from interchangeable parts, which would also make repairs easier to carry out under battlefield conditions. His protégé, Honore Blanc, attempted to implement the "Systeme Gribeauval" in France, but never succeeded.

Gribeauval's idea was conveyed to the United States by two routes: First, Blanc's friend Thomas Jefferson sent copies of Blanc's memoirs, and papers describing his work, to Secretary of War Henry Knox. Second, an artillery officer named Louis de Tousard, who had served with the Marquis de Lafayette in the Revolutionary War, was an enthusiast of Gribeauval's ideas. After the Revolution, Tousard wrote two influential documents touting interchangeable parts. One was used as the blueprint for the West Point Military Academy and the other became its officers' training manual.

The War Department, which included officers trained at West Point on Tousard's manual, established armories at Springfield, Massachusetts and Harper's Ferry, Virginia. These officers directed the army to create rifles with interchangeable parts. Captain John H. Hall finally accomplished this in the 1820s. Between the 1820s and the Civil War, American gun makers developed a production process mechanized and precise enough to produce standardized interchangeable gun parts. The American manufacturing system is also known as "armory practice" because of its development in the Springfield and Harper's Ferry armories. During the Civil War, the Springfield Armory started to mass-produce guns using interchangeable parts on a large scale.

The idea of interchangeable parts migrated from the armories to other industries as machinists trained in the armory system were hired by other manufacturers. Soon after the war, American watchmakers showed that these techniques could be successfully applied even when very high precision was required. Other key manufacturers influenced by the American system of interchangeable parts included the Singer sewing machine manufacturer and the McCormick Harvesting Machine Company.

Agricultural Inventions Accelerate Westward Expansion

The invention of the mechanical reaper by Cyrus Hall McCormick in 1831 was an important milestone in America's Industrial Revolution. After refining his reaper and taking out a patent in 1834, he produced the machines in the blacksmith's shop of his father's farm in Walnut Grove, Virginia. In 1847, he moved to Chicago to be closer to his main market, the vast grain fields of the Midwest. He and his brothers William and Leander formed the McCormick Harvesting Machine Company in 1848. McCormick's "Virginia Reaper" hastened the westward expansion of the U.S. by greatly reducing the labor needed to reap standing grain.

The reaper and subsequent farm machinery allowed fewer and fewer people to produce more and more food. It opened a new era in agriculture – an age of mechanization that changed life on the farm and made it possible for millions of people to leave the land and enter industrial society. Instead of 90 percent of the population farming to meet the nation's needs, as was the case in 1831, less than two percent of the U.S. population is directly involved in farming today.

Locomotives Expand Growth and Open New Markets

Locomotives began the next phase of American manufacturing, putting the U.S. at the cutting edge of technology. Richard Trevithick's invention, in 1799, of a high-pressure steam engine with improved boilers permitted engines to be compact enough to be used on locomotives, steamboats, and ships. Robert Fulton's first steamboat, the *Clermont*, made its maiden run on the Hudson River in 1807, marking the first commercial application of steam to transportation. The first commercial railroad in America was launched in 1828, only three years after its British counterpart. An improved steam engine for trains, the *Rocket*, was imported from England and copied by John Stevens. He and his son, Robert L. Stevens, made their own contributions to improved engine design and created the modern Trail.

For 120 years, the major locomotive manufacturers were the Baldwin Locomotive Works, Rogers Locomotive Company, and the American Locomotive Company.

Matthias Baldwin founded what became the Baldwin Works in 1831 in Philadelphia. John Stevens provided technical information for his first engine, the *Ironsides*, built in 1832. Various partnerships during the next 80 years resulted in a number of name changes until it was finally incorporated as the Baldwin Locomotive Works in 1909. Baldwin made its reputation building steam locomotives for the Pennsylvania Railroad, the Baltimore and Ohio, the Atchison, Topeka and Santa Fe, and many others in North America and England, France, India, Haiti, and Egypt. Westinghouse Corporation bought Baldwin in 1948, and in 1950 the Lima-Hamilton Corporation and Baldwin merged. In 1956, the last of 70,541 locomotives was produced after the company failed the transition to diesel power.

Thomas Rogers had been designing and building machinery for the textile industry for nearly 20 years when he sold his interest in Godwin Rogers & Company in 1831 to form the Jefferson Works to build textile and agricultural machinery. A year later, he and his partners Morris Ketchum and Jasper Grosvenor founded the Rogers Locomotive and Machine Works in Paterson, New Jersey. The company started out manufacturing springs, axles, and other small parts for railroad use. In 1835, it assembled a locomotive built in England and shipped disassembled to the United States.

They received their first order, for two locomotives, in 1837. The first was the *Sandusky*, which became the first locomotive to operate in Ohio. The company's most famous locomotive was the *General*, built in 1855 and one of the principals of the Great Locomotive Chase in the American Civil War. Most railroads in the 19th century U.S. had at least one Rogers-built locomotive. It was the second largest manufacturer, behind Baldwin, among almost a hundred companies. The company avoided being part of the merger of seven smaller locomotive builders with the Schenectady Locomotive Works to form the American Locomotive Company (ALCO) in 1901, but was sold to ALCO in 1905.

ALCO was formed to compete against the largest locomotive builder of the day, Baldwin Locomotive Works. In 1902, the Locomotive & Machine Company of Montreal joined the company, and in 1905, the Rogers Locomotive Works was merged into ALCO, which in its history (before and after the mergers) produced about 75,000 locomotives. During World War II, ALCO produced army tanks, tank destroyers, shells, bombs, gun carriages, and gun mounts, in addition to 4,488 locomotives. In 1955, it became known as ALCO Products, and it was bought by the Worthington Corporation in 1964.

These first two American industries – textiles and locomotive manufacturing – started the standard pattern of industry explosion and consolidation. In a new industry, a large number of companies start off manufacturing some new technology. But through business failures, mergers, and acquisitions, the industry narrows down to three or four major companies that control the entire market.

Light Increases Productivity

Another major industry of the first Industrial Revolution was gas lighting. The process consisted of the large-scale gasification of coal in furnaces, purification of the gas (removal of sulfur, ammonium, and heavy hydro-carbons), and its storage and distribution. Again, this industry began in England, when William Murdock invented a gas light in 1792, lighting up his cottage. By 1798, he was using gas to light his entire factory. In 1804, he built a gas works to light an entire cotton mill in Manchester.

Gas lighting spread to the United States and in 1816, Baltimore was the first city to light its streets with gas. Rembrandt Peal founded the first American gas company in Baltimore. The company manufactured gas, laid pipes in streets, and provided street lighting. Gas lighting had a big impact on social and industrial organization because it allowed factories and stores to remain open longer than with tallow candles or oil lamps. With the discovery of natural gas in Fredonia, New York, in 1820, natural gas competed with the gasification of coal.

The Second Industrial Revolution began around 1850. Railroads ignited this second phase as their construction created a large market for mass-produced items such as iron rails, wheels, and spikes. More importantly, they provided the means by which to transport goods to a larger national market. This Second Industrial Revolution gradually grew to include the chemical industries, petroleum refining and distribution, electrical industries, and, in the 20th century, the automobile.

Modern business procedures were introduced starting in the 1840s and 1850s. This included the accounting innovations of Louis McLane, president of the Baltimore and Ohio Railroad, and the organizational overhaul of the Pennsylvania Railroad launched by its president J. Edgar Thompson in 1853. By the time of the Civil War, competent technicians and pro-ductivity-minded administrators were revolutionizing one industry after another, a process that became general after 1870. Organizers and inventors came together to achieve historic goals. For example, Alexander Holley built the most modern steel mill in the world for Andrew Carnegie in 1875.

Sometimes, the innovative organizer and the investor were one and the same, as in the case of Thomas Edison, who set up an experimental laboratory in Menlo Park, New Jersey, in 1875. His inventions are too numerous to be described in this brief history, but his invention of electric lighting in 1879 moved industrialization to the next level. Edison's achievement was inventing not just the bulb itself, but a whole system that contained all the elements necessary to make incandescent lighting practical, safe, and economical. (He had to invent a total of seven system elements critical to the practical application of electric light as an alternative to gas.) He went on to invent many small appliances and other modern conveniences, such as the phonograph and motion picture camera, which run on electricity.

Electricity Transforms Industry

The modern electric utility industry began in the 1880s. It evolved from gas and electric carbon-arc commercial and street lighting systems. In 1882, Thomas Edison's Pearl Street electric generating station went into operation, providing light and electricity to customers in a one square mile area of Lower Manhattan. By the end of the 1880s, small central stations dotted many U.S. cities, each limited to a few blocks because of the transmission inefficiencies of direct current (DC).

Edison's various electric companies were brought together to form Edison General Electric in 1889. The tremendous capital needed to set up electricity generating systems required the involvement of investment bankers like J. P. Morgan. When Edison General Electric merged with its leading electricity-distribution competitor, Thompson-Houston, in 1892, Edison was no longer in control of the company and "Edison" was dropped from the name of the company, which became simply General Electric.

Edison's system was based on DC (direct current). George Westinghouse, on the other hand, promoted the AC (alternating current) invented by Nikola Tesla, a young engineer and inventor who had emigrated from Croatia. Tesla was working for Thomas Edison at the time, but Edison wasn't interested in AC. So Tesla went to work for

Westinghouse, who could see the advantages of AC. AC could be stepped up to very high voltages with transformers, sent over thinner and less expensive wires, and stepped down again at its destination. It eventually replaced DC in most generation and distribution, greatly extending range and efficiency.

While the modern electric utility industry changed the lives of people across the country, it also had a dramatic effect on industry. Electric lighting was safer (no gas line explosions) and cheaper than gas lighting, enabling manufacturers to economically extend the working day to two or even three shifts.

Another invention that had a major impact on manufacturing was the electric motor. While early versions had existed since the 1830s, they had failed to be commercially successful because of the high cost of battery power. The modern DC motor was invented by accident in 1873 when ZenobeGramme connected a spinning dynamo to a second similar unit, driving it as a motor. There was no practical commercial market at first, but in time, the Gramme machine was the first industrially useful electric motor.

In 1882, Nikola Tesla identified the rotating magnetic field principle and pioneered the use of a rotary field of force to operate machines. He used the principle to design a unique two-phase induction motor in 1883 and was granted a patent in 1889 for his AC electromagnetic induction motor. The introduction of his motor into factories to power manufacturing equipment fueled the Second Industrial Revolution, made possible by the efficient generation and long-distance distribution of electrical power using the AC transmission system.

To increase the volume of goods being produced by factories in the United States, the problem of mass distribution needed to be solved. Most Americans still lived in rural areas and relied on agriculture for their livelihoods. For many Americans, a single general store was their main source of supplies. Merchandise went through many wholesalers on the way from manufacturer to end user. While general stores along the growing network of railroads received their shipments relatively quickly, merchandise was transported by wagon to towns from railheads.

Mail-Order Catalogs Expand Markets

One solution to expanding mass distribution was the mail-order catalog. In 1872, Aaron Montgomery Ward founded the world's first mail order company. He had spent several years as a traveling salesman in rural America, and had observed that rural customers wanted "city" goods but were often victimized by monopolists who provided no guarantee of quality. He believed he could cut costs and make a wide variety of goods available by cutting out the middlemen and having his customers purchase goods by mail and pick them up at the nearest train station.

Ward produced his first catalog in August 1872, with 163 articles for sale. Despite opposition from rural retailers, his business grew quickly over the next several decades, primarily from rural customers who were attracted by the wide selection of items unavailable locally. By 1883, the company's catalog had grown to 240 pages and 10,000 items, and by 1904, the company was mailing 3,000,000 catalogs a year. (Montgomery Ward stopped producing catalogs in 1985, and closed all of its 250 stores in 2001 after struggling for years in an increasingly crowded field against companies like Target and Wal-Mart. It was the largest retail bankruptcy in U.S. history.)

A second mail-order catalog helped further increase mass distribution. Richard Sears was a railroad station agent in North Redwood, Minnesota when he received a shipment of watches from a Chicago jeweler that were unwanted by a local jeweler. He purchased them himself and sold the watches at a nice profit to other station agents. He ordered more for resale and started a business selling watches through mail-order catalogs. In 1893, Richard Sears and Alvah Roebuck founded Sears, Roebuck and Company in Chicago. Within a year, their catalog had grown to 322 pages, featuring sewing machines, bicycles, sporting goods, and a host of other items. Chicago clothing manufacturer Julius Rosenwald bought into the company in 1895 and shortly thereafter, Roebuck had to resign due to ill health. Rosenwald kept the Sears and Roebuck name, but reorganized the company so it could handle orders economically and efficiently. By 1900, it had sales of $10 million, exceeding Montgomery Ward's $8.7 million. Its catalog was sometimes referred to as "the Consumers' Bible." The Christmas catalog was known as the "Wish Book," perhaps because of the toys in it. Sears diversified and became a conglomerate during the mid-20th century. It established several major brands, like Kenmore (appliances), Craftsman (tools), DieHard (batteries), Silvertone (electronics) and Toughskins (clothing). In 1993, it stopped producing its general merchandize catalog, but it continues to produce specialty catalogs and the Holiday Wish Book.

Mass Production Increases Efficiency

A major breakthrough in manufacturing came from innovations in assembly-line techniques by the Ford Motor Company. Henry Ford founded Ford Motors in 1903 with $28,000, 11 men, and himself as vice president and chief engineer. Skilled workers were scarce in America, so it was beneficial to follow production strategies that needed them as little as possible. Using new and more productive methods, they produced three cars per day, with up to three men working on each car. In 1908, the company produced the Model T, a reliable and affordable vehicle for the mass market.

To keep up with demand, Ford built a new factory in Highland Park, Michigan in 1913. This factory used standardized interchangeable parts and a conveyor-belt assembly line. This was the beginning of what is called mass production. This new technique used a moving assembly line, which allowed workers to stay in one place and perform the same task repeatedly on multiple vehicles that passed by. Unskilled labor could thus be substituted for skilled labor.

The assembly line proved tremendously efficient, helping the company far surpass the production levels of its competitors and making the vehicles much more affordable. The factory was able to build a car in just 93 minutes, producing around one million vehicles a year at a reasonable cost, paving the way for the cheap automobiles that turned the United States into a nation of motorists. By 1918, half of all the cars in the United States were Model T Fords. The factory had everything needed to construct the vehicles, including its own steel mill and glass factory.

Mass production provides economies in several ways. First, there is the reduction of nonproductive effort on the part of workers. They no longer have to move about a shop to get parts and locate and use many tools. Second, the probability of human error is reduced when tasks are mostly carried out by machinery. Each worker repeats one or a few related tasks, using the same tool to perform identical or nearly identical operations. The exact tool and parts are always at hand.

In addition, there are jigs, gauge blocks, and fixtures to ensure that parts are made to fit a particular setup during assembly, and parts are made to specifications which ensure they fit with the mating parts. Each workbench or assembly-line station along the assembly line is different, and each set of tools at each station is limited to those necessary to perform that stage of the assembly. Mass production would never have been possible without factories that were electrified and had sophisticated machinery to automate the various production steps.

However, mass production is inflexible because it is difficult to alter a design or production process after a production line is set up. Also, all the products made on one production line will be identical or very similar, so introducing variety to satisfy individual tastes is hard. (Some variety can be achieved by applying different finishes and decorations at the end of the production line.)

Mass production is also very capital intensive, as it uses a lot of machinery per worker. The machinery is so expensive that there must be some assurance that the product will be successful enough for the company to get a return on its investment. Thus, mass production is ideally suited for products that serve markets large enough to satisfy the long production runs required.

Ford cut the workday from nine hours to eight so his factory could convert to a three-shift workday and operate 24 hours a day. He paid wages nearly triple the going rate for unskilled workers ($5.00/day vs. $1.75). The main reason was to reduce turnover—from 370 percent in 1913 to 16 percent by 1915—but he also wanted his employees to be able to afford to buy the cars they were making. He said, "There is one rule for the industrialist and that is: Make the best quality of goods possible at the lowest cost possible, paying the highest wages possible."

Over the next 30 years, most manufacturers of high-volume products for the consumer market adopted Ford's assembly-line system, producing things like radios, phonographs, telephones, washing machines, refrigerators, and stoves. Mass-production conveyor systems also began to be used in food manufacturing.

Manufacturers then faced a problem. Once a market had been saturated, replacement demand was lower than during the initial expansion of the market. So they faced the problem of figuring out how to add value to the product so consumers would not simply replace but upgrade. Because manufacturers could not sell them the original product a second time, they had to figure out some way to sell customers an improved version.

Alfred Sloan at General Motors solved the problem for automobiles by making the "guts" of the cars the same but putting those guts in differently colored boxes or chassis and changing the style elements so that consumers could buy a car that wasn't identical to every other car on the street.

Manufacturers of other consumer products adopted this strategy by creating new styles and models with added-value features and technological improvements.

Manufacturers of lower-volume products developed a modified assembly-line system. For example, aircraft manufacturers arranged the workflow in their plants in "lines" of aircraft being assembled. Obviously, they couldn't use a conveyor system, but they could transport heavy subassemblies to the aircraft being assembled via an overhead monorail or crane.

During this period – the 1930s and 1940s – many manufacturers wanted to have complete control over a product's production, from raw materials to final assembly. This came to be called vertical integration, and it worked best for products that were fairly simple, small, and easy to ship.

But as products became more complex and the machinery needed to make their parts and sub-assemblies became more complicated and expensive, it became cost prohibitive for most manufacturers to continue with vertical integration. For example, to set up an in-house sheet metal fabrication department today, the equipment might cost between $500,000and $1,000,000, depending on whether you buy used or new machines. It is less expensive to set up an in-house machine shop ($50,000 to $100,000), but there is also the cost of the skilled machinists you have to hire to run it. If your product doesn't use enough sheet metal or machined parts to keep the operators busy for eight hours a day, five days a week, then you face the cost of employees standing around with nothing to do. This problem is compounded by some computer-controlled machines for plastic injection molding, which take only seconds to minutes to make each part. The volume required to keep these machines busy full-time is in the hundreds of thousands of parts per year.

Small and Medium-Sized Companies Fill a Need

Small and medium-sized companies, specializing in manufacturing different parts and sub-assemblies for the major automobile manufacturers and other mass producers of consumer goods, sprang up to solve this problem, starting in the 1930s but increasingly since the 1950s. By having a variety of customers, they could keep their machines and employees busy year-round.

Some of these companies became known as "job shops" because they shopped their specialty manufacturing services to larger manufacturers, who became known as Original Equipment Manufacturers (OEMs). Examples of these services include rubber molding, plastic forming and molding, precision machining, sheet metal fabrication, metal stamping, and printed circuit board fabrication. Other small- and medium-sized manufacturers became "contract manufac-turers" to larger manufacturers, providing subcontract fabri-cation and assembly of sub-assemblies and even whole pro-ducts. Sometimes the contract manufacturers used materials and parts consigned to them by their customer; sometimes they procured materials and parts themselves.

Some of these contract manufacturers specialized in a particular type of product, which they might produce for a larger manufacturer using that company's "private label." An example of this is a company that makes welding equipment sold under its own label while also making other models under the label of one or more customers. Contract manufacturers that specialize in producing a whole product for other manufacturers, also called "turnkey" manufacturers, started to form in the early 1990s. They handle everything from procuring parts and materials to drop shipping the product to the end customer.

Today, there are even manufacturers of products, including high-tech products, that I call "virtual manufacturers." These have no manufacturing capability in-house. Sometimes they don't even have the personnel to *design* the product. The founders of the company may have a concept of the new product they wish to develop and market, but they don't have the technical expertise to do the design and development themselves. They may hire outside consultants to design and develop the product, or subcontract the design, development, and prototyping to a company specializing in these services. At the extreme end, they subcontract out everything from start to finish, including engineering design, procurement of parts and materials, assembly, test, inspection, and shipping to the end customer. They may handle marketing and customer service themselves, but sometimes they even subcontract these functions to marketing and customer service firms. Virtual manufacturers have become common for consumer products with a limited life span sold to the mass market, or for company founders who just want to make a quick fortune and are not interested in building a company to last with follow-on products. Examples of fad products that had a limited life include the Hula Hoop, Cabbage Patch Kids, and Pokemon. If a product has been designed for ease of manufacturing, the location of the vendors who produce its parts and sub-assemblies doesn't matter so much. However, ease of communication and the cost of transportation for parts play a big role in determining where it will be made.

Technology Drives Modern Manufacturing

Modern manufacturing systems greatly depend on computers, process new, trickier-to-handle materials, and operate in an environmentally sensitive world that gets smaller every day.

Modern technology has impacted manufacturing to the point where planning is a necessity for competing. Manufacturing techniques used today include computer-aided design (CAD); computer-integrated manufacturing (CIM); computer-aided process planning (CAPP); computer-aided manufacturing (CAM); just-in-time (JIT) delivery of materials, components, and subassemblies; flexible manufacturing systems (FMS); and computerized inventory-control systems.

Computer-aided design or computer-aided drafting (CAD) began by using computer technology to aid in the design of products. Current software packages range from 2D drafting systems to 3D solid and surface modelers. Some allow the incorporation of all design requirements, down to individual electronic components, with the computer searching through a listing of proven component designs and selecting the most qualified.

Computer-integrated manufacturing (CIM) is the complete automation of a manufacturing plant, with all processes under computer control and a digital network tying them together. Computer-aided manufacturing (CAM) enables machines to make parts based on the data supplied by CAD.

Computer-aided process planning (CAPP) provides a means to electronically store a process plan that translates design information into the steps and instructions needed to efficiently manufacture the product.

Critical Path Analysis is used to organize and plan projects so they are completed on time and within budget. Tasks that are dependent on each other are noted so that critical tasks can be identified. Starting with manual wall charts of this kind, computerized programs of this kind have played a key role in organizing the development of complex space and defense programs.

ISO Registration

Since 1990, it has become increasingly important for companies to become ISO registered. ISO stands for the International Standards Organization, headquartered in Geneva, Switzerland. The original purpose of the ISO was to develop common standards of performance worldwide. ISO standards are a quality-management system that addresses a company's ability to ensure that its product or service consistently meets customers' written and implied expectations. The generic nature of the standard allows companies to develop quality systems around their unique products and processes. The unique feature of the ISO quality standards is their provision for third-party assessment and the subsequent registration of companies fulfilling the standards' requirements.

At first, only large companies could afford the expensive and intensive process of being audited by third-party registrars to become ISO registered. But within the last five years, costs have dropped to the point that many small- and medium-sized companies can now afford it. ISO registration has dropped from more than $250,000 to below $10,000, depending on the size of the company and its number of plants.

Lean Manufacturing

In the past 20 years, a growing number of manufacturers have implemented "lean" manufacturing based on the Toyota Production System (TPS) developed in Japan as a result of severe resource constraints after World War II. The founders of TPS had to do more with less, so this became the guiding philosophy behind lean thinking at Toyota.

This system was developed to produce smaller batches with just-in-time delivery, producing only the necessary units, in necessary quantities, at precisely the right time. This resulted in reducing inventory, increasing productivity, and reducing costs. In the 1990s, this highly efficient system became known as lean manufacturing.

"Lean" has evolved into a system-wide management process that continually seeks to increase profits by stripping out wasted time, materials, and manpower ("non-value added" steps in what is referred to as a "value stream map" of the manufacturing process). It began at large companies because of the costs of training and the time involved to implement the process. But today there are many affordable training programs for small- and medium-sized manufacturers.

The days are gone when manufacturing companies could have machines and building space sitting idle for days or weeks on end. Today's manufacturing companies must operate in an efficient manner to make a profit and must account for every dollar invested in the business.

2

The Role of Unions in Shaping America's Industrialization

The brief history of the development of manufacturing in the United States covered in the previous chapter may have sounded smooth and straight-forward. But in reality, it was a story rich in human drama and tragedy. The United States actually has the bloodiest labor-movement history of any industrialized nation. People died in the struggle for American workers to earn a voice in the workplace and increase their share of the economic pie.

The Revolutionary Era: 1763-1789

During the colonial period, the independent craftsmen who participated in the representative governments of the Northern and Middle colonies gave the common man a voice. There was a growth in political organization and action in the latter years of this period, leading up to the Revolutionary War.

Workers and their interests played an important role in the success of the Revolution. One example is the Boston

Massacre of 1770. British troops had been sent to Boston to maintain order and to enforce the Townshend Acts of 1767, one of a series of unpopular taxes. The troops were constantly tormented by groups of colonists. The event had roots in the unhappiness of Boston rope-makers over competition from off-duty British soldiers, who sought casual work to supplement their wages. What began as a verbal confrontation between a rope maker and a soldier grew into a confrontation between workers and sentries in which British soldiers fired into the rioting crowd, killing five men. The British captain and his men were tried for murder in the colonial courts; two were convicted, but the captain and eight men were acquitted. The "massacre" was a legendary event of the American rebellion and became a battle cry for the Revolution.

Further evidence of the importance of common people in the movement is the success of Thomas Paine's 1776 pamphlet *Common Sense*, which was written for the masses, not the upper class. He made several points: on government being a necessary evil, on why we should break free from British rule, and on how an American revolution would eventually occur anyway. *Common Sense* reached a large audience and helped to sway the undecided to support independence. Its tremendous sales (three printings and more than 150,000 copies) indicate the level of interest the average person had in the emerging ideology of independence.

After 1776, the fighting shifted to the South and the British destroyed buildings, crops, and livestock. They seized slaves and lured them into British lines with promises of freedom. British privateers (ships) damaged the New England fishing and whaling fleets and the British market for whale oil was lost. However, people continued to work during the war and domestic manufacturing increased, causing the Thirteen Colonies to become more self-sufficient.

An articulate middle class composed of lawyers, merchants, and planters led the American patriots, but most of the soldiers were commoners – farmers, apprentices, laborers, fishermen, craftsmen, ex-slaves, and even women. Workers united to better their condition. They fought wartime monopolies and price controls. The involvement of workers and the common people truly made this more a revolution than a rebellion.

In theory, the Revolution created a government and society based on the equality of free men. In reality, it maintained an elitist system that favored the educated upper class. It didn't change working conditions for the common people, and slavery was deliberately not addressed by the Declaration of Independence and continued as an institution.

Growth of a New Nation: 1789-1830

President Jefferson warned of the evils of an industrial society where wealth separated men. He and his supporters hoped America would remain a rural agricultural society where ties to the land would maintain men's equality and civic virtue. An industrial class system, they feared, would erode democracy. But the Jeffersonians lost the struggle to retain their vision of America in the face of industrialization.

A pattern of hard times (depression and recession) followed by periods of prosperity began to emerge, also referred to as "boom and bust." Labor was weak in hard times. But it had the power to increase wages and improve working conditions in periods of prosperity, when labor was in short supply.

In the early republic, workers were differentiated by skill, income, type of workplace, living conditions, property ownership, freedom or servitude, and opportunities for advancement. Most workers were not paid solely in the form of money, but also in goods, crops, meals, and living quarters. The unskilled fared poorly, receiving one dollar or less per day, which was too low to maintain even a minimal standard of decent living. Skilled workers, variously known as craftsmen, artisans, or mechanics, received wages 75 to 100 percent higher. Their tools, and their proficiency in using them, gave them marketable assets. Working independently, or with others as journeymen in small shops directed by master craftsmen, they could realistically anticipate becoming masters themselves someday. The working day for skilled workers paralleled the traditional working day on American farms: sunup to sundown.

The trade union movement in the U.S. originated during this period, the 1790s, when skilled workers were the first to organize and form unions. These were not so much trade unions in the modern sense as benevolent organizations. They were concerned with providing death benefits to widows, assisting members who were ill or unemployed, providing loans and credit, maintaining libraries, perpetuating high standards of craftsmanship, and settling disputes among their members. Some of these journeymen societies had objectives that went beyond benevolence to seeking shorter hours and higher wages.

During the 1790s, the carpenters and shoemakers of Philadelphia, the tailors of Baltimore, the printers of New York City, and craft workers in other large cities formed unions. These were usually small and organized to conduct particular strikes, called "turnouts," after which they dissolved.

In 1790, cabinet and chair makers in Philadelphia fought an attempt by employers to blacklist union members and in 1791; Philadelphia carpenters struck (unsuccessfully) for a 10-hour day and overtime pay. This was the first American building trades strike.

In 1794, shoemakers in Philadelphia formed the Federal Society of Journeymen Cordwainers. (Cordwainers made boots and shoes, in contrast to cobblers, who repaired them.) They organized in self-defense against their masters' attempts to reduce their wages. In 1806, eight members of the Cordwainers were tried for conspiracy after a strike for higher wages. They were charged with joining to raise wages and injure others. At issue was the right of journeymen to organize themselves to negotiate the price of their labor. The contending forces were arrayed along political lines, with Federalists defending the interests of the employers and Jeffersonians those of the journeymen.

The legal basis employers used to challenge the organized journeymen was the old English common-law doctrine of conspiracy. (English courts treated labor combinations as illegal conspiracies.) Although English common law had no formal standing in America, lawyers still often used English precedents in their arguments. Faced with an unsympathetic judge and jury of nine employers and only three journeymen, the Cordwainers lost and were forced to disband after being fined and going bankrupt. This was the first union to be tried for conspiracy, and its outcome set a legal precedent that affected labor issues in the United States for years.

In 1823, the Hatters of New York City were tried and found guilty of conspiracy in joining to deprive a non-union man of his livelihood. In 1827, the Tailors of Philadelphia were tried for conspiracy and convicted. The verdict stressed the "injury to trade" aspect of their organization.

So far, we have dealt only with trade societies, not a true labor movement. A true labor movement presupposes a feeling of solidarity that goes beyond the boundaries of a single trade and extends to other workers. The true American labor movement began in 1827 when several trades in Philadelphia formed the Mechanics Union of Trade Associations. This was originally an economic organization, but it changed to a political one the following year when it unsuccessfully struck for a 10-hour workday.

Other cities soon had similar local trade federations, like the Working-men's Party of New York, formed in 1829. The members of these organizations were generally craftsmen or mechanics, rather than laborers or factory workers. Fear that the spread of the factory system would jeopardize the status of skilled workers drove them to unite. Another reason was that their incomes were threatened by inflation and employer pressure to cut wages. These unions were subject to savage attacks by a hostile press and were referred to as "anarchists," "rabble," "levelers," and a "mob."

As factories sprang up in one industry after another, machines and unskilled workers replaced the skilled workers of the small shops. The search for cheap factory labor led to a heavy reliance on child labor. In the 1820s and 1830s, children under 16 constituted one-third to one-half of the industrial labor force of New England. While adults might earn as much as $2.50 a week in the mills, children's wages hovered between 33 and 50 cents.

Girl Textile Worker, 1910

Industries like cotton spinning and weaving were particularly hard for workers to endure long hours of labor in. Some worked up to 19 hours a day with only a one-hour total break. It was common for workers to work 12 to 14 hours a day in hot and exhausting work places. Children as young as six worked long, hard hours for little or no pay. They were paid only a fraction of what an adult would get, and orphans were sometimes paid nothing, with factory owners justifying this by saying they provided food, shelter, and clothing.

Children were often employed to move between dangerous machines, as they were small enough to fit between tightly arranged machinery. This led to their being placed in a great deal of danger, and death rates were high. Long hours added to the dangers, as exhaustion led to workers becoming sluggish, which made them more vulnerable to accidents.

Thankfully, not all factories were as bad as this. For example, the founders of the Lowell factory described in Chapter One sought to preserve America's agricultural base by employing rural women who would supplement their incomes on the farm. The factory started by Francis Cabot Lowell and his partners in 1820 had clean, comfortable, and well-lit rooms, with boarding rooms for the women workers.

Lowell and his partners were regarded as good employers in this respect. They were among a group of people, known as reformers, who wanted to change the way factories were run. They faced opposition from other mill owners, who knew that reforms would cost them money and give the workers more rights. Although the Lowell experiment eventually failed in its original form, reformers did gradually managed to force changes to the way factory workers were treated.

Expansion and Sectionalism: 1831-1860

This was a significant period of reform in American history. Emerson and Thoreau were contemplating the essentials of life and William Lloyd Garrison founded the abolitionist movement. Out of this climate came the 10-hour movement, which achieved legislative success in several states. However, these laws contained a loophole that employers used: employees were allowed to contract with their employers for longer hours *if they wanted*. Employers manipulated this to apply to all workers, and those who refused were fired or blacklisted. Increased immigration, mainly from Ireland during the potato famine that lasted from 1845 to 1851, fed an expanding and eager labor pool and weakened workers' bargaining power on this and other issues.

Reform organizations sought a wide range of changes, from the abolition of slavery to child labor restrictions and a 10-hour day. Some organizations called for equal distribution of land, the abolition of imprisonment for debt, a tax-supported public school system, reform of a militia system that let the rich avoid service, and simplification of the legal system. Women's labor organizations increased their voice and militancy during this period.

Transportation improvements like turnpikes, tolls roads, canals, steamboats, and railroads opened up opportunities for large-scale manufacturers. Limited custom orders and local trade gave way to a huge national market. Merchant capitalists increasingly assumed control over not only the sale of goods but also over their production. They supplied the raw materials to craft shops, so shop owners became small contractors employed by merchant capitalists. The shop owners, in turn, employed journeymen, and introduced the "sweating" system, demanding greater productivity from their workers. The apprentice program broke down as skilled labor was replaced by the unskilled – women, children, and even prisoners.

The first nationwide labor federation, the National Trades Union, was formed in New York City in 1834, but was short lived due to the Panic of 1837, when banks failed and stopped paying in gold and silver. The ensuing depression temporarily halted the labor movement. One-third of the nation's workers were unemployed due to the economic downturn. President Andrew Jackson declared a 10-hour day in the Philadelphia Navy Yard to quell discontent caused by the panic.

In 1836, the National Cooperative Association of Cordwainers, the first national union for a specific trade, was founded in New York City. The same year, a convention of mechanics, farmers, and workingmen met in Utica, NY. They wrote a Declaration of Rights that opposed paper money and the arbitrary power of the courts, and they called for legislation to guarantee the right to organize to increase wages. They formed the Equal Rights Party to be free of control by the existing parties.

Journeymen house carpenters, weavers, cordwainers, and printers took steps to create national societies. The *New York City Union Journal* claimed in 1836 that unions had 200,000 members. However, the Panics of 1837 and 1839, and the long depression that followed the latter, led to the failure of most unions when workers found it impossible to afford their dues. In 1845, *The New York Tribune* estimated that one-third of the male population was unemployed.

Workers did not do well during the prosperity that returned in the late 1840s. Between 1837 and 1858, the wages of skilled ironworkers in Pennsylvania were reduced by one-third to one-half. The wages of unskilled workers dropped even lower; for example, female needle workers earned less than a dollar per week.

In 1842, the threat of conspiracy lawsuits was lifted by the reversal of previous court decisions in Commonwealth vs. Hunt, in which the Massachusetts Supreme Court ruled that strikes to improve labor conditions were lawful, not illegal conspiracies. The same year, Connecticut and Massachusetts passed laws prohibiting children from working more than 10 hours per day. (This was 40 years after England had limited the working hours of children aged nine to 13 to a maximum of eight hours, and adolescents between 14 and 18 years to a maximum of 12 hours, with the Factory Act of 1802.)

The 10-hour movement grew and in 1840, President Martin Van Buren proclaimed a 10-hour day, without reduction in pay, for all federal employees on public works. In 1844, 200 delegates formed the New England Workingmen's Association to fight for the 10-hour day. The same year, Sarah Bagley helped form the Female Labor Reform Association (an auxiliary of the New England Workingmen's Association), in Lowell, Massachusetts, also to work for a 10-hour day.

In 1845, female workers in five cotton mills in Allegheny, Pennsylvania struck for a 10-hour day. Workers in Lowell, Massachusetts and Manchester, New Hampshire supported them. Finally, after nearly 50 years of effort by the labor movement, New Hampshire in 1847 became the first state to make 10 hours the legal workday, and Pennsylvania passed a 10-hour law in 1848. Pennsylvania also passed a child labor law in 1848, making 12 the minimum age for commercial occupations.

While business boomed in the 1850s, prices soared and wages lagged, causing a wave of strikes. These did not result from negotiations breaking down between labor and management, as would happen today. Instead, unions would decide on their objectives and announce that a strike would be called for a particular day if their demands were not met. If the employer accepted the terms, a "trade agreement" was concluded.

If not, the workers did not show up for work until their demands were accepted.

The National Typographical Union, the earliest national workers organization that has endured to the present day, was founded in 1852. That same year, Ohio passed the first state law limiting women's working days to 10 hours. The depression that followed the Panic of 1857 again destroyed most unions, and only two survived: the NTU and the Machinists and Blacksmiths' International Union. An Iron Molders Union was formed in Philadelphia in 1859 during the depression, and in 1860 there was a successful strike of 20,000 shoemakers in New England. President Abraham Lincoln, in support of New England shoemakers, said, "Thank God that we have a system of labor where there can be a strike."

The Civil War and Reconstruction: 1861-1877

By the eve of the Civil War, the United States had a manufacturing output second only to Great Britain. An elaborate railroad system, iron-hulled steamships, and electric telegraphs linked the northern and central parts of the country into a single market. Factory production prevailed in textiles, paper, and farm equipment.

Obviously the institution of slavery was a major cause of the Civil War. Yet it was not solely a moral issue. Northern workers did not want to compete against slave labor. How could they? As Northern workers sought to increase their share of the nation's wealth, black workers in the South labored without any compensation at all. Northern labor leaders and industrialists thought the South was trying to destroy capitalism and spread its Slave Power aristocracy across the nation. Unfortunately, there was no solution except war, but with the North's victory and passage of the 13th Amendment, slavery was abolished. For blacks, the struggle was not over. A long road toward complete freedom was ahead, as for all workers.

Industry was especially spurred by the needs of war, and wartime labor organizing led to the formation of 12 national unions, as labor was in high demand and thus had more leverage. In 1863, the Working Women's Union and the present-day Brotherhood of Locomotive Engineers were founded. In 1864, the legality of importing immigrants by holding a portion of their wages or property was upheld in the Contract Labor Law. Employers often used immigrants as strikebreakers. Though this law was repealed in 1868, the practice was not outlawed until the passage of the Foran Act in 1885.

After the Civil War, industrialization accelerated dramatically. This period was marked by the development of large enterprises employing thousands of workers, most of whom no longer expected to eventually escape their working-class status. As a result, unionization advanced rapidly. More than 30 national craft unions were established during the 1860s and early 1870s. The National Labor Union formed in Baltimore in 1866 as a federation of national and local unions and city federations. Within two years, it had more than 600,000 members, but its emphasis on political action alienated many of the constituent unions and it collapsed in 1872 after several groups withdrew.

In 1868, the movement for an *eight*-hour workday began with a general strike of Chicago unions. Congress passed a law enacting a federal eight-hour day the same year, but it applied only to laborers, mechanics, and workmen employed by the federal government.

The first local chapter of the Knights of Labor was founded in Philadelphia in 1869, though it maintained extreme secrecy. (Membership later became open to blacks and women.) The Knights opposed strikes on principle, and sanctioned them only in cases where their members were victimized or employers refused to arbitrate. These two exceptions, however, allowed hundreds of strikes to be waged under its auspices. The same year, the Black National Labor Union was founded in Washington, D.C. under the leadership of Isaak Myers, and the first national female union was organized: the Daughters of St. Crispin, which held a convention in Lynn, Massachusetts and elected Carrie Wilson as president.

The 1870s were a period of widespread labor agitation and unrest. Numerous unions struck against wage cuts and the displacement of workers by laborsaving machinery. Most employers vigorously opposed trade union activity.

The Panic of 1873 began with the failure of the largest investment-banking firm of the day, Jay Cooke and Company. Cooke was the principal backer of the Northern Pacific Railroad, a prime investor in other railroads, and an agent for the federal government's financing of railroad construction. The New York Stock Exchange closed for 10 days, credit dried up, and foreclosures and factory closings were common. Of the country's 364 railroads, 89 went bankrupt, more than

18,000 business failed, and unemployment reached 14 percent in 1876.[1]

This depression hit industrial America harder than earlier depressions, when the agrarian nature of society had allowed more workers to provide for themselves. By this time, most of America's industrial workers had been born in the cities, not on farms. Most lived near the factories where they worked, and countless chimneys belched black smoke into the air from the coal furnaces that powered the factories. The smaller factory towns were often worse than the notorious filth of the tenements in New York and Chicago because raw sewage was dumped into their rivers, canals, and ponds.

By 1877, wage cuts, distrust of leaders, and poor working conditions had built up a bitter antagonism between workers and employers. The Great Railroad Strike of 1877 started on July 14 in Martinsburg, West Virginia in response to the cutting of wages, for the second time in a year, by the Baltimore & Ohio Railroad. The strike spread to Cumberland, Maryland, stopping freight and passenger traffic. Maryland's Governor Carroll sent National Guard regiments to put down the strike, but citizens from Baltimore attacked the troops. The 6th Regiment fired on the crowd, killing 10 and wounding 25.

The strike spread to Pittsburgh where militiamen killed another 40 strikers after they set fire to buildings and destroyed 104 locomotives and 1,245 freight and passenger cars. On July 21 and 22, President Rutherford B. Hayes sent federal troops to restore order in Maryland and Pittsburgh. This did not stop the spread of the strike to Philadelphia, where much of the city center was set on fire before federal troops intervened and put down the uprising. In Reading,

Pennsylvania, home of the Reading Railroad, workers had already been on strike since April and blocked rail traffic, committed arson in the train yard, and burned down a bridge that was the railroad's only link to the west.

The strike then spread to the Midwest and the West, where strikers halted all freight traffic for a week in East St. Louis, Illinois. Rail traffic was paralyzed in Chicago on July 24 when angry mobs of unemployed citizens wrecked the rail yards. Demonstrators shut down railroad traffic in Bloomington, Aurora, Peoria, Decatur, and other rail centers throughout Illinois. In San Francisco, crowds of people sacked railroad property and attacked Chinatown. On July 25, 1,000 men and boys, mostly coal miners, looted the Reading Railroad depot in Shamokin, Pennsylvania.

The strike began to lose momentum when President Hayes sent federal troops from city to city, until it ended 45 days after it had started. After the strike, union organizers planned for the next battles, while politicians and business leaders took steps to ensure that such chaos could not recur. Many states enacted conspiracy statutes. Some states formed new militia units and constructed National Guard armories in a number of cities. The Workingmen's Party and the Greenback Party merged to form the Greenback Labor Party in an attempt to have more influence in national politics. However, Republicans and Democrats eagerly snatched up prominent workers to be candidates, which hindered the development of a national labor party.

The six-year depression finally ended in 1879 and another boom period began. Wages leveled off and food prices starting falling, improving the lives of working-class families.

The Second Industrial Revolution and the Progressive Era

This period was a time of amazing growth in America. In 1860, the U.S. population was 31 million, but it doubled to 63 million by 1890, and then nearly tripled to 92 million by 1910. Railroads, the epitome of industrialization, expanded from about 30,000 miles of track before the Civil War to nearly 270,000 miles by 1900. And the industrial labor force nearly tripled between 1880 and 1910, to about eight million.

Large factories, which had existed only in the textile industry before the Civil War, became increasingly common in a variety of industries. Labor was in high demand to work in these new industries. Unfortunately, population growth spurred by immigration helped keep the price of labor low. Still, workers continued to organize and resist when their way of life or health were threatened. Unions focused on securing safe working conditions and reasonable compensation.

Twelve million immigrants came by ship to America between 1865 and 1900. About half were German or Irish, and almost a million were British, many of whom had gained industrial experience in Europe. American steamship and railroad agents combed southeastern Europe with promises of work in America. Young men from the villages of Croatia, Galicia, the Carpathians, and Italy came in search of industrial wages. Settled communities of Ukrainians, Italians, Poles, and Hungarians soon became familiar sights in the United States as immigrants sent home for their families. After 1890, these new arrivals came to outnumber those from Germany and Ireland. Norwegians, Swedes, and Danes immigrated at rates reaching 100,000 a year in the 1880s. Lured by the promise of work, tens of thousands of French Canadians immigrated to work in the textile, shoe, and paper factories of New England, where they lived in cramped tenements.

Several trade unions combined in 1881 to form the Federation of Organized Trades and Labor Unions as a means of influencing legislation on behalf of labor. At its convention in Chicago in 1884, the Federation resolved that "eight hours shall constitute a legal day's labour from and after May 1, 1886."

When May 1, 1886 approached, American labor unions prepared for a general strike in support of the eight-hour day. On Saturday, May 1, rallies were held throughout the United States. There were an estimated 10,000 demonstrators in New York and 11,000 in Detroit. In Milwaukee, 10,000 turned out. The movement's center was Chicago: Albert Parsons, founder of the International Working People's Association, led a march of 80,000 people down Michigan Avenue and an estimated 40,000 workers went on strike. Nationwide, estimates of the total number of striking workers range from 300,000 to a half a million. Many strikes succeeded, at least in part: some workers gained shorter hours (eight or nine) with no reduction in pay; others accepted pay cuts with the reduction in hours.

Two days later, May 3, 1886, there was a rally at the McCormick Harvesting Machine Company's Chicago plant in support of molders who had been locked out since early February. When workers confronted strike-breakers at the end of the workday, police fired into the crowd, killing six. Outraged by this act of police violence, local anarchists printed and distributed fliers calling for a rally the next day at Haymarket Square. The rally was peaceful during the speeches, but when police later ordered the crowd to disperse, a pipe bomb thrown at the police exploded, killing a policeman. The police opened fire and in the ensuing melee, eight policemen and at least four workers were killed. Eight people connected directly or indirectly with the rally were arrested and charged with murder. As a result of a highly sensationalized trial in 1887, seven of the accused were sentenced to death. The case was appealed all the way to the U.S. Supreme Court, where the petition was denied. Five of the seven were executed, though two had their sentences commuted to life in prison by Illinois Governor Richard James Oglesby.

The Haymarket Affair was a setback for American labor and its fight for an eight-hour day. It highlighted the ineffectiveness of the Federation of Organized Trades and Labor Unions and the Knights of Labor. As a result, delegates from both organizations met in Columbus, Ohio in December 1886 and established the American Federation of Labor, electing Samuel Gompers, president of the Cigarmakers International Union, as its first leader. Samuel Gompers had led the New York labor movement's push to end child labor in the cigar industry by sponsoring legislation that banned the tenements where thousands of young children worked in the trade. The initial membership of the AFL was estimated at about 140,000 workers, grouped in 25 national unions.

The AFL was a loose confederation of autonomous unions, each with exclusive rights to deal with workers and employers in its own field. It concerned itself primarily with organizing skilled workers. Instead of campaigning for sweeping reforms, as had been advocated by the Knights of Labor, the AFL pursued attainable goals like higher wages and shorter hours. At its first convention, it passed a resolution calling on states to ban children under 14 from employment. It renounced identification with any political party and urged its members to support candidates who were friendly to labor, regardless of party affiliation.

During the 1880s, there were nearly 10,000 strikes and lockouts. The first Labor Day celebration was held in New York City in 1882 and in 1884, the Federal Bureau of Labor was established as part of the Department of the Interior. In 1888, AFL president Samuel Gompers urged the International Workingmen's Association to endorse May 1, 1890 as the day that American workers should work no more than eight hours. The IWA endorsed this date at its second international meeting, in Paris in 1889, starting the international tradition of May Day. The first international May Day, on May 1, 1890, was a spectacular success.

By the end of the 1880s, an income of roughly $500 a year was necessary for an average-sized family of five in a mid-sized industrial town to live in comfort. In good times, about 45 percent of workers, like carpenters, molders, machinists, mule spinners (textiles), and coal miners earned that much. But about 40 percent of working-class families earned less. These families, crowded into one or two rooms in poor tenements, depended heavily on the earnings of their children.

Incomes ran from $800 to $1,100 yearly for the most prosperous workers (about 15 percent), which included iron rollers, locomotive engineers, pattern makers, and glass blowers. Some of these higher-paid workers were able to leave the smoky cities for the quiet suburbs, and their wives and children didn't have to work. Popular recreation in this era included cards, dominoes, baseball, horseshoes, and picnics. Textile towns abounded in reading rooms, gymnasiums, lodges, and debating clubs.

In 1892, 700 craftsmen of the Amalgamated Iron and Steel Workers Lodge were locked out of Andrew Carnegie's steelworks in Homestead, Pennsylvania. More than 3,000 non-union workers stood by them in a sympathy strike for six months. Four other Carnegie plants and several outside mills also stopped work in sympathy but in the end, strikebreakers were brought into the Homestead plant under protection of state militia and Pinkerton detectives and the union was forced to surrender.

Early in 1893, the bubble burst again. Dozens of railroads went bankrupt and more than 20 banks failed. Immigration fell off by more than one-third and tens of thousands of newcomers returned to their home countries. Unemployment passed 16 percent. Private charities provided bread, soup, and old clothing, but many unemployed workers were too proud to accept charity and wandered from town to town in search of work. The depression lasted until 1897.

The American Railway Union grew rapidly during this depression and strikers at the Pullman Palace Car Company near Chicago requested that the union boycott all Pullman cars, allowing none to move on American railroads. The ARU pledged support for this sympathy strike and began a nationwide action. The General Managers' Association of the railroads got a federal injunction against the strike based on the Sherman Antitrust Act of 1890, which made a combination in restraint of trade illegal. The strike stopped railroad traffic and federal troops were stationed at all vital junctions. Battles between troops and strikers broke out in 26 states, martial law was declared in Chicago, and the strike's leaders were imprisoned, putting an end to it. Thereafter, employers used injunctions with increased frequency and effectiveness as an antistrike weapon, and the power of sympathy strikes was defused.

The depression of the 1890s softened public attitudes toward organized labor. Between 1897 and 1904, union membership climbed from 447,000 to 2,072,700.In the same period, the number of craft unions affiliated with the American Federation of Labor rose from 58 to 120.

Congress passed the Erdman Act in 1898, signed into law by President William McKinley. This was an outgrowth of the American Railway Union's strike, after which general managers for the railroads used a blackball system to keep strikers from returning to work. This law provided for arbitration of disputes between interstate railroads and union workers. Its most significant provision was a prohibition on railroad companies demanding that workers not join a union as a condition for employment, though the law only applied to workers on moving trains, not those at stations and railroad yards. While arbitration was voluntary, if all sides agreed to it, the results were binding

After the formation of U.S. Steel Corporation in 1901, a convention of the Amalgamated Association of Iron and Steel Workers resolved to require all U.S. Steel subsidiaries to sign a union contract. When no agreement was reached, the union called a strike at three U.S. Steel subsidiaries. J. P. Morgan, Charles Schwab, and Elbert Gary, the heads of U.S. Steel, refused to recognize unions at their unorganized mills and replaced strikers at these plants. After three months, the strike was settled on terms disastrous to the union, according to which it lost 14 mills and could not seek to organize any more. After this defeat, the union steadily lost strength and influence.

At the annual AFL convention in 1903, blue-collar and middle-class women united to form the National Women's Trade Union League. Mary Morton Kehew was elected president and Jane Addams vice-president.

In 1903, "Mother Jones" (Mary Harris Jones) organized children working in mills and mines in the Children's Crusade, a march from Kensington, Pennsylvania to Oyster Bay, New York, home of President Teddy Roosevelt. They carried banners demanding "We want time to play!" and "We want to go to school!" Many of the children were victims of industrial accidents. Though the president refused to meet with the marchers, the incident brought the issue of child labor to the forefront of the public.

The National Child Labor Committee was formed in 1904 to abolish child labor. Years later, on January 25, 1909, President Roosevelt hosted the first White House Conference on Children, at the suggestion of a Washington lawyer named James West who had spent his childhood in institutions and was concerned about the state of children. The conferences were held every decade through the 1970s.

The eight-hour movement moved forward in 1906 when the International Typographical Union won a strike for an eight-hour day in the printing trades. Then, in 1908, in Muller v. Oregon, the Supreme Court ruled that female maximum-hour laws were constitutional, due to a woman's "physical structure and… maternal functions." The same year, in U.S. vs. Adair, the Supreme Court declared Section 10 of the Erdman Act unconstitutional. This act had legalized "yellow dog" contracts, which forbade an employee from organizing or joining a union. This ruling thus forbade a person being fired for belonging to a union.

In 1911, 146 workers, mostly young women, died in the Triangle Shirtwaist Company fire in New York City. This company was on the 8th floor of a building and its doors were bolted from the outside. When firemen got to the site, their ladders only went up to the 6th floor. Some women jumped to their deaths out of the windows, and the charred bodies of scores of women were found piled against the locked doors. This catastrophe led to establishment of the New York Factory Investigating Commission to monitor factory conditions.

The U.S. Department of Labor was established in 1913, and the Secretary of Labor was given powers to "act as a mediator and to appoint commissioners of conciliation in labor disputes."

The United Mine Workers of America had attempted to organize the Colorado coalfields since the early 1900s without success. The coal companies, led by the Rockefeller-owned Colorado Fuel and Iron Company, refused to deal with the union. In September 1913, miners voted to strike for an eight-hour day, wages of $3.45 a day, the right not to buy from the company store, and a union man to check the weight of the coal, as they felt the company was cheating them. The local sheriff commissioned several hundred deputies and the company sent its own guards, in a specially built armored car, to the tent camps established by the UMWA. Governor Elias Ammons also sent the National Guard to the strike area in Ludlow, Colorado.

On April 10, 1914, Lt. Linderfelt of the National Guard attacked the tent colony, spraying it with bullets and setting fire to the tents. Eleven children and two women died in the flames, and strike leader Louis Tikas and two others were killed. In the ensuing ten-day battle, 46 people died, most of them company guards. Eventually, President Woodrow Wilson sent in federal troops and the battle ended. In the subsequent court-martial, the troops were absolved and Lt. Linderfelt was given a light reprimand. In the end, the strike failed to achieve the objectives of the United Mine Workers. However, President Wilson did appoint the Colorado Coal Commission to investigate the Ludlow Massacre and labor conditions in the mines.

The First World War: 1914-1920

Mobilization for war brought thousands of women and blacks into industrial plants to replace the men who went off to war. Thousands of women and children of the lower working class had been working in the factories since the 1700s. But now women from the middle class went to work in industry and experienced the deplorable conditions that the working class had suffered. Also, many women from the upper class volunteered at hospitals, the Red Cross, and other charitable organizations and thus gained more exposure to the realities of working class life.

Before the United States entered the war in 1917, three key pieces of legislation were passed. The first was the 1914 Clayton Act, which limited the use of antitrust injunctions against unions in strikes. The second was the La Follette Seamen's Act of 1915, which regulated the working conditions of seamen. The third was the Adamson Act of 1916, which established an eight-hour day for railroad workers, averting a nationwide strike. A federal child-labor law was also enacted, but declared unconstitutional before it could take effect.

In 1917, President Wilson created a mediation commission, headed by the secretary of labor, to adjust wartime labor difficulties. The federal government took control of the railroads until early 1920 under legislation that allowed government operation during wartime.

On September 11, 1919, Boston policemen went on strike when a plan for adjusting their wages and working conditions failed. This was the first strike by public safety workers in American history. The absence of police was followed by 24 hours of rioting, looting, and violence. At the request of city authorities, Governor Calvin Coolidge sent 5,000 militiamen to keep order. Clashes between mobs and soldiers resulted in the death of eight civilians.

On September 22, 1919, the Amalgamated Association of Iron, Steel and Tin Workers called a strike against U.S. Steel, and 367,000 steelworkers responded. U.S. Steel refused to meet with union representatives and the strike ultimately failed after 20 people, 18 of them strikers, were killed.

After keeping their no-strike pledge during World War I, the United Mine Workers voted to strike on November 1, 1919. An estimated 425,000 to 450,000 coal miners nationwide went on strike, completely shutting down coal mining. President Wilson declared the strike unlawful and federal troops were ordered into the mining areas of several states. After arbitration with a presidential commission, the miners earned a 27 percent wage increase (they had demanded 60 percent), though they were denied the six-hour day and five-day workweek they had asked for. (As before, they were required to work eight hours a day, six days a week.)

The Roaring Twenties: 1921-1929

During the 1920s, the trade union movement declined. A major cause was the postwar depression of 1921-1922, when unemployment rose sharply. Competition for available jobs was so keen that unions in many industries were unable to prevent wage reductions and speedup methods, which forced workers to work faster.

Many employers vigorously opposed unionization. They made workers sign "yellow dog" contracts forbidding them from joining unions and encouraged them to join company-controlled employee associations instead. They developed paternalistic health and welfare plans and helped workers in other ways, like supporting low mortgage rates to enhance home ownership, subsidizing lunches, encouraging personal savings, and creating profit-sharing plans. Systems of grievance procedure, through which employee complaints could be considered, were established, but employers usually had the right to make the final decision. The growth of these associations seriously affected union membership, which declined from a high of 5.1 million in 1920 to 3.5 million in 1929. Membership in company-sponsored associations rose to about 1.5 million in the same period.[27]

In 1922, the United Mine Workers was held not responsible for a local strike action, and striking was held not to be a conspiracy to restrain trade under the Sherman Antitrust Act, in Coronado Coal Co. v. UMWA.

An amendment to the Constitution restricting child labor passed Congress in 1924, but not enough states ratified it for it to become law.

The Railway Labor Act of 1926 required employers to bargain collectively and not discriminate against employees who wanted to join a union. It also provided for mediation and voluntary arbitration in labor disputes. And in the event of a shutdown of rail service that might affect the public interest, it provided for the appointment of an emergency board of inquiry appointed by the President.

Coal miners faced an extended crisis in the 1920s as mine owners sought to reduce costs and pressured unionized miners to accept wage cutbacks and even abandon their union. In the summer of 1927, the United Mine Workers called a strike based on a policy of "no backward step" to protest downward wage adjustments demanded by mine owners.

In Colorado, the strike successfully shut down 113 of the state's 125 coal mines, but Rocky Mountain Fuel's president, Josephine Roche, settled with the UMWA after a massacre at their Columbine mine in which several miners were killed by machine guns wielded by mine guards. Compromises were reached with mine operators in Illinois and other areas, but more than 200,000 miners decided to resist in Ohio and western Pennsylvania. After a bitter struggle, in which some families were evicted from their homes, the union admitted defeat and the strike ended in July 1928.

The relative prosperity of the 1920s ended with the stock market crash in October 1929, beginning the longest depression in American history.

The Great Depression: 1929-1939

The Great Depression was devastating to the common workingman, but saw dramatic growth in the labor movement. The use of a sit-down strike strategy brought recognition of unions in several large industries, notably automobiles. Many of the labor movement's key battles were fought and decided in the courts.

Mass unemployment had a profound impact on American workers and their families. Immigration from abroad virtually stopped, and the long-term shift from farm to city slowed significantly. (In fact, there was some reverse migration because people living on farms or in rural areas could at least grow some of their own food.) People migrated from one part of the country to another as opportunity in their city, town, or region dried up. "In the middle of the decade when dust blew in the Great Plains, wiping out their farms, whole families of 'Okies,' 'Arkies,' and 'Mizoos' migrated west, especially to California...The destitute often lost their homes or farms because they were unable to make payments on mortgages."[2]

In an attempt to deal with nationwide epidemic unemployment, a Republican-controlled Congress passed the Davis-Bacon Act, which President Herbert Hoover signed on March 3, 1931. This established a requirement to pay prevailing wages on public works projects. All federal construction contracts, and most contracts for federally assisted construction over $2,000, were required to pay no less than locally prevailing wages and benefits.

After the election of Franklin D. Roosevelt in 1932, a Democrat-controlled Congress passed a body of pro-labor legislation. The first was the Norris-LaGuardia Act, which outlawed yellow-dog contracts and "deprived federal courts of jurisdiction to issue injunctions against peaceful striking, assembling, patrolling, or publicizing facts in connection with a labor dispute."[3]

While the federal government did not systematically collect statistics on unemployment until 1940, the Bureau of Labor Statistics later estimated that 12,830,000 persons had been unemployed in 1933 – about 25 percent of a civilian labor force of 51 million. To address this massive unemployment, Congress passed the Wagner-Peyser Act in 1933, creating the U.S. Employment Service within the Department of Labor to establish a national employment system in cooperation with the states. The Act provided federal matching funds for the operation of state employment offices, federal supervision of their operations, and employment services for veterans.

In the summer of 1933, the UMWA launched a massive drive in the Ohio, Illinois, West Virginia, western Pennsylvania, and southern Appalachian coal fields. Miners responded immediately and almost unanimously, and a new structure of bargaining, the so-called Appalachian Agreement, was signed on September 21, 1933. This applied only to "commercial" mines, but after a strike at the "captive" mines owned by the steel corporations, and some intervention by President Roosevelt, successful elections were also held at several captive mines.

While 1933 had seen dramatic growth of unions and many serious strikes, another great wave of strikes occurred across the country in 1934, in the form of citywide general strikes and factory takeovers. Violent confrontations occurred between workers trying to form unions and police and private security forces defending the interests of anti-union employers. There were no fewer than 1,856 work stoppages that year nationwide. One of the largest occurred in Minneapolis, where a citywide strike of truck drivers led to the recognition of the Teamsters in that city. A strike by dock-workers in San Francisco led to a coast-wide maritime shutdown, resulting in recognition of the Longshoremen's and Harbor Workers Union. The largest strike occurred during the fall, when 376,000 textile workers, in hundreds of mills across New England and the South, walked off the job. The Great Uprising of 1934 led to the first National Labor Legislation Conference, called by the secretary of labor to obtain closer federal-state cooperation in working out national labor legislation.

The strikes of 1934 also convinced Senator Robert Wagner (D-NY) that the nation needed a new labor policy. So he proposed the National Labor Relations Act (the Wagner Act), signed into law by FDR on July 5, 1935. The broad intention of the Act was to guarantee employees "the right to self-organization, to form, join, or assist labor organizations, to bargain collectively through representatives of their own choosing, and to engage in concerted activities for the purpose of collective bargaining or other mutual aid and protection." The Act created the National Labor Relations Board to arbitrate deadlocked labor-management disputes, guarantee democratic union elections, and penalize unfair labor practices by employers. Employers tied it up with injunction suits for almost two years, but on April 12, 1937, the Supreme Court upheld its constitutionality. It then afforded unprecedented opportunity to the American labor movement.

Congress passed several key pieces of legislation in 1936. The first was the Walsh-Healey Act (the Public Contracts Act), administered by the Department of Labor. For goods manufactured under government contracts worth at least $10,000, it required an eight-hour workday and a 40-hour week, with time-and-a-half pay for additional hours. It also prohibited employment of convicts and children under 18, authorized the secretary of labor to set minimum wages based on locally prevailing rates, and established sanitation and safety standards on all federal contracts. The second was the Byrnes Act of 1936 (the Anti-Strikebreaker Act), which made it a felony to transport any person in interstate commerce who was employed for the purpose of using force or threats thereof against non-violent picketing in a labor dispute, or against organizing or bargaining efforts.

The Committee for Industrial Organization (CIO) split off from the AFL in 1936, taking with it 10 affiliated unions. The Amalgamated Association of Iron, Steel and Tin Workers merged with the newly formed Steel Workers Organizing Committee and by the end of the year; workers from U.S. Steel left the company union to join the new union. A collective bargaining agreement was signed on March 2, 1937, followed by agreements at many smaller firms. Workers won a 10-percent wage increase, an eight-hour day, and a 40-hourweek. However, the so-called "Little Steel" companies – Bethlehem, Republic, Youngstown, National, and Inland – refused to negotiate, so the union was forced into a strike. There was much violence, and at Republic's South Chicago mill, police killed 10 people and wounded many others. The five-week strike was broken when Inland Steel employees went back to work without union recognition or other gains.

The same year, the United Auto Workers established a new strategy of sit-down strikes, which emerged as an effective organizing weapon. In Flint, Michigan, the UAW began a sit-down strike at General Motors. The largest manufacturing corporation in the world was forced to stop production. The strike continued for six weeks, and Michigan governor Frank Murphy called in the National Guard to keep the peace. Murphy moved to mediation involving union president John Lewis, GM's top officials, Secretary of Labor Frances Perkins, and President Roosevelt. On February 11, 1937, an agreement was reached and GM agreed to recognize the UAW as the bargaining agents for autoworkers and not to discriminate against union members.

This great victory by the UAW was followed by agreements at Hudson, Packard, Studebaker, Chrysler, and many auto parts manufacturers. Henry Ford was utterly opposed to collective bargaining and, after two UAW organizers were beaten unmercifully, the union deferred its campaign to unionize Ford.

After numerous concessions on standards and coverage, Congress passed the Fair Labor Standards Act (FLSA) in 1938. This Act covered a restricted number of industries engaged in interstate commerce and established a maximum of 44 hours per week (to be reduced to 40 hours within seven years), set a minimum wage of 25 cents per hour, and prohibited most child labor under 16 years. The FLSA has since been altered and amended on at least 43 subsequent occasions.

Nearly 700,000 workers were affected by the wage increase initially, and some 13 million more were ultimately affected by the maximum hours provision. Those affected by the Act were mostly white males (39 percent) compared with only 14 percent women. During the Depression, labor unions made efforts to exclude blacks and women from unionized Industrial jobs due to the scarcity of those jobs. Therefore, the FLSA did not affect the millions of blacks and women engaged in agricultural and domestic sectors.

The Second World War: 1939-1945

The outbreak of war in 1939 transformed the position of American labor. The mass unemployment of the 1930s melted away as the nation turned to arming and supplying Britain and the Soviet Union, in addition to building up its own military. By the time of Pearl Harbor, there were shortages of skilled labor, and the nation reached full employment in 1942. Women and blacks entered the work force in large numbers as white males went to war.

However, jobs at defense plants were still closed to blacks. A. Philip Randolph, president of the Brotherhood of Sleeping Car Porters, whose members were black, organized a demonstration for July 1, 1941. Through First Lady Eleanor Roosevelt and Mayor Fiorello H. LaGuardia of New York, President Roosevelt attempted to persuade Randolph to cancel the march, but Randolph refused. Invited to the White House, Randolph told Roosevelt that his price for calling off the demonstration was an executive order dealing with discrimination in defense plants. So, on June 25, 1941, the President issued Executive Order No. 8802, which barred discrimination in employment in defense industries and created the Committee of Fair Employment Practices to investigate complaints and correct valid grievances.

The Steel Workers Organizing Committee took advantage of the tight labor market and the need for steel to launch an organizing campaign against the "Little Steel" companies, selecting Bethlehem Steel as its prime target. This led to National Labor Relations Board (NLRB) elections at Bethlehem's mills in New York, Pennsylvania, and Maryland. The union won all plants by large majorities. These victories broke down opposition at Republic, Youngstown, and Inland and by November, the union had won elections at all four corporations.

Between 1937 and 1940, the United Auto Workers filed a series of unfair practice charges against the Ford Motor Company with the NLRB. The company won only one case, in which Henry Ford had stated: "Labor union organizations are the worst thing that ever struck the earth," a statement that was deemed free speech under the First Amendment. But the other cases were UAW victories. The UAW felt the time was right to organize Ford, and launched a major drive in the fall of 1940. On April 2, 1941, workers struck at Ford's River Rouge plant; Governor Van Wagoner of Michigan mediated a settlement in which they returned to work in return for Ford's consent to NLRB elections. The results shocked Ford: only 2.6 percent voted for no union. To avoid NLRB hearings on Ford's violence against the UAW, Ford recognized the union and signed a union-shop agreement, the first in the auto industry.

After the United States entered World War II, the AFL and CIO announced a no-strike pledge for the duration of the war.

But this didn't mean disputes between labor and management disappeared. On January 12, 1942, President Roosevelt issued an executive order creating a National War Labor Board with 12 members, four each from labor, industry, and the public. The NWLB then established a procedure for wartime wage adjustments.

During the war, two unions did not honor the no-strike pledge of the AFL and CIO: the UMWA and the Railway Workers. In the spring of 1943, the Mine Workers demanded an increase of two dollars a day and compensation for travel time between the mine entrance and the coal face. The UMWA's president refused to appear at a War Labor Board hearing, and the miners began to strike. President Roosevelt seized the mines and named Interior Secretary Harold Ickes as administrator. When no agreement was reached at the NWLB, the miners resumed their strike. There was a great public outcry against the UMW, and Congress was moved to pass the punitive Smith-Connally War Labor Disputes bill, which restricted the right to strike and authorized plant seizures, if needed to avoid interference with the war effort. The President seized the mines again and said he would ask Congress for authority to draft the striking miners into the Army. Finally, an agreement was reached, in which the miners won an increase of a dollar and a half a day, and they returned to work in November 1943.

Similarly, the Railway Workers of America called a strike on December 30, 1943, but President Roosevelt directed the Army to take over the railroads, ending it.

By 1943, tight labor markets had forced defense plants to shift from a 40 to a 48-hour week, with time-and-a-half pay for more than 40 hours, as required by the Fair Labor

Standards Act. Wartime tight labor markets significantly improved the economic status of two groups that had suffered historic discrimination: women and blacks. The number of females employed soared as "men's" jobs opened up, particularly in the blue-collar categories. And the NWLB's policy of equal pay for equal work eliminated wage differentials based on sex.

The sharp increase in employment during the war caused a dramatic growth in union membership. By the end of the war, the trade union movement was big and had established firm collective-bargaining bases in most important industries. When the war ended in August 1945, there were 18,600,000 union workers in the United States, 3,500,000 of who were women.

Post-war America: 1946-Present

In 1946, the largest strike wave in American history occurred as pent-up labor grievances were unleashed. Four and one-half million workers went on strike in the railroad, maritime, coal, oil, auto, electrical, telephone, meat-packing, and steel industries. Unions sought to make up cuts in take-home pay caused by unemployment, reduced overtime, price increases, and increased productivity.

The first, largest, and longest postwar strike, from November 1945 to March 1946, was by the UAW against General Motors. The union won a contract providing for automatic wage increases linked to rises in the cost of living.

These strikes were generally successful, leading conservative legislators to denounce the growing power of labor. One response was restrictive legislation like the Lea

Act, which prohibited musician "featherbedding" (requiring employers to hire more workers than necessary) in radio stations and the 1946 Hobbs Anti-Racketeering Act, which prescribed heavy criminal penalties for robbery or extortion that affected interstate commerce.

In 1947, a Republican Congress enacted, over President Truman's veto, the Labor-Management Relations Act, also known as Taft-Hartley. This contained a number of provisions designed to curb the power of organized labor. It amended the National Labor Relations Act (the Wagner Act) and restricted certain union activities, like wildcat strikes, solidarity or political strikes, secondary boycotts, closed shops, and union donations to federal political campaigns. Union shops were heavily restricted and states were permitted to pass "right-to-work" laws that outlawed union shops. In addition, the President could obtain a strikebreaking injunction if an impending or current strike "imperiled the national health or safety," a test that has been interpreted broadly by the courts.

For several years prior to 1948, most affiliated unions of the Congress of Industrial Organizations (CIO) were critical of the pro-Communist policies of some of the other affiliates. When the CIO affiliated with the newly created World Federation of Trade Unions in 1945, the AFL did not join because it felt the labor organizations of the Soviet Union were not "free and democratic." At the CIO convention of 1948, an overwhelming majority voted to support the domestic program of President Truman and those aspects of his foreign policy designed to contain Communism. A minority accused the Truman foreign policy of being a cover for U.S. imperialism and announced their support for presidential candidate Henry Wallace of the Progressive Party.

The CIO's anti-Communist drive led to the expulsion of the United Electrical, Radio, and Machine Workers, with 450,000 workers, at its annual convention in 1949. In subsequent months, the CIO expelled another 10 other unions after long hearings. In some cases, it chartered new organizations, notably the International Union of Electrical Workers, to absorb workers who resigned from the Communist-leaning unions. Free, democratic trade unions from various countries withdrew from the World Federation of Trade Unions, which came to be dominated by Communists. Instead, labor representatives of 51 countries formed the International Confederation of Free Trade Unions in London.

A new wave of strikes developed in the steel, coal mining, and railroad industries in 1949 and 1950, but every effort was made to reach an agreement before the strikes crippled the American economy and hampered the national effort in the Korean War, which began in June 1950.

In 1952, the number of work stoppages due to strikes was greater than in every other postwar year except 1946. The most serious strike was one called by the United Steelworkers in the winter of 1951-1952. The union agreed to postpone the strike until the Wage Stabilization Board made its recommendations, but the steel companies rejected these. A strike was called for April 8, but to forestall it, President Truman instructed the secretary of commerce to take possession of the steel companies. The companies then went to the courts seeking an injunction against this. The case went all the way to the Supreme Court, which ruled that the President's action was unconstitutional. An eight-week strike followed, until the plants were returned to their private owners on June 2. A new contract was finally signed on July 24.

In 1955, George Meany became president of the AFL following the death of William Green. Walter Reuther, a former UAW president, became president of the CIO following the death of Philip Murray. This change of leadership paved the way for a merger of the two organizations in December 1955, healing a 20-year breach in the American labor movement. The head of the AFL, George Meany, became the first president of the new organization. This brought together about 85 percent of all union members.

The AFL-CIO's main challenge was eliminating racketeers, individuals who participated in illegal business practices. In January 1956, the AFL-CIO's Executive Committee adopted three ethical practices codes intended to rid the labor movement of racketeers and unethical union leaders. In January 1957, the AFL-CIO expelled the Bakery Workers, Laundry Workers, and Teamsters for corruption after the U.S. Senate's Select Committee on Labor and Management Practices found evidence of widespread wrong-doing. The revelations of the Senate committee intensified public hostility toward organized labor and created additional support for state right-to-work laws and federal legislation subjecting union finances to public audit.

Organized labor won a significant victory in the elections of November 1958, when right-to-work laws, or proposals to amend state constitutions to permit them, were defeated in a number of states, including California, Colorado, Ohio, and Washington. In 1959, the Labor-Management Reporting and Disclosure Act (the Landrum-Griffin Act), which regulates the internal affairs of unions to prevent corruption, passed Congress. This Act guarantees the right of union members to union meetings, free speech, assembly, and to vote by secret ballot for union officers at periodic elections. It also requires labor and management organizations and labor consultants to file detailed reports of their financial dealings.

In 1962, federal employee unions won the right to bargain collectively with government agencies as a result of President Kennedy's executive order. This triggered an eruption of public-employee unionism that has continued to the present. The decade-long economic expansion from 1960 to 1970 gave governments the revenues with which to meet their demands for increased salaries and permitted the unions to demonstrate the value of collective bargaining to their members.

Legislation related to workers' rights during the 1960s was mainly directed at eliminating various forms of discrimination. In 1963, the Equal Pay Act prohibited wage differences for workers based on gender. In 1964, the Civil Rights Act prohibited discrimination in employment based on race, color, religion, sex, or national origin. In 1968, the Age Discrimination in Employment Act made it illegal to discriminate in hiring or firing persons between 40 and 65 on the basis of age.

In 1973, the major steel companies and the United Steelworkers approved an Experimental Negotiation Agreement in which the union gave up the right to strike in favor of binding arbitration. The companies, in return, agreed to end stockpiling of their products.

In 1975, 80,000 members of the American Federation of State, County and Municipal Employees (AFSCME) went on strike in the first legal, large-scale strike of public employees.

In 1981, President Reagan fired most of the nation's air traffic controllers, and then decertified their union, in response to an illegal strike. This was a defining moment for the labor movement, as subsequent decisions by the National Labor Relations Board created more obstacles for unions attempting to organize non-union workers.

In the 1990s, a trend developed for the merger of unions in related occupations. Unions with no apparent connection merged to form larger associations. This mirrored the trend of business consolidations to achieve economies of resources.

Membership in American unions has been steadily declining since the late 1940s. At the peak in 1945, almost 36 percent of American workers were represented by unions, but by the end of 2009, the figure was around 12 percent. And the growth of public-employee unions since the 1960s has masked the even more dramatic decline in private sector union membership: private sector union membership has plummeted to around seven percent, while public sector union membership has grown to 36 percent.

Conclusion

As the 20th century ended, the American workforce was much better off than it had been at the beginning. Wages had risen, fringe benefits had grown, and working conditions had improved. As a whole, U.S. per capita income (in 1999 dollars) was $4,200 in 1900 and $33,700 in 1999[3]

The size of the U.S. workforce increased roughly six-fold during this period: it was estimated at 24 million in 1900, counting those aged 10 and above; in 1999, it was 139 million aged 16 and older.

The composition of the labor force shifted from industries dominated by primary production to those dominated by professional, technical, and service workers. Employment in goods-producing industries decreased from 31 percent in 1900 to 19 percent in 1999.

Women composed only 19 percent of the workforce in 1900, but 60 percent in 1999.

Child labor was common at the turn of the century and many families needed the income to survive. The 1900 census counted 1.75 million children aged 10 to 15 who were employed, and children composed six percent of the labor force. There were no national laws governing child labor. But America today heavily restricts child labor, prohibiting it outright in many occupations, especially outside agriculture.

Since Independence, our economy has experienced more than 30 recessions (called panics in the 1800s) and one Great Depression. During recessions, workers have often had to give up the gains they made in good times. Parts of the U.S. economy began experiencing another recession in late 2007, which soon spread to almost every other sector. After the collapse of the financial sector in the fall of 2008, some economists feared the recession would turn into a depression comparable to the Great Depression of the 1930s, though this did not happen.

It took 150 years of struggle, and the deaths of many workers, for unions to bring about the working conditions Americans today take for granted. It is important for Americans to remember that unions can be credited with the end of child labor, improved worker safety, increased wages for both union *and* non-union workers, reduction in the work day from more than 10 hours to eight, and the raising of our entire society's standard of living. In essence, unions raised the lower class of workers up into the middle class.

People don't realize that we would have to roll back to the wage levels of 1938 (25 cents an hour!), and give up everything we take for granted, in order to compete with the wages of our current global competitors China and India and others that may develop in the future.

The American people have a choice to make. We can accept the continuing destruction of America's industrial base and allow the gains achieved by America's past workers to be wiped out. Or we can choose to secure a future for American industry and American workers.

3

What Is Happening To
Manufacturing in the United States?

For nearly 70 years, American manufacturing dominated the globe. It was responsible for turning the tide for the Allies in World War II and defeating Nazi Germany and Japan. It then helped rebuild Germany and Japan after the war, and enabled the United States to win the Cold War against the Soviet Empire, while simultaneously meeting the material needs of the American people.

The United States was the world's largest producer of manufactured goods and led the world in innovation. American companies like General Motors, Ford, Boeing, Maytag, IBM, and Levi Strauss were household names worldwide. American manufacturing was synonymous with quality and ingenuity.

Fast-forward to the present. GM was rescued from bankruptcy in 2009, Maytag was bought by Whirlpool, IBM sold its personal computer division to the Chinese company Lenovo, and Levi jeans are now made in China like every other brand. America runs huge trade deficits in both manufactured goods and high technology.

Manufacturing is the foundation of the American economy and has been responsible for the rise of our middle class over the last 200 years. High-paying manufacturing jobs helped spur a robust and growing economy that had little dependence on foreign nations. American families, and entire communities, depend on our strong manufacturing base for their standard of living.

In the 1960s, about 25 percent of American workers were in manufacturing, but this number has decreased every year since 1990, plummeting by almost a fifth since 1996.[1] In 1953, manufacturing accounted for 28.3 percent of U.S. GDP. It dropped to 20 percent by 1980, and by 2009 it had dropped to only 11.2 percent, before climbing back up to 11.7 percent in 2010, the latest period for which data is available. Our trade deficit in goods has worsened steadily since 1979, growing from $25.5 billion in 1980 to $737.1 billion in 2011 (down from a record high of $835.7 billion in 2006).

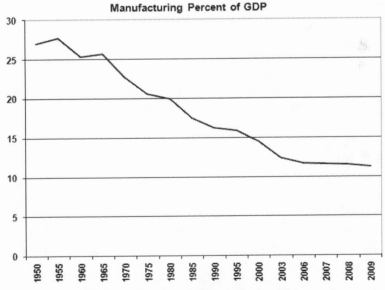

Manufacturing Percent of GDP

Source: Bureau of Economic Analysis

Recent manufacturing job loss has hit the South, rural areas, and minorities the hardest. In 2004, William Julius Wilson of Harvard's Kennedy School of Government stated that since "2001, over 300,000 black males have lost jobs in the manufacturing sector – the highest rate of any ethnic group."[2] The heaviest job losses for Hispanics are concentrated in manufacturing and retail trade, which together account for 40 percent of all Hispanic unemployment; according to one July 2006 report.[3]

There has been some controversy about whether recent data is accurate because of a 2002 change in the way industry classifications are reckoned. Before 2002, The Department of Labor used the Standard Industrial Classification (SIC) system to classify industries. The new system, the North American Industry Classification System (NAICS), was supposed to provide a more accurate assessment. However, under NAICS, manufacturing includes fewer subcategories. Research and development firms, like San Diego's cell phone systems maker QUALCOMM, and book publishers are no longer classified as manufacturers. Using the new system, manufacturing's share of the San Diego Gross Regional Product went from 23.7 percent in 2003 to just below 15 percent in 2004.[4] But local economists don't believe manufacturing went down by eight percent in one year, so the statistics may be misleading.

From 1999 to 2009, more than 57,000 U.S. manufacturing facilities closed. And the U.S. lost 5.5 million manufacturing jobs between 2000 and 2011, going from more than 17 million jobs to less than 12 million. According to the Bureau of Labor Statistics, the number of people employed in manufacturing fluctuated between 17 and 19 million during the 30-year period from 1969 to 1999. But manufacturing employment dropped to less than 12 million by the end of 2009 – the lowest since 1950 – and hasn't recovered since. A recent study by the Economic Policy Institute showed that at least 58 percent, and possibly up to 88 percent, of manufacturing workers in selected states who lost their jobs between 2000 and 2004 did so because of international trade and our trade deficit.[5]

So after dominating the globe for decades as the largest, most productive, and most technologically advanced in the world, America's manufacturing sector is in decline in nearly all industries. Our lead in a number of industries vanished years ago, and nearly all industries are facing potentially dangerous erosion.

No single indicator perfectly encapsulates all manufacturing capabilities and trends. But several key indicators, taken together, provide strong evidence that American manufacturing has greatly weakened in the last decade: share of GDP, capacity, employment, the number of manufacturers, our balance of trade in goods, and our import penetration rate.

The recession of 2001 to 2004 hit U.S. manufacturers and their workers the hardest. While the overall U.S. economy expanded strongly in 2005 and 2006, much of the manufacturing sector continued to operate well below its previous peak. So few jobs were created in the recovery that some economists called it a "jobless recovery." And when the economy slowed again at the beginning of 2007, manufacturers felt even greater pain.

Source: St. Louis Federal Reserve Bank

The collapse of the U.S. housing market that triggered a meltdown in the banking and financial industry in fall of 2008 worsened the woes of manufacturers. Hardly a day went by without announcements in newspapers and online news sources about one manufacturer after another going out of business, closing plants, or reporting financial losses. It would take pages to name just the best known of the many companies that went out of business or closed plants in 2008.

The manufacturing recession intensified in the last half of 2008, according to Daniel J. Meckstroth, Chief Economist of the Manufacturers Alliance for Productivity and Innovation. Manufacturing production declined at a 7.8 percent annual rate in the third quarter of 2008.Meckstroth said, "The vicious circle of financial crisis, decline in wealth, consumer spending cuts, and job loss continues to spiral into a severe recession – certainly the worst since the early 1980s...The 2008-2009 recession will go down in the economic cycle record books as one of the most severe, in terms of job loss, in the post-World War II period."

The next year, in 2009, manufacturing firms reported 504 layoff events, involving the separation of 83,691 workers. Manufacturers were responsible for 25 percent of all private nonfarm extended layoff events, and 26 percent of related separations, in the fourth quarter of 2009. The largest number of separations in manufacturing was associated with transportation equipment (mostly automobile manufacturing) and food (mostly fruit and vegetable canning).

In 2009, manufacturing job losses hit 1,200,099, the worst year since the Great Depression. The U-6 unemployment rate, which counts part-time workers who want full-time jobs and those who have stopped looking for work, reached 17.2 percent by October 2009. The official (U-3) unemployment rate rose to a high of 10.0 percent the same month and stayed above 9 percent for the 16 months before dropping to 8.9 percent for one month, staying above 9 percent for another six months, and then finally leveling off at 8.9 percent and below in October 2011.

What about capacity and import penetration? These are tied together because the capacity of American companies is impacted by import penetration of U.S. markets for their products. There was an across-the-board increase in the import penetration rate for 114 high-tech and capital-intensive manufacturing sectors – from 21.4 percent of domestic consumption to 34.3 percent – between 1997 and 2007. Let's take a look at some specific industries.

For example, if you went to buy a set of drinking glasses, you'd have trouble finding a set made in the U.S. That's because one of America's oldest industries, glassware, is down to two companies: Libbey Glass of Toledo, Ohio, and

Anchor Hocking of Lancaster, Ohio. By 2009, every major domestic competitor was either out of business, in Chapter 11, or up for sale. The U.S. glass industry has been swamped by imports: in 1996, imports from China and Turkey accounted for 12 percent of the U.S. market, but by 2006, imports were up to 53 percent of the U.S. market.[6] Libbey Glass CEO John Meier blamed unfair trade and the fact that the U.S. government is allowing foreign governments "to get away with subsidizing their producers and not enforcing their laws."

According to the U.S. International Trade Commission, another U.S. industry has virtually disappeared – the manufacture of travel goods out of textiles. In 2006, the total U.S. market for travel goods with an outer surface of textile materials was estimated at approximately $3 billion wholesale. The nine remaining U.S. firms identified by the USITC reported totaled revenues of $37 million in 2006. So U.S. producers commanded only a one percent share of the U.S. market! These nine companies said that at least 70 percent of their business goes to the U.S. military and government, markets that represents less than five percent of domestic consumption. China has become the preferred source for offshore production since the removal of import quotas on textile travel goods in 2002 because of its low-cost labor, fabric, and accessories; in 2006, it accounted for 80 to 90 percent of imports.

The USITC also reports that the U.S. has completely lost the ability to make high-tech warm and water-resistant clothing, often called performance outerwear, for the commercial market. Skiers, hikers, mountain climbers, bikers, firemen, policemen, military personnel, and those in hazardous environments wear these garments. The USITC identified 13 companies making high-tech jackets and pants, but six said they produce strictly for government and military use. Only two said they produce for the commercial market. Conflicting estimates of the U.S. share of the commercial market range from 1.3 percent to less than five percent. The USITC notes that most companies in this industry have moved production offshore, primarily to Asia, namely China and Vietnam, where the technology, such as seam sealing and laser cutting, used to produce such garments is prevalent.

The decline is even more serious in manufacturing industries that supply products, components, and technologies the Pentagon considers important to defense. University of Texas at Austin engineering professor Michael Webber has evaluated the economic health of 16 industrial sectors within the defense industrial system. Of the 16 industries he examined, 13 showed significant signs of erosion, especially since 2001.[7]

The American machine tool industry, for example, is facing intense competition from foreign competitors, especially China. (Machine tools are used to cut and form metal and are used in nearly all manufacturing involving metals, from autos to airplanes.) Foreign penetration of the U.S. market rose from about 30 percent in 1982 to 72 percent in 2008. The U.S. fell from the world's third largest machine tool producer in 2000 to seventh in 2008, behind Japan, Germany, China, Italy, Taiwan, and Korea.

The U.S. loss of competitiveness in the manufacturing of five-axis machine tools exemplifies the erosion of this industry. Five-axis machine tools are technologically advanced and used in the production of components in the aerospace, gas and diesel engine, automobile part, medical, and heavy industrial equipment industries. Only six U.S. companies capable of making five-axis machines remain compared to at least 20 in China and 22 in Taiwan.

The importance of semiconductors to today's military is well understood, and preserving a world-class domestic semiconductor industry is vital to our national security. However, this industry lost nearly 1,200 plants of all sizes between 1998 and 2000, a 17 percent drop. The U.S. share of global semiconductor capacity fell to 17 percent in 2007 and 14 percent in 2009. Of the 16 semiconductor fabs under construction around the world in 2009, only one was being built in the United States. The U.S. led the world in closure of fab plants between 2008 to 2009 – 19 out of 42.[8] These losses have been driven by the migration of microelectronic manufacturing to low-cost foreign locations like Taiwan, Singapore, China, and Korea.

These are just a few examples of the erosion of U.S. industries. Hardly a day that goes by without news of some company closing a plant, having a mass layoff, or going completely out of business.

Free Trade or Unfair Trade?

Some believe the crisis of American manufacturing is mainly caused by our massive trade imbalance.

Since the U.S. joined the World Trade Organization in 1995, our trade deficit in goods has exploded. It set records for six straight years (2002-2007). It dropped to $374.9 billion in 2009 due to the worldwide recession, and our China deficit dropped to $226.8 billion.[9] But the overall deficit popped back up to $558 billion in 2011, and the deficit with China reached $295.5 billion.[10] Of particular concern is that the U.S. had a record $94.2 billion trade deficit in Advanced Technology

Products (ATP) with China in 2010, an increase of 45.5 percent in only three years. By contrast, the U.S. in 2010 had a $13.3 billion *surplus* in ATP with the rest of the world.

In 2006, billionaire investor Warren Buffet warned that the U.S. trade deficit was a bigger threat to the domestic economy than either consumer debt or the federal budget deficit. "In my view it will create political turmoil at some point," he said. "Pretty soon, I think there will be a big adjustment." He also pointed out that 15 years ago, the U.S. had no trade deficit with China, but by 2006, it was over $200 billion.[11]

Even though the United States has the largest trade deficit of any country in the history of the world, the World Trade Organization has ruled against us in 40 out of 47 cases. Some of the cases lost by the U.S. required major changes of U.S. laws and administrative rules. Robert Lighthizer, a partner specializing in international trade at the elite law firm Skadden Arps, has stated, "Rogue WTO panel and Appellate Body decisions have consistently exceeded their mandate by inventing new legal obligations that were never agreed to by the United States."[12]

In an article entitled "The Death of Manufacturing," conservative commentator Pat Buchanan wrote, "Free trade is a bright shining lie. Free trade is the Trojan Horse of world government. Free trade is the murderer of manufacturing and the primrose path to the loss of national sovereignty and the end of our independence." He also wrote that "The U.S.-China relationship cannot truly be described as trade. It is rather the looting of America by China and its corporate collaborators in the United States."[13]

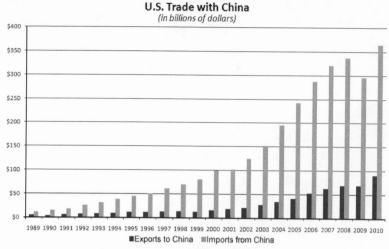

Source: Bureau of Economic Analysis

Trade Problems Ripple Through Our Economy

It is sometimes hard to understand why some companies are experiencing a slowdown without probing further. For example, one company I know in San Diego makes equipment used in dental labs, and their business has been slow since the summer of 2007. The company's best guess is that when money gets tight in other sectors of the economy, people put off getting dental work done, which slows down work at dental labs, which, in turn, delays those labs in buying new equipment.

The off-road vehicle industry has also experienced a slowdown, which started in early 2007. The reasons behind this are a bit more complicated. Inquiries reveal that a majority of people who purchase off-road vehicles like dune buggies, quad wheelers, and dirt bikes work in the building and housing industry. With the housing market in a slump, fewer homes, condos, and apartments are built. People working in supporting industries put off buying off-road vehicles or keep the vehicles they already have. Over the past 15 years, the industry has changed from low-cost home kit models to expensive custom-built vehicles made by companies specializing in the field. Today, the price of new custom-built off-road vehicles ranges from $50,000 to $70,000. Many people took advantage of their increased equity as home values doubled or tripled over the past decade by using a portion of their equity from home equity loans to purchase off-road vehicles. Some of these loans were subprime loans and now the owners are in financial trouble. Often the first things to go is the "toy," so used off-road vehicles have flooded the market. This, in turn, hurts the market for new vehicles.

Another company I know in San Diego makes specialized equipment to cut metal tubing and metal sheet stock to specific lengths after it has been formed. The equipment's controllers can be programmed to make up to 100 cuts of different lengths while the tubing or sheet stock is fed continuously through the machine. In 2006, 30 of the company's customers went bankrupt due to intense competition from China, which, in turn, significantly impacted their sales of equipment. The bulk of their business in 2009 and 2010 was selling electronic controllers to upgrade old cutting machines.

The intense foreign competition American machine tool companies are facing was highlighted recently in an article, "That Blur in the Rearview Mirror is China," in *American Machinist*. The author, Dr. Paul Freedenberg, writes that "the U.S. machine tool industry has lost 38.8 percent of its market share to China over the last decade." He adds that, "The United States currently has 175 manufacturers of metal-cutting machinery. By contrast, China has two-and-one-half times that number, with 415 metal-cutting machine tool builders."[14]

The air conditioning industry is facing the same challenge. The September 28, 2008 issue of *Manufacturing & Technology News* reported that "The last U.S. manufacturer of air conditioning window units is moving its production to Mexico. Friedrich Air Conditioning Company has announced its intention to close its San Antonio manufacturing plant and move the work to Monterrey, Mexico...The company says that low-priced air conditioners from China are forcing it to move out of the United States." This was only two months after Lennox International announced that it would shift production of its air conditioners from two U.S. plants (Marshalltown, Iowa and Grenada, Mississippi) to a new plant in Saltillo, Mexico. Lennox CEO Todd Bluedorn said, "We must produce quality products at lower costs to compete and grow our business."[15]

The U.S. textile industry is in a similar situation. For example, in July 2007 Springs Global, a producer of bed fabrics and sheets, announced that it was closing two major manufacturing plants in South Carolina and would lay off 750 employees. CEO Crandall Bowles said, "This marks the end of 120 years during which Springs has manufactured bedding in South Carolina. The closing of these plants reflects the global nature of the textile industry, which has made U.S. textile manufacturing uncompetitive."

The stories above are just a few examples of the thousands of stories that could have been included in this chapter.

Chinese Dumping

"Dumping," as this word is used in the context of trade law, is defined as a manufacturer in one country exporting a product at a price below either its cost of production or the price it charges in its home market. While dumping is not prohibited outright by the World Trade Organization, Article VI of GATT allows countries to act against it where there is "material" injury to their domestic industry. They are thus allowed to act in a way that would normally break the basic GATT principles of binding tariffs (committing to keep them below a certain rate) and not discriminating between trading partners. Typically, antidumping actions involve charging an import duty on a product to bring its price up to the "normal" value.

There are many different ways to calculate whether a particular product is being dumped, and a detailed investigation has to be conducted according to specific rules. In the U.S., the U.S. International Trade Commission (USITC) conducts these investigations when a company or industry makes a dumping petition. If the domestic industry is able to establish that dumping is injuring it, then antidumping duties are imposed.

Provisions of China's WTO accession agreement of 2002 offer U.S. industries the possibility of imposing temporary trade barriers, called "safeguards," against a surge of imports. This agreement made available two safeguard provisions: the product-specific safeguard, which expires in 2013, and the China Textile Safeguard, which expired in 2008. The USITC makes recommendations to the President on these safeguard requests.

In the last five cases, the USITC has recommended against import relief in two cases, and the President decided against imposing safeguards in the others: ductile iron waterworks fittings, steel wire garment hangers, and pedestal actuators. The number of U.S. dumping cases against imports from China is up, and more than 50 categories of goods from China are now subject to antidumping duties. These products include steel fence posts, iron pipe fittings, hand trucks, ironing tables, wooden bedroom furniture, crepe paper, plastic shopping bags, shrimp, and saccharin.

Despite the USITC slapping antidumping duties on steel pipes used in plumbing and heating systems in 2007, steel companies are still pressing for legislation to make it easier to win import relief against China. Since 2000, Chinese steel production has grown 289 percent, Chinese steel exports have grown 1,276 percent, and the Chinese government's energy subsidies to its steel industry have grown 1,365 percent. In addition to energy subsidies, there have been thermal coal subsidies, coking coal subsidies to Chinese steel mills, and favorable power rates and water distribution rates.[16]

Stricter Environmental Regulations

Do you remember playing a game when you were a child where you tried your best not to walk on any cracks in the sidewalk? Well, businesses are forced to play a similar game with the government today, and the "cracks" are getting so close together that it's almost impossible to tip-toe through the maze of "cracks" that come in the form of taxes and regulations. One of the most troubling indicators is the increasingly tough environmental regulations imposed at the federal and state levels on various sectors of manufacturing. The following describes three of the tougher environmental regulations:

Clean Water: As authorized by the Clean Water Act of 1972, the Environmental Protection Agency oversees the National Pollutant Discharge Elimination System (NPDES) Regulations for Storm Water Discharges. In most cases, NPDES is administered by the states. In turn, many states have set up regional water-quality control boards to develop and administer regulations. The San Diego regional board, for example, issued 62 pages of new regulations in August 2002. These have proven onerous and expensive for manufacturers. For example, rain water falling on a parking lot surrounding a manufacturing plant must be monitored so that toxic pollutants, oil, grease, waxes, chemicals, and visible floating materials are prevented from entering storm drains connecting to the local sewer system.

Hazardous Air Pollutants: In 2005, the Occupational Safety and Health Administration (OSHA) proposed new emission standards, to go in effect January 1, 2006. However, Congress didn't approve them as stringently as written. The proposed standards would have drastically reduced, for example, allowed emissions of hexavalent chromium (used in chrome plating and a known carcinogen) from 52 mg. of per cubic meter of air down to 1 mg. (The standard of 52 mg. that went into effect in 1998 in California to comply with Federal OSHA requirements was already a 97 percent reduction from the previous standard.) In May 2006, Congress finally approved slightly less stringent regulations, which went in effect in January 2007. The new standard set the time-weighted average for the amount of chromium that a worker could be exposed to during an eight-hour period at 5 mg.

Metal plating, including chrome plating, provides significant support to electronic, machine equipment, defense, and automotive aftermarket manufacturing. The new standards have forced existing chrome plating facilities to purchase new environmental control equipment in order to maintain compliance. Because the new standards affect chrome plating nationwide, they seriously affect all sectors of domestic manufacturing and will accelerate the offshoring of products requiring chrome plating.

In San Diego County, six metal processors have already gone out of business in the past two years, and a remaining one closed down its plating line in anticipation of the stricter regulations. There are now only two metal processors that do chrome plating in all of San Diego County, which is stretching lead times for locally machined and fabricated parts that require chrome plating.

Air Quality: Particulate matter is fine particles, such as soot, dust, and liquid droplets, which are too small to see. Exposure to particle pollution is linked to a variety of significant health problems. This pollution is also the main cause of visibility impairment in the nation's cities and national parks. In September 2006, the EPA approved new air quality standards that reduced the previous standard by nearly 50 percent, from 65 micrograms of particles per cubic meter of air to 35. (The EPA retained the current standard for long-term exposure at

15 micrograms.) Electric utilities and manufacturers objected to the new regulations, saying that they would cost billions of dollars. Dan Reidinger of the Edison Electric Institute said, "The industry will spend more than $50 billion to cut emissions." The National Association of Manufacturers cautioned that these new regulations could levy significant burdens on U.S. manufacturers, creating new international competition.[17]

A 2001 study by the Regulatory Studies Program at George Mason University's Mercatus Center, "A Review and Synthesis of the Cost of Workplace Regulations," found that these regulations impose a significant cost. The researchers surveyed 100 manufacturers in the United States, ranging from seven employees to 65,400 employees. The survey reported that,

> Complying with workplace regulations cost an average of $2.2 million per manufacturing firm, or about $1,700 per employee. Smaller firms (fewer than 100 employees) faced higher costs than large firms (500 or more) with costs of $2,573 per employee and $1,530 per employee respectively.

The survey revealed which types of regulations affect manufacturers the most. Worker health and safety regulations, including OSHA rules, accounted for one-third the cost of compliance. Regulations governing employee benefits ranked second, making up 27 percent. Civil rights, labor standards, and labor-management relations regulations each made up about 10 percent. If these amounts were extrapolated to all manufacturing firms in the U.S., the total cost would be about $32 billion.

A 2005 study, "The Impact of Regulatory Costs on Small Firms," by Prof. W. Mark Crain of Lafayette College for the Small Business Administration's Office of Advocacy showed that small businesses continue to bear a disproportionate share of the regulatory burden. The cost of compliance with federal regulations was an average of $5,633 per employee for all sizes of firms. However, for companies under 20 employees, the cost was $7,647, compared to $5,282 for companies with more than 500 employees. In the manufacturing sector, the cost per employee for all sizes of firms was $10,175, nearly double the average for all firms. But for small manufacturers, the cost was $21,919, compared to $8,748 for large firms. For medium-sized firms, the compliance cost per employee was $10,042. In the service sector, interestingly, regulatory costs differed little between small and larger firms.

A survey by the National Association for the Self-Employed found that the self-employed and micro-businesses (under 10 employees) are "expecting this new regulatory burden to greatly or somewhat increase the amount they spend on tax preparation." With more than 40 percent of survey respondents preparing their own taxes, this added workload will significantly increase the time business owners spend on tax preparation or force them to hire an outside accountant, adding to their costs. This is an example of how the indirect costs of complying with government rules and regulations are as burdensome as the direct costs of taxes and regulatory fees.[18]

Manufacturing firms in this country also pay more taxes, on average, than firms in other sectors. While manufacturers pay an average of 26 percent, financial services firms pay only 20 percent, real estate firms 19 percent, and mining firms a mere 6 percent, according to a recent study by Prof. Douglas Shackleford of the University of North Carolina.

A recent National Association of Manufacturers study showed that U.S. manufacturers face a 22 percent cost premium, compared to our trading partners, due to taxes, employee benefits, litigation costs and environmental controls. American manufacturers cite government regulations imposed on them, especially environmental regulations, as one of the prime reasons they have offshored manufacturing. Countries like China may have environmental and labor regulations on the books, but government officials have been told to look the other way and do not enforce them. If our elected representatives want to save American manufacturing, they need to wake up to the fact that adding burdensome government laws and regulations will actually *reduce* the tax revenue the federal government receives, by driving manufacturers overseas.

Impact of War on Terrorism and Recession

Most wars of the past, like World War I, World War II, the Korean War, and the Vietnam War, had a stimulative effect on U.S. manufacturing. However, the Gulf War of 1991 and the War on Terror have not had this effect. The Gulf War was too short to have much effect, and took place at the beginning of drastic cutbacks in defense as a result of the breakup of the USSR.

One reason the War on Terror is not stimulating the economy as past wars have is that the Defense Department no longer mandates that all systems, assemblies, subassemblies, and components be made in the U.S. After the Gulf War in 1991, the DOD allowed prime contractors and their subcontractors to utilize what was termed "dual technology," i.e. components, products, assemblies, and systems that were made to commercial standards, not more costly and stringent military standards. The result is that companies located offshore, even in China, now make an unknown percentage of these products. And American manufacturers are not reaping the same benefits from increased defense spending as they did in the past.

With the War on Terror continuing, the ship-repair industry is now in its 10th year of recession. Navy ships are out to sea longer and the Navy only contracts out the repairs that are absolutely necessary when they come back into port, delaying major overhauls so they can go back out to sea as soon as possible. The contracts to build new ships that companies like San Diego's General Dynamics/NASSCO have received are the only bright spot in the industry. Unfortunately, small ship repair companies haven't benefitted from the contracts for new ships, as the large companies have expanded their in-house capabilities and subcontract out less work than they used to. Even defense and aerospace companies have felt an adverse effect from the war because, with so much of the defense budget being spent on troops, supplies, weapons and munitions, other defense-related needs, especially research and development, are getting less money.

A 2005 report by the American Electronics Association, "Losing the Competitive Advantage?" noted that "Congress cut funding for the first time in 16 years for the National Science Foundation (NSF), the leading public supporter of R&D" in fiscal year 2005. The report also noted that total

R&D funding by the federal government has declined over the past two decades since its peak in 1987. The report observed that "R&D funding is vital in supporting innovation and the advancement of the technology industry, which bolsters the U.S. economy and even the military." The report opines that "These reductions in federal R&D spending will directly harm the competitiveness of the United States in the world economy."[19]

A March 2007 follow-up report, "We Are Still Losing the Competitive Advantage," noted that "In 1985, federal R&D funding represented 1.25 percent of U.S. GDP, nearly a half percentage point higher than in 2004, when R&D represented only 0.80 percent of GDP." The report argued that, "Technology R&D remains vital to the economic health of the nation. It fosters the cutting edge technologies that bolster the economic and industrial strength of the United States... Increasing federal R&D spending is crucial to maintaining American competitiveness in a global economy."[20]

The federal government did begin to respond to these concerns. Its FY 2008 budget called for dramatic increases in NSF funding for long-term basic research. The 2009 budget increased funding another seven percent, the 2010 budget increased 6.7 percent, and 2011 increased by 8.8 percent. Unfortunately, budgetary pressures blunted this trend for several subsequent years, and the present direction is unclear as of 2012.

Case Study: California's Aerospace Industry

The U.S. aerospace industry generated $211 billion in sales worldwide in 2010. "In 2011, the industry contributed $87 billion in export sales to the domestic economy. The industry's positive trade balance of $57.4 billion places aerospace in the lead, representing the largest positive trade balance of any manufacturing industry."[21]California is responsible for about 25 percent of the industry in the U.S. Besides a strong supplier presence, it has more NASA centers than any other state and a higher education system that provides a pipeline of skilled workers. There are also four Air Force bases that support research, design, and testing of commercial and military aerospace systems: Edwards, Vandenberg, Los Angeles, and Air Force Plant 42. California's clustering of aerospace supplier industries promotes knowledge transfer and innovation, reduces operating costs, and attracts new aerospace businesses to the state.

A few large firms, like Northrop Grumman and Lockheed Martin, which produce aircraft for the military and the private sector, dominate the industry. These large firms subcontract with smaller suppliers to manufacture or design parts. The industry is composed of the following subgroups:

- Aircraft manufacturing
- Aircraft engines and engine parts
- Other aircraft parts and equipment
- Aircraft support
- Missiles, space vehicles, and parts
- Search, detection, and navigation instruments

In 2008, there were about 5,300 aerospace companies in the state, with the majority located in Los Angeles County (1,850), followed by Orange County (790), Silicon Valley

(610), and the San Diego and Imperial County region (450). The industry generated more than $27 billion in sales in 2009, with the Los Angeles region generating 42 percent of that total.

The industry in California has fared relatively well recently, compared to manufacturing overall, according to a recent study by the Northern California Center of Excellence and the Center for Applied Competitive Technologies at Cerritos College. Between 2004 and 2008, it added more than 5,500 jobs. Between 2004 and 2009, the industry declined by only five percent, compared to 12 percent for the manufacturing sector as a whole. But then it experienced a sharp decline in 2009, with the loss of nearly 14,500 jobs.

The study divided the state into 10 regions, with Los Angeles, Orange, San Diego/Imperial County, the Inland Empire, and South Central providing the most jobs. While four of the top five regions lost jobs, my own San Diego/Imperial County region gained more than 3,000, indicating a unique competitive advantage relative to other regions. Aerospace manufacturing was projected to experience slow growth in the next five years, regaining fewer than half the jobs it had lost in the previous five. Orange County and the San Diego and Imperial County regions were expected to experience the largest gains, with the addition of about 1,550 and 1,630 jobs respectively. Unfortunately, the region with almost half of current employment, Los Angeles, was projected to decline by about four percent, or nearly 3,300 jobs, by 2014.

Between 2009 and 2014, the 10 fastest-growing aerospace occupations were projected to be machinists, aircraft mechanics and service technicians, computer-controlled machine tool operators, industrial engineers, computer software engineers, business operation specialists, aerospace engineers, and engineering and other managers. A bachelor's degree is required for six of these 10 occupations, with the remaining four requiring work experience, on-the-job training, or a vocational training certificate.

A few defense contractors, like General Atomic Aeronautical and Northrop Grumman, which build unmanned aerial vehicles (UAVs), have a good backlog of orders and should be busy for two to three more years based on existing contracts. In turn, their trickle-down dollars will benefit their suppliers. Component manufacturers like ITT Cannon and Sabritec, both in Orange County, are running seven days a week, 24 hours a day, and have 26-week lead times for new orders. These companies build Mil. spec. connectors for many defense contractors, including Boeing, Raytheon, General Atomic, and Northrop Grumman.

Higher Costs

In addition to offshore competition, other major causes of the downturn in manufacturing are higher fuel and energy costs, higher taxes, higher material and processing costs, and higher benefit costs, especially for health insurance. A 2007 report by the National Association of Manufacturers reports that "The domestic environment for manufacturers is dominated by concerns about rising external costs that make manufacturing from a U.S. base difficult. These costs for corporate taxes, health care and pensions, regulation, natural gas, and tort litigation add more than 30 percent to manufacturers' costs."[22]

The NAM report also pointed out that the price of natural gas, the primary fuel used in manufacturing in the U.S., rose dramatically after hurricanes Katrina and Rita. Yet in their aftermath, prices did not return to previous levels. For consumers, fuel costs went up by 45 percent between early 2005 to mid-2007, and since then there have been only brief periods of dropping and stabilizing before prices rise to the next higher level.

Raw materials prices have been on the rise and are impacting every company in the supply chain. Costs for metal and plastic rose dramatically nearly every month from mid-2006 to early 2008, after which they dropped due to recession. But as demand built up again in 2009, they rose again, and are now equal or greater than the peak prices of early 2007. For example, the price of 304 stainless steel went from $1.89/lb. in 2005 to $3.53/lb. in 2010, and even the less-expensive cold rolled steel went from $.30/lb. to $.55/lb. Little has changed since. Plastics, being petroleum byproducts, have been greatly impacted by the rising cost of oil in recent years. This situation will only get worse as time passes because there is a finite supply of oil worldwide and as the rest of the world industrializes, its demand for plastic will increase. Suppliers have, in fact, publicly blamed rising prices on increasing demand for these materials in China and India. Rising health care costs are another challenge for manufacturers. When companies are spending more money on materials, fuel and energy, health insurance, and so on, they have less money for R&D, new product development, and investments in capital equipment and systems. This, in turn, affects the companies that provide such equipment and services.

Trade Unions

Most labor unions in the United States are members of the American Federation of Labor-Congress of Industrial Organizations (AFL-CIO) or the Change to Win Federation, which split from the AFL-CIO in 2005. Both organizations advocate for policies and legislation favorable to workers; the AFL-CIO is especially concerned with trade issues.

Many people have cited high union wages and benefits as a major reason for American companies being uncompetitive with offshore companies. They say that the outsourcing of work to Asia, Latin America, and Africa has been driven by increasing costs of unionized labor, making it more efficient to perform labor-intensive work in those countries.

In the past, lower labor costs were one of the main reasons Northern manufacturers moved to the Southern states, where trade unions were relatively weak. All the states of the Deep South, and a number of traditionally Republican states in the Midwest, Great Plains, and Rocky Mountains, have right-to-work laws. (Arizona, Arkansas, Florida, and Oklahoma go one step further and enshrine these laws in their state constitutions). These laws prevent unions from negotiating contracts requiring companies to fire workers who refuse to join the union.

Unions became a larger issue in the 2008 economic crisis when the automakers sought billions of dollars in loans in order to stay viable. Many people blamed the United Auto Workers for the automotive industry crisis. Some said that costly labor agreements, including pension and health plans, put U.S. automakers at a disadvantage to foreign automakers.

Critics cited the fact that unionized employees of American automakers made about $20 to $30 more per hour, depending on how fringe benefits are calculated, than the non-union employees at Honda, Nissan, and Toyota plants in the U.S.

While it's true that union wages are higher than non-union wages, even the lowest-paid American workers cannot compete with workers in countries like China, India, and Vietnam. At the very least, American workers are paid 10 times what a Chinese worker earns. The difference in standard of living and quality of life is incomparable. Would any American worker want to live the same way as a Chinese worker? Of course not! No company owner should want his employees to reduce their standard of living tenfold or more to live on wages comparable to offshore workers.

The Supply of Skilled Workers

As far back as the early 1990s, there were warnings that American manufacturers would not have enough skilled workers in the future. A study by the Manufacturing Institute, "2005 Skills Gap Report," indicated that 81 percent of companies reported a moderate-to-severe deficit of qualified workers. This tight labor market will only get worse, according to the report. "The Baby Boom generation of skilled workers will be retired within the next 15 to 20 years.... The result is a projected need for 10 million new skilled workers by 2020." Similarly, when Eric Mittlestadt of the National Council for Advanced Manufacturing addressed the 2007 American Welding Society Conference, he said, "By 2018, 70 million baby boomers will retire and 40 million new workers will enter the workforce, creating 30 million fewer available workers."

The American Association of Engineering Societies estimates that there are currently 1.3 million engineering and engineering technology jobs available in the U.S. without trained people to fill them. According to the Department of Labor, between 2002 and 2012 there will be two million job openings in computer science, math, engineering and physical sciences, and 2.4 million skilled production jobs for machinists, machine assemblers and operators, systems operators, and technicians. At the same time, the current science and engineering workforce is getting older. More than half of these workers are already older than 40, and 28 percent are older than 50.[23]

For example, in San Diego there has been a severe shortage of journeymen machinists, particularly lathe operators, in the past few years. There are a few large companies that pay above-average wages for machinists, like General Dynamics/NASSCO, BF Goodrich (formerly Rohr Corp-oration), and Caterpillar's Solar Turbines. The rest of the small- and medium-sized manufacturers with in-house machine shops, and the even smaller independent machine shops, are reduced to poaching qualified workers from each other.

In a market economy, of course, labor "shortages" only exist relative to the wage employers are willing to pay. The real problem is that the entry-level wage for a machinist completing college training is only $12/hour, and journeyman wages range from $18 to $25/hour, depending on the size of the company. There is only one training program for machinists in San Diego County: a 600-hour course offered at San Diego

City College. That entry-level wage isn't even double the current minimum wage ($7.15/hour) in California, so taking a 600-hour course to become a machinist isn't attracting a large number of takers. Solar Turbines has had an apprentice program for entry-level machinists to become journeymen for many years and is considering establishing an apprenticeship program for entry-level machinists to address this problem.

A highly skilled workforce is the lifeblood of our national economy, but the U.S. workforce is increasingly unprepared for the 21st century. In the past, the skills workers learned were good for decades. Now, they need to constantly learn new skill sets, which will require continuous education and retraining programs to prepare them and their employers to compete in the knowledge-based economy.

The education of a knowledge workforce starts with grades K-12. Without a strong background in math and science at the K-12 level, students will struggle later to earn degrees in scientific and technical fields. When comparing American K-12 students to their international counterparts, U.S. 8th grade students ranked ninth in science and 15th in math, according to the International Association for the Evaluation of Educational Achievement.

American colleges and universities also aren't graduating enough scientists and engineers to fill the gap left by the retiring Baby Boom generation. A 2007 American Electronics Association report, "We Are Still Losing the Competitive Advantage– Now is the time to Act," warned that China graduates almost six times as many engineers as the U.S. The European Union, Japan, Russia, and India also graduate more engineers than the United States, and South Korea, with one-sixth our population and one-twelfth our GDP, graduates slightly more than we do.

However, these numbers have been questioned by Pratt School of Engineering Professor Vivek Wadhwa and Duke sociologist Gary Gereffi. They argue that many Chinese and Indian "engineers" would only qualify as technicians in developed nations, and that, in an apples-to-apples comparison, in 2004, "Looking strictly at four-year degrees, the U.S. graduated 137,437 engineers vs. 112,000 from India and 351,537 from China. All of these numbers include information-technology and related majors." They noted a difference between what they called "dynamic engineers" and "transactional engineers." They defined dynamic engineers as "capable of abstract thinking and high-level problem-solving. These engineers thrive in teams, work well across international borders, have strong interpersonal skills, and lead innovation. Transactional engineers may possess engineering fundamentals but not the experience or expertise to apply this knowledge to larger problems. These individuals typically perform rote tasks." They conclude that the vast majority of graduates in China and India are transactional engineers and that both countries may actually face severe shortages of dynamic engineers.

Prominent Deniers of the Problem

Harvard Business School professor Michael Porter, the main author of the Council on Competitiveness's "Innovation Index: Where America Stands," believes that the U.S. is not losing its edge in innovation, nor is it particularly important for the nation to worry about losing its manufacturing. In

2006, he told a press conference in Washington that the U.S. remains the world's largest manufacturing economy and that it is not losing manufacturing but manufacturing *jobs*, and "that is a fundamental distinction." Porter asserted that the American economy faces four primary challenges: education, energy, health care, and legal costs. He added that the problem is not jobs, but the skills workers need for better jobs. He claimed that education remains the number one weakness of the U.S. economy.[24]

Editor-in-Chief of *American Machinist* publications Bruce Vernyi agrees with Porter, commenting in an article entitled "Where are the Real Problems in Manufacturing?" that "the U.S. remains the world's largest manufacturer – and has lost only 1.1 percent in global market share since 1984." While he admits that manufacturing jobs are declining, he wrote, "Every time a productivity increase is reported, it means that jobs have been lost." He described visiting machine shops that run CNC machine tools unattended during night shifts, concluding, "That's productivity. That's the current state of the art for U.S. manufacturing. And that is something to be proud of." In conclusion, he writes, "I think the future remains bright for manufacturing in the United States."[25]

Unfortunately, while increased productivity from advances in technology and implementation of such practices as lean manufacturing have indeed resulted in the loss of many jobs, the other causes mentioned previously in this chapter are still cause for concern. The future remains dim for U.S. manufacturing if it continues on the same path.

General Electric's chairman and CEO Jeffrey Immelt recently commented, "Over the last five years, we have really positioned ourselves as a global company... the world has never been more independent from the U.S. economy.... The U.S. economy is still important, but not like it was five, 10 or 20 years ago." Immelt said that globalization is "profound. It's irrefutable and it's irreversible." He later added that the fate of the U.S. economy "is going to be decided in the next three to five years. You've got to have a real game plan for health care and energy and you've got to have a tax and public policy that tries to create the right mechanism for exports."[26]

I, too, believe that the fate of the U.S. economy will indeed be decided in the next three to five years. The question is whether we will remain a First World country, with a strong manufacturing base, or descend to the status of a Third World country, importing finished goods and exporting raw materials.

4

What Are the Effects
Of Offshore Outsourcing?

This is a period of major disruption in the economy of the United States. We are in the middle of a worldwide economic revolution that will take another 20 to 30 years to fully complete. Some say that the Industrial Revolution has ended and that we are now in the Information Technology Revolution. But I believe that we are actually in the final phase of the Industrial Revolution, wherein Third World countries are becoming industrialized and manufacturing is being transferred from the First World to the Third. Historically, First World countries imported raw materials from Third World countries and transformed them into manufactured products. But with the export of so much of our industry and the outsourcing of so much of our engineering, the United States is on the fast track to becoming a Third World country. We already are in some commodities, like textiles.

The United States long encouraged other countries to adopt free-market principles. The good news is that many countries listened and opened their doors to American products and services. The bad news is that many countries listened, entered the global economy, and are now competing aggressively against American companies. In this new global economy, American companies aren't just competing against their rival down the street or in another part of the country; they are competing with companies in China, India, Malaysia, and elsewhere.

Other countries are adopting and utilizing technology to drive their growth and enhance their competitiveness. Utilizing the latest innovations allows developing countries to leapfrog over yesterday's technology faster and cheaper. For example, it took nearly a century for the industrialized world to provide 90 percent of its population with telephone service, mainly via copper lines to households. Wireless and satellite technologies are accomplishing this in a fraction of the time and cost. Because offshoring has given away technology that took decades to develop, the U.S. risks losing its dominance in science and technology.

One major effect of offshoring manufacturing is the loss of jobs in the U.S. According to the Economic Policy Institute, between 2001 and 2010, "the trade deficit with China eliminated or displaced 2.8 million jobs, 1.9 million (69.2 percent) of which were in manufacturing."[1] EPI reported that the computer and electronic parts industry was hardest hit, with 909,400 jobs displaced, 32.6 percent of the total. Apparel and accessories lost 178,700 jobs, textile fabrics and products lost 92,300, fabricated metal products lost 123,900, plastic and rubber products lost 62,000, motor vehicles and parts lost 49,300, and miscellaneous manufactured goods lost 119,700. The states with the biggest losses were California, Texas, New York, Illinois, Florida, North Carolina, Pennsylvania, Ohio, Massachusetts, and Georgia. (These job displacement estimates are conservative and represent only direct and indirect jobs displaced by trade, excluding jobs in wholesale and retail trade and advertising.)

For the purposes of this book, "offshoring" refers to relocating one or more processes or functions to a foreign nation. The five main forms of offshoring are:

1. Wholly-owned facilities built or acquired.

2. Wholly-owned facilities built and managed with assistance of a partner.

3. Facilities set up by someone else to facilitate speed of entry into market, reduce risk, and protect intellectual property.

4. Facilities managed by a partner initially and transitioned to captive at a later stage.

5. Facilities fully managed by some other company.

In less than a decade, offshore outsourcing evolved from a little-used practice to a mature industry. Even conservative companies are now willing to experiment with it to gain a competitive edge.

The June 2008 issue of *Industry Week* published the results of a survey by SAP and IW Custom Research investigating the strategic objectives of subscriber companies with annual revenues over $10 million when they expanded overseas. The top objectives for the 170 respondents were to increase market share, increase profitability, reduce costs, provide a superior customer experience, and increase revenue. Companies with annual revenue of $1 billion or more met 58 to 74 percent of these objectives, while companies with less than $1 billion annual revenue met 37 to 47 percent.

Ease of communication via the Internet was the initial driver of offshoring, but the use of collaborative tools like web chatting, Lotus Notes, and virtual whiteboards is burgeoning. Companies such as IBM, Intel, AMD, Motorola, Cisco, and Siemens have even opened R&D centers in India, drawn by payroll costs a quarter of those in the U.S. and Europe.

More companies are relying on offshore entities for core business processes. This entails increased risk of piracy, security breaches, theft of information, intellectual property theft, and patent infringement. All of these increase the risks involved with offshore outsourcing. Outsourcing relationships often morph into defacto partnerships without the analysis, reporting, visibility, and control that typically characterize true partnerships.

Mark Zandi of Moody's Economy.com calculates that 20.5 percent of the manufactured goods bought in America in 2007 were imported, up from 11.7 percent in 1992. However, Alan Tonelson, a research fellow at the U.S. Business and Industry Council, writes,

Using the same data and the same methodology as Mr. Zandi, but delving into individual industries, we found that the United States is importing more than 50 percent – and in some cases close to 90 percent – of the machine tools used in this country, the aircraft engines and engine parts, the parts that go into cars, trucks, the industrial valves, the printed circuits, the optical instruments and lenses, the telephone switching apparatus, the machines that mold plastics, the broadcasting equipment used for radio, television and wireless transmissions.[2]

The cost of counterfeiting to the U.S. economy is estimated to be as much as $250 billion a year. The U.S. Customs and Border Patrol reports that a loss of more than 750,000 jobs is attributed to counterfeit merchandise. This growth in IP theft and counterfeiting is tied to the growth in outsourcing product development and manufacturing. Bob Wright, CEO of media and entertainment giant NBC Universal, says, "This issue needs to be moved up on the agenda of every business leader, every trade organization and every policymaker. At risk is every sector of our economy where creativity, innovation and invention drive the creation of economic value and of high-wage jobs."[3]

The U.S., UK, Germany, and France are the top performing countries in addressing the problem of Intellectual Property (IP) theft and counterfeit products, while China and Russia are the worst. The International Anti-Counterfeiting Coalition reported that global trade in counterfeit goods today is $600 billion, i.e. five to seven percent of world trade.

What Has Driven Manufacturing Offshore?

The search for lower cost areas for manufacturing is nothing new. As previously noted, sixty years ago Northern and New England companies started moving manufacturing to the Southern states. Southern states were right-to-work states, and had less burdensome government and environmental regulations in the years before the establishment of the national EPA and OSHA. And most of the Southern states had lower personal and corporate tax rates.

Thirty years ago, American manufacturers, particularly West Coast manufacturers, started moving high-volume production to Hong Kong, Singapore, and the Philippines for the same reasons: wages and less regulation. About the same time, manufacturers started assembling in Mexico, in the maquiladoras, for the same reasons.

The next area for lower cost manufacturing was mainland Asia, predominantly China and India. At first, U.S. manufacturers outsourced specific parts and components of products with offshore vendors. Then they outsourced whole product lines. Finally, they built their own plants after the Chinese government's policies changed to allow foreign investment and private ownership of companies.

Many people believe that unions played a big role in driving manufacturing offshore, but this is not actually the case. First, as noted in Chapter Two, unions today represent only about seven percent of our private sector workforce. Second, the first industries to set up manufacturing offshore were not unionized – electronic components and assemblies and toys. I've worked in San Diego's electronics and manufacturing industries since I was 18 years old, and I've never worked for a company that was unionized. At most, there were only a dozen or so companies that were unionized and today, I know of only two: General Dynamics NASSCO (shipbuilding) and Solar Turbines (gas turbine engines, compressors, and power generator sets). California's high-tech industry in Silicon Valley was never unionized, and virtually all of California's technology-based manufacturing is non-union. The only union that still has any significant membership in California manufacturing is the International Association of Machinists and Aerospace Workers, and its membership has dropped dramatically in the past 20 years.

In my opinion, the main reasons U.S. companies have offshored manufacturing are labor costs, environmental regulations, less government regulation of building construction, lower taxes, and the global free-trade mentality.

America's National Security at Risk

A 2007 report by the 12-member, bipartisan U.S.-China Economic and Security Review Commission (USCC) reported that "At the present time, U.S. officials are neither carefully tracking the persistent attrition of the U.S. defense industrial base as more and more manufacturing is outsourced offshore, nor identifying and justifying on national security grounds an irreducible minimum defense industrial base that the United States should retain regardless of the cost or effort required to do so." So our Defense Department does not know the extent to which its parts and components are being sourced from China. The report sums up the problem as follows: "U.S. defense contractors have merged and moved some manufacturing outside the United States. Sources of defense components are becoming scarcer in the United States, and the supply of American workers skilled in manufacturing these components is diminishing."

The USCC found that "China's mercantilist policies are taking a huge toll on small and medium-sized manufacturing facilities and their workers in the United States." U.S.-based multinational companies have moved production to China, but smaller firms are not able to and thus "face the full brunt of China's unfair trade practices...This is significant because small and medium enterprises represent 60 percent of the manufacturing jobs in the United States." The report concluded that:

DOD is not a sufficiently large customer to many of its suppliers to be able to influence their supply chain decisions... There are potential security risks to the United States from using foreign-made parts and components in weapons systems important to U.S. defense. These can result from:

- Tampering with or specially engineering foreign-manufactured parts and components.

- Inadequate quality that leads to failure or substandard performance.

· Interruption of the supply chains, thus depriving U.S. forces of the weapons and equipment on which they depend to defend U.S. interests."[4]

According to a story on this issue in *Manufacturing and Technology News,*

The Department of Defense and its prime contractors are not responsive in providing information about the source of parts in its major weapons systems...USCC contractor Synthesis Partners made repeated attempts to contact key personnel in more than 50 organizations who might have information on sources of parts and components... for three weapons systems: the UH-60 Blackhawk helicopter; the F-22 Raptor fighter; and the DDG 1000 Destroyer. It was provided with no information worthy of reporting...'A single authoritative source covering the complete supply chain to the third tier supplier level does not exist,' says the study.[5]

According to a report by the National Research Council entitled "Minerals, Critical Minerals, and the U.S. Economy,"

"Decision makers in both the public and private sectors need continuous, unbiased and thorough information on the uses and possible supply restrictions of nonfuel minerals, but currently the federal government and the industries that use these materials do not collect these data with enough detail or frequency."[6]

The lead article in the January/February 2008 issue of the Metals Service Center Institute's *Forward* magazine says, "The United States has lost critically needed capabilities to arm itself for future wars." Rear Admiral Kathleen M. Dussault, Deputy Assistant Secretary of the Navy for Acquisition and Logistics Management, says, "The Navy does not have visibility into commercial items indirectly purchased (from China) via second- and third-tier producers." The article points out that as a consequence, a range of essential materials, used to make everything from ordinary ammunition to propellants for missiles and components of submarines, are no longer made in the United States. In some cases, essential materials are available almost exclusively from China.[7]

In this same vein, Rep. Duncan Hunter (R-CA), former chairman of the House Armed Services Committee, reported two experiences that shook him up in 2008.

The first was when this committee was seeking solutions to the deadly surge of improvised explosive devices (IED's) in Iraq by addressing the need to improve the armor on military vehicles. He "sent a team from his committee to find manufacturers that could produce high-grade armored steel as quickly as possible. The team found only one company left in the United States."

The second experience involved the Joint Direct Attack Munition, when a Swiss company refused to provide the crystals needed for the guidance system of America's most important smart bomb. When the committee sought out U.S. sources of the crystal, it found only one company left making this essential technology. Hunter said, "We're down to one-sies and twosies on critical aspects of the defense industrial base. This is a security problem!" He went on to say, "For practical purposes, many of the multinational corporations have become Chinese corporations."[8]

Remember that a portion of the profits of every Chinese company goes to a Communist government with the stated goal of dominating the United States. Their game plan is to render America completely dependent on Chinese production, innovation, and financing. They won't even have to wage a military war against us if they win the economic war. The management of American companies needs to wake up to the fact that they are funding their country's future enemy by outsourcing their production to China, instead of just worrying about their next quarter's return on investment for stockholders and stock incentives and bonuses for themselves. And our political establishment and government leaders need to open their eyes to the disastrous consequences of "free" trade that is really unfair trade.

American Lives at Risk

A few years ago, McWane Inc. of Birmingham, Alabama, the country's largest provider of ductile waterworks fittings, brought a case to the U.S. International Trade Commission under Section 421 of the Trade Act, declaring that Chinese producers were dumping fittings into the U.S. The USITC ruled in favor of McWane in a six-to-zero vote and determined the industry worthy of import relief, consisting of duties of up to 50 percent on fittings from China. However, President Bush overruled the decision in 2004. As a result, the company started reducing production at its plants in Alabama, Texas, and Ohio. McWane closed its U.S. factories in 2008 and shifted its production to a 400,000 sq. ft. plant in China it had built on a 50-acre site. Executive Vice President David Green said,

> We have been forced to build facilities in China and import that product back into the United States because of government inaction here and the lack of any kind of protection for the investments we have made here to comply with U.S. environmental and safety laws and regulations.... There are no U.S. environmental regulations in China.[9]

Besides 500 people losing their jobs, what are the potential long-range effects on the American consumer of producing water fittings in China? One of these types of water fittings is installed in every new home built in America. There are no standards in China regulating arsenic in the coking coal used to make piping and components that carry fresh water, and the Chinese have no certifiable radiation-testing systems. In addition, they have been found to be using asbestos to coat pipes and fittings in an attempt to minimize leakage. Thus death by arsenic or radiation poisoning or asbestos ingestion could be a long-term consequence of sourcing water fittings from China.

Case Study: North Carolina's Textile Industry

North Carolina has a greater percentage of its workforce in manufacturing than any other state, and has therefore been more vulnerable to competition from imports than other states. North Carolina's manufacturing economy is made even more vulnerable by its concentration in import-sensitive sectors like textiles, apparel, and furniture.

The North Carolina Employment Security Commission followed the employment prospects of 4,820 workers laid off from bankrupt Pillowtex in 2003, the largest mass layoff in state history. An article in *Manufacturing and Technology News* reported that North Carolina has been the state most impacted by trade-induced layoffs. "Between 2004 and 2006, almost 39,000 North Carolina workers have been certified by the Trade Adjustment Assistance program as having lost jobs to trade, more than 10 percent of the U.S. total of 387,755." Furthermore, "About 40 percent of the laid-off workers had not yet found work, three years after they lost their jobs, and for those who have, take-home pay isn't as much as they were making at Pillowtex."[10] And the problem isn't just people losing jobs and not being able to find other employment that pays as well as their former job: "hundreds of small towns throughout North Carolina impacted by plant closures are dying."

During the period 2001-2007, the proportion of jobs in North Carolina's services sector increased. This put downward pressure on wages because manufacturing paid substantially higher wages. This shift also reduced the number of workers receiving fringe benefits like retirement and health insurance, in part because many displaced workers were only able to find part-time jobs, which usually lack benefits.

In its 2007 annual report to Congress, the U.S.-China Economic and Security Review Commission included a case study of the local impact of trade with China on North Carolina. It said,

> The accelerating decline in North Carolina's manufacturing employment is due in large measure to increasing competition from imports mostly from China...The combination of China's 2001 admission to the World Trade Organization (WTO), which gave it quota-free access to U.S. markets for its textile and clothing exports, and the subsequent U.S. grant of Most Favored (Trading) Nation status that lowered most tariffs on Chinese imports, battered North Carolina's textile and apparel industries, and they never recovered.

According to the Social Science Research Institute of Duke University, in 1996 there were 2,153 textile and apparel plants in North Carolina, employing 233,715 people. But by 2006, the apparel industry had experienced a 70 percent decline in jobs and a 55 percent loss of plants. And the textile industry had lost 63 percent of its jobs and 32 percent of its plants. As the study notes,

> Trade agreements can profoundly affect state and regional economies and particular industries. While trade agreements that lower import barriers among America's trading partners have the potential to benefit American exporters, North Carolina appears to have realized few if any substantial benefits from China's admission to the WTO, and the net effect of trade with China since its accession appears to be negative overall for North Carolina's economy.

How does this downturn in the textile industry in the South affect other regions, like San Diego? Well, the San Diego region has a large number of companies manufacturing sporting vehicles, like dune buggies, go-karts, mini-motorcycles, etc. The Southeast has traditionally been the largest market for go-karts, and a majority of U.S. textile companies are located there. One San Diego company that has manufactured parts for go-karts for more than 40 years told me that their sales had dropped significantly in the past 10 years in the Southeast. Go-karting is mainly a hobby of blue-collar workers, like textile workers. The workers who lost their jobs have not been able to find equally well-paid jobs in other sectors. The average weekly salary for a U.S. textile worker was $487 in 2002, 38 percent more than the average salary for a worker in a retail store. When a family's disposable income drops drastically, money for nonessentials is cut or goes away altogether.

Many experts felt that as long as Americans were designing the products, it was alright to let other countries produce them. The danger is that invention and production are intertwined. Stephen Cohen, co-director of the Berkeley Roundtable on the International Economy at the University of California, Berkeley, says, "Most innovation does not come from disembodied laboratories. In order to innovate in what you make, you have to be pretty good at making it – and we are losing that ability." Franklin Vargo, Vice President for International Economic Affairs of the National Association of Manufacturers, echoes this sentiment, saying, "If manufacturing production declines in the United States, at some point we will go below critical mass and then the center of innovation will shift outside the country and that will really begin a decline in our living standards."

Even the biotech industry is feeling the effects of offshoring. U.S. pharmaceutical and biotech companies are beginning to do more of their research work through companies in China, India, and Eastern Europe, where labor is cheaper. San Diego-based Discovery Partners International, a chemistry research services business, closed its doors in September 2007 after failing to win a competitive bid that would have renewed its contract with Pfizer. They were bidding against providers in India, China, and Eastern Europe. Former CEO Michael Venuti said, "Offshoring is what destroyed our business, literally."

Information Technology and Service Sector Jobs

The IT industry has not proved to be the panacea for job creation that some thought it would be. American workers in the professional and high-tech sectors have learned that they can be increasingly easily replaced by engineers, IT workers, accountants, and even medical professionals like radiologists overseas, especially in India.

At a recent hearing of the House Science Committee, former Vice-Chairman of the Federal Reserve Board of Governors Alan Blinder said, "Shipping electrons is a lot easier and cheaper than shipping physical goods. ... There is little doubt that the range and number of jobs that can be delivered electronically is destined to increase greatly as technology improves and as India, China and other nations educate more and more skilled workers." Now a professor of economics at Princeton University and director of the

University's Center for Economic Policy Studies, he says that "the preponderance of service sector jobs to be lost in coming years will be those that do not require face-to-face contact with customers." Earlier in 2007, he declared that between 30 million and 40 million jobs were potentially offshorable.[11]

A study entitled "Next Generation Offshoring: The Globalization of Innovation," by Duke University's Fuqua School of Business and the consulting firm Booz Allen Hamilton, states that China is the preferred location for offshoring procurement and product development projects to support manufacturing operations already established there. The study noted that more than 50 percent of companies are now engaged in offshoring. Information technology projects being offshored increased by an average of 27 percent per year between 2001 and 2005. And product development, including software product development, is the second-largest function being moved offshore.[12]

In October 2006, Duke University's Masters of Engineering Management program presented a summary of its research on "Industry Trends in Engineering Offshoring" at a National Academy of Engineering Workshop. This report was the result of a detailed industry questionnaire submitted to Fortune 1000companies on former CNN anchor Lou Dobbs' list of companies that are "Exporting America." Respondents indicated that India and China remain the top offshoring destinations, with Mexico in third place. Types of engineering work sent offshore ranged from simple drafting of drawings and computer programming to engineering design and software development. While a majority of respondents indicated the offshoring trend would continue and expand over the next three to five years, the top three potential barriers to offshoring were reported to be intellectual property theft, language or cultural barriers, and wage inflation.

It is encouraging to note some of the report's conclusions, like "The productivity of American engineers is almost always higher or equal to those hired offshore. Engineering jobs in the U.S. are more technical in nature. The quality of work done by U.S. workers is generally higher than or equal to what is done overseas." Also, respondents highlighted "the superior communication and business skills of American workers and their creativity and ability to challenge the status quo."

As a result of so much offshoring, American companies specializing in engineering design and product development are forced to spend more time looking for their next projects. One San Diego-based engineering design consultant recently emailed me that he is "very frustrated at having to spend so much time looking for projects. That isn't what I went to school for or expected when I went out on my own."

Trade Shows

Manufacturing trade shows and exhibitions in the United States are also affected by the shift of production offshore, according to the publication *Trade Show Week and Skyline Exhibits*. Its 2007 report, "Manufacturing & Industrial Exhibition & Event Marketing Trends & Outlook," reveals that manufacturers are exhibiting at fewer events in North America and are heading to China to participate in shows there. Companies are also scaling down the size of their booths and placing fewer people in them. "Two out of three exhibitors believe that demographics are impacting their industry and shows and about half of this group indicates that attendance levels are lower as waves of executives and managers retire."[13]

For decades, trade shows for the manufacturing industry were events at which you either exhibited or attended every year. If you didn't, you would be missing out on the latest trends, new sales leads, and networking opportunities. For show managers, it was easy to sell booth space because trade shows were the "in" thing to do, and attendance at some shows, like COMDEX, was as high as 250,000.

According to Steven Prahalis, VP for Strategic Alliances at the Society of Manufacturing Engineers, two major things changed trade shows forever: the Internet and 9/11. It became possible to keep up with industry trends and find out information about potential sources for equipment, products, and services on the Internet. And if 9/11 and the subsequent recession caused you to miss a show, you discovered it didn't matter as much as you thought it would. You may have missed the networking opportunities, but LinkedIn and Facebook became the replacements.

Lower attendance at trade shows caused the demise of the WESCON show that had alternated between Southern California and the San Francisco Bay Area. At one time, WESCON was the largest electronics show in the world, but the last stand-alone show was held in Anaheim in 2004. There was a WESCON conference at the 2006 Consumer Electronics Show in Las Vegas, but no WESCON conference was listed for the 2007 or 2008 CES shows. The owners of the Pacific Design Show saved this show by combining it with the well-attended Medical Design and Manufacturing Show and four other small shows to become six shows in one. The 2008 show added a Green Manufacturing Expo in an attempt to increase attendance.

The granddaddy of all electronics manufacturing trade shows, NEPCON West, finished a 37-year run in 2002. For more than 30 years, NEPCON West was held at the Anaheim Convention Center, one of the largest venues in the U.S., nearly filling it to capacity. In July 2003, Kelvin Marsden-Kish, Reed Exhibitions' vice president, wrote in a press release, "At this time, the Northern California market is not strong enough for NEPCON West to provide the return on investment desired by exhibitors." Among reasons cited were "the continued recession in the electronics manufacturing industry... the trend for OEMs to outsource manufacturing, and the migration of the electronics manufacturing industry to China."[14]

While the demise of trade shows was expected because of the Internet and offshoring, shows like the Design-2-Part show produced by The Job Shop Company have been the exception. The Design-2-Part shows are held regionally and feature design and contract manufacturers located in the U.S. (While some of these companies may also have a plant offshore, no offshore-only companies are allowed to exhibit.) The mission of The Job Shop Company that puts on the dozen different shows around the country is to support and feature American companies. There is no substitute for the face-to-face interaction provided by trade shows. At the Design-2-Part shows, engineers get to see and touch actual parts built by the exhibitors. This gives them ideas for new products they are designing and shows them how other people have solved problems.

I have been attending the Design-2-Part show since 1982, when I started in sales, and the show in Long Beach in October 2010 was exciting. It was the best-attended show since the fall of 2007, before the recession. Show management said it was one of the best Southern California shows in the history of the company, with attendance up 21 percent over last year's show and up 10 percent over 2008. In fact, it was so well attended that many exhibitors had trouble talking to all of the attendees visiting their booths. The attendees weren't just browsing, and many exhibitors had far more leads from this show than the two previous shows.

What made it even more exciting this year was the number of attendees who came to the show looking for domestic sources for parts for new products or for a domestic source to replace an existing offshore vendor. Some even brought prints to quote. We heard several stories about quality problems with offshore vendors that are making it no longer advantageous to source the parts offshore. One company mentioned that because parts coming from China didn't meet dimensional specifications, they had to rework them and modify assembly steps at their own cost. When they contacted the Chinese vendor to return the bad parts, the vendor said, "We'll be happy to accept a new order," but wouldn't give credit for the defective parts.

More recently, I attended the imX (interactive manufacturing eXperience) in Las Vegas on September 12-14, 2011. This show is jointly sponsored by the Society of Manufacturing Engineers and the American Machine Tool Distributors' Association. The event had eight partners: DMG/Mori Seiki U.S.A., Fanuc, Kennametal, MAG IAS, Makino, Methods Machine Tools, Okuma America, and Sandvik Coromant, as well as a strategic media partner, *Manufacturing Engineering,* and three media sponsors: CNC-West.com, *Micro Manufacturing,* and *Cutting Tool Engineering.*

It was different from any other trade show I have attended in the past 30 years. What made it special was that the whole focus was on benefits for the attendee, instead of focusing primarily on benefits for the exhibitors. Traditional shows concentrate on drawing as many attendees as possible to be sales leads for the exhibitors, though they may offer some technical sessions as an added draw. But to attend imX, you had to be invited by one of the sponsors, the eight partners, or other exhibitors in the event.

The goal was to chart a new course for the future of domestic manufacturing industry by fostering collaboration among American manufacturers of all sizes. For the first time, the manufacturing industry came together not as competitors, but as collaborators with the common goal and focus of long-term industry viability. Participants had the opportunity to meet to discuss and foster an understanding of the challenges and opportunities facing their customers and their competition and to explore the latest manufacturing technology.

SME President Paul Bradley said this event was in development for five years. The imX team spoke with members and customers to discover what they wanted and needed from an event. AMTDA and the eight eXperience partners identified the needs of their members and customers. Individual meetings and group discussions between exhibitors and attendees were identified as key needs to provide more customer engagement. ImX event manager Steve Prahalis said that their survey of exhibitors and buyers revealed that some hadn't been to a show in as long as five years. Instead, they were attending corporate technical sessions at plants around the country. So they got together a roundtable of CEOs over a period of three years to come up with ideas for a new kind of event that would be invitation-only and incorporate the kind of experiences that corporate technical sessions provided, but in one location and at one time.

This is why education received major emphasis at imX, in the form of Learning Labs presented by the eight eXperience partners and Knowledge Bars provided by other exhibitors. The Learning Labs provided a small setting where buyers and sellers could share information on business-critical solutions. Each partner had from one to four theaters scheduled at one to five time slots during the three days of the event. A few of the topics: "Delivering Productivity from Art to Part," "Tooling Trends and Technologies," "The Fearless Use of Today's Technology," and "Training within Industry." The Knowledge Bars were intimate sessions to discuss such trends and topics as manufacturing software, automation, machining, energy, aerospace and defense manufacturing, and medical manufacturing.

Manufacturers' Sales Reps Losing Business

Manufacturers' representatives were seriously hurt by the effects of the long 2001-2003 recession, and they continue to be hurt by the shrinking base of prospective customers going out of business or moving manufacturing offshore.

This was first evident at the Del Mar Electronics Show held in San Diego County in April 2005. Previously, it was a show where the majority of exhibitors were manufacturers' representatives exhibiting their product lines. The number of representatives exhibiting has dwindled every year, until their exhibits comprised less than 10 percent of the booths at the 2005 show. (It has been about the same at subsequent shows.) The reduced number of representatives in the show wasn't just due to companies choosing not to participate. It was also because a significant number of rep agencies have gone out of business since 2001. From a high of 70 rep agency members in the San Diego Chapter of the Electronic Representatives Association in 1994, there are now only 30. Many older reps decided to shut down their businesses before they had spent all their "nest eggs" trying to keep their businesses going. Some sold their homes and moved out of state to retire. Some who stayed in business gave up their offices and went back to working out of their homes.

The reduced number of reps could become a serious problem for job-shop companies and electronic component manufacturers because independent reps provide the least expensive method of marketing and sales outside of a company's home territory. Very few job shops can afford a direct sales force and if they can, this sales force cannot cover as much of the country as a network of sales reps. In the competitive global economy, job shops cannot survive, much less succeed, by only marketing through word of mouth, direct sales in their home territory, trade show participation, directory listings, and through their websites.

Long-Range Consequences of Outsourcing

In an opinion article entitled "Outsourcing Jobs Offshore: Short and Long-Term Consequences," Prof. William Raynor of the State University of New York comments that in the past, when manufacturing jobs were lost to foreign countries, American "workers were able to retrain and find new positions. Sometimes, they found professional jobs in the white-collar sector after completing degrees, continuing education programs, etc." Then he asks, "But what jobs will professional workers retrain to after the new wave of high-tech outsourcing? My question is — from where will the new high-paying jobs come?"[15] Paul Craig Roberts, former Assistant Secretary of the Treasury under President Reagan, is also very concerned about the potential consequences of outsourcing: "Trade implies reciprocity. It is a two-way street. There is no reciprocity in outsourcing, only the export of domestic jobs."[16]

One example of this lack of reciprocity is Harley-Davidson's experience. The Wisconsin-based motorcycle manufacturer announced on April 17, 2008 that it planned to cut its motorcycle production, slashing 370 production jobs and 360 non-production jobs, because the sluggish U.S. economy had slowed demand. But if China were willing to let its people buy Harley-Davidson motorcycles, then exports could keep these workers employed. The Chinese motorcycle market is huge: about 24 million in 2007. Harley-Davidson has been hoping to sell in China without building a factory there, and expanded its sales efforts by opening a dealership in Beijing in April 2006. However, its sales have been low because China charges a 30 percent tariff on foreign vehicles, including motorcycles, and manipulates its currency to keep the yuan low.[17]

What I call the global economy mentality is starting to be questioned, although some prominent people in the past 20 years have warned of its perils. The late Sir James Goldsmith, a billionaire international business leader, wrote two books, *The Trap* (1993) and *The Response* (1995), warning of the perils of globalization. He even gave a speech to the U.S. Senate in 1994 warning about it. He "predicted that the working and middle classes in the United States and Europe would be ruined by the greed of Wall Street and corporations, who would boost corporate earnings by replacing their domestic work forces with foreign labor, which could be paid a fraction of labor's productivity as a result of the foreign country's low living standard and large excess supply of labor."[18]

Roger Milliken, who led Milliken and Company for 71 years, during which it grew to become the world's largest privately owned textile and chemical manufacturer, shared the same opinion. One of the last in the tradition of those great industrialists who built America's manufacturing success; he believed America's manufacturing leadership was the found-ation of his nation's economic achievements.

Ralph Gomory, an American applied mathematician, former IBM executive, and president of the Alfred P. Sloan Foundation for 18 years, has written extensively on the nature of technology development, industrial competitiveness, models of international trade, and the function of the corporation in a globalizing world. In 2007, he joined the Stern School of Business at New York University as a research professor. He currently focuses on the increasing complexities of the globalized economy and the differing goals of countries and companies. In his 2001 book *Global Trade and Conflicting National Interests*, co-written with economist William Baumol, he wrote, "A country that ends up producing little value will have little to consume at home and little to trade abroad, and will have a low standard of living."[19] This book also argues that the famous free trade theory of "comparative advantage" of David Ricardo was merely a special case, not a general theory. In a 2007 interview with *Manufacturing & Technology News*, Dr. Gomory stated that the traditional theory of free trade has broken down because companies are no longer bound to the interests of their home countries. Multinational corporations are now highly profitable, but by shifting their production offshore, they are no longer adding to the nation's GDP. "The country and companies are going off in two different directions," he said. "We are going into debt to the tune of 6 percent of our GDP each year, and we are not finding a way to pay it back... A country cannot forever consume more value than it creates."[20] Gomory's books and papers, and those of similar economists, are gradually starting to reshape the national debate on the roles and responsibilities of corporations in the modern American economy.

Economist Dr. Paul Craig Roberts is of like mind. In an article in the June 20, 2011 issue of *Manufacturing & Technology News*, he wrote, "Anytime there is an excess supply of labor, or the ability of corporations to pay labor less than its productivity, the corporations bank the difference, share prices rise, and Wall Street and shareholders are happy." In this article, he commented on the key points made by Nobel prize-winning economist Michael Spence and Sandile Hlatshwayo, a researcher at New York University, in their report "The Evolving Structure of the American Economy and the Employment Challenge." Spence and Hlatshwayo show that "U.S. industries are separated into internationally tradable and non-tradable components." Non-tradable goods and services cannot be offshored or produced in locations distant from their market, and thus government and health care have become the largest employers in the past 20 years. Tradable jobs produce goods and services that can be produced in locations distant from their markets and can be exported. This has resulted in "the adverse movements in the distribution of U.S. income over the past 20 years, particularly in the middle of the income range.... The evolution of the U.S. economy supports the notion of there being a long-term structural challenge with respect to the quantity and quality of employment opportunities in the United States."

Jobs paying the $20 per hour that historically enabled American wage earners to support a middle-class standard of living are leaving the U.S. Only 16 percent of today's workers earn the $20 per hour baseline wage, down 60 percent since 1979.This is expected to get worse, according to the Department of Labor's report "Occupational Outlook for 2006-2016," which predicts that 70 percent of jobs created between 2006 and 2016 would be service jobs paying low wages. Of course, it was written before the start of the Great Recession, and we've lost another one and a half million manufacturing jobs since.

State employment data released January 24, 2012 by the Bureau of Labor Statistics shows that American workers continue to pay a staggering price for the lack of concerted action to create jobs. In December 2011, nonfarm employment increased in 25 states and the District of Columbia, decreased in 24 states, and was unchanged in one state. However, eight states and the District continued to have unemployment of nine percent or higher, and four states and the District had rates of ten percent or more. Four states and the District have continued to lose jobs since June 2009, even though the economy has technically been in a recovery.[21]

Unsurprisingly, Americans today are pessimistic about our country's economic standing. According to a Gallup Poll on Feb. 11-14, 2008,

Four in 10 Americans consider China to be the world's leading economic power; only 33 percent chose the

United States. By contrast, in May 2000, the United States dominated public perceptions to this question, with 65 percent saying it was No. 1.[22]

Although this perception is not yet quantitatively true, the public's pessimism shows that the American people are well aware of what's going on – which holds out hope that they may yet vote for a solution.

5

How Has Industrialization Affected China and India?

Manufacturing in America developed over a period of more than 200 years. It developed gradually, so there was the opportunity to learn about the hazards of industrialization on a smaller scale than has been possible with the rapid industrialization of developing countries. Pollution caused by specific industries affected small geographic areas, like West Virginia's coal mining and Pennsylvania's steel regions. The Bill of Rights provided freedom of speech, freedom of the press, and the right to assemble, enabling affected communities and workers to address unsafe working conditions and pollution. Residents spoke out against pollution's health effects in their communities. Workers formed unions to fight for better working conditions and higher wages, especially in hazardous occupations. Newspapers, and later radio and TV, made the public aware of what was happening. After sufficient pressure was put on elected officials at the local, state, and federal levels, laws were passed that improved working conditions, protected worker safety, and reduced pollution.

As a result, great strides on these issues were made in the U.S. in the 20th century. These efforts culminated in the establishment of the Environmental Protection Agency in December 1970, consolidating 15 components from five agencies for the purpose of grouping all environmental regulatory activities in a single agency. Since then, the U.S. has developed a comprehensive body of law to protect the environment and prevent pollution. The EPA enforces more than 15 statutes or laws, including the Clean Air Act; the Clean Water Act; the Federal Food, Drug, and Cosmetics Act; the Endangered Species Act; the Pollution Prevention Act; and the Insecticide, Fungicide, and Rodenticides Act. In turn, each of the 50 states has its own body of law to comply with federal laws and regulations.

Cleaning up the nation's air, water, and land hasn't come cheap. Since passing these laws, the U.S. government has spent trillions of dollars to clean up and prevent pollution. Individuals, small businesses, and corporations paid the taxes that funded these programs. But businesses were hit with a double whammy. They not only had to pay taxes for the government to carry out its end of these programs, they had to pay cleanup costs for their own sites and buy the equipment to prevent future pollution. In addition, they had to hire and train personnel to implement and maintain mandated pollution prevention systems and procedures.

This is why the National Association of Manufacturers estimates that the cost of complying with federal regulations is more than $10,000 per employee for manufacturers. According to the report "Pollution Abatement Costs and Expenditures," based on a Census Bureau survey of 20,000 plants, U.S. manufacturers spent $5.9 billion on pollution equipment, and another $20.7 billion on pollution prevention in 2005.

The EPA has achieved some major successes:

- More than half of large American cities now meet air-quality standards.

- Emissions of common air pollutants have dropped an average of 24 percent.

- Levels of lead in children's blood have declined 75 percent.

- Sixty percent of the nation's waterways are safe for fishing and swimming.

- Ocean dumping has been banned.

- Wastewater standards have been established for 50 industries.

- DDT has been banned and safer pesticides introduced.

- Toxic emissions in the air have been reduced 39 percent.[1]

As a result, we now have cleaner air in our cities, and cleaner and safer water in our streams, rivers, lakes, bays, and harbors, than at any time since the Industrial Revolution began more than 200 years ago.

In contrast, India and China have been getting more polluted in the last 30 years as they have industrialized. Four cities in India, and six in China, are listed in the "Dirty 30" list of the most polluted sites in the world compiled by the New

York-based Blacksmith Institute.[2] This list is based on scoring criteria devised by an international panel including researchers from Johns Hopkins, Harvard, and Mt. Sinai Hospital. (Specialists from Green Cross Switzerland also participated in assessing more than 400 polluted sites.) "Children are sick and dying in these polluted places, and it's not rocket science to fix them," said Richard Fuller, Blacksmith's founder and director. "There has been more focus on pollution in the media, but there has been little action in terms of new funding or programmes."[3] The Institute highlights health threats to children, like the stunting effect of lead poisoning on intellectual development. Some 12 million people are affected in the top 10 sites, says the report.

Pollution in China

It's hard to describe the horrors of pollution in these cities. Imagine living in Xiditou (pronounced shee-dee-tow), China, about 60 miles east of Beijing, where the Feng Chan River that runs through the town is now black as ink and clotted with debris. The local economy has doubled in just four years, but at a terrible cost. More than 100 factories occupy what were once fields of rice and cotton. These include dozens of local chemical plants, makers of toxins including sulfuric acid, and these factories disgorge wastewater directly into the river. Industrial poisons have leached into groundwater, contaminating drinking supplies. The air has a distinctively sour odor. The rate of cancer is now more than 18 times the national average. "People regard their drinking water as little better than liquid poison, but unable to afford bottled water for all their daily needs, most adults continue to drink it. They buy mineral water only for their children."[4]

Tianying, in Anhui province, is one of the largest lead production centers in China, with an output of half of the country's total. Low-level technologies, illegal operations, and a lack of air-pollution control measures have caused severe lead poisoning. Lead concentrations in the air and soil are 8.5 to 10 times national standards. Local crops and wheat at farmers' homes are also contaminated by lead dust, at 24 times the national standard.

The ironic note to these statistics is that China actually has more stringent restrictions on lead than the U.S. The difference is that neither the local nor the national government is enforcing the laws. Residents, particularly children, suffer from lead poisoning, which causes encephalopathy, lower IQs, short attention spans, learning disabilities, hyperactivity, hearing and vision problems, stomachaches, kidney malfunction, anemia, and premature births. The number of people potentially affected in Tianying alone is 140,000.[5]

Or perhaps you would like to live in Wanshan, China, termed the mercury capital of China because more than 60 percent of the country's mercury deposits were discovered there. Mercury contamination extends throughout the city's air, surface water, and soils. Concentrations in the soil range from 24 to 348 mg/kg, 16 to 232 times the national standard. To put this into perspective, the mercury from one fluorescent bulb can pollute 6,000 gallons of water beyond safe levels for drinking, and it only takes one teaspoon of mercury to contaminate a 20-acre lake – forever. Health hazards include kidney and gastrointestinal damage, neurological damage, and birth defects. Chronic exposure is fatal.

Or you could go live in Linfen and experience what it was like to live in the coal towns of the United States in the early 20th century. Linfen, in Shanxi province, is at the heart of China's enormous and expanding coal industry, which provides about two-thirds of the nation's energy. China's State Environment Protection Agency (SEPA) has branded Linfen as having the worst air quality in the country. You wouldn't need to bother to hang clothes out to dry after washing them, because they would be black before you finished hanging them up. Residents say they literally choke on coal dust in the evenings. Water has been diverted from agriculture to industry, with tight rationing programs that make water available to residents and farmers only a few hours a day. Pollution is taking a serious toll on the health of Linfen's residents, with growing cases of bronchitis, pneumonia, and lung cancer. More than 3,000,000 people are affected.[6]

Coal-Fired Power Plant in China

On November 13, 2005, Jilin Province became polluted with benzene, aniline, and nitrobenzene when an explosion at a petrochemical plant led to a spill of an estimated 100 tons of toxic substances into the Songhua River. The Songhua joins the Heilongjiang and forms the border with the Russian Federation. The river continues into Russia, where it is renamed the Amur and flows into the Sea of Okhotsk. The explosion forced the temporary evacuation of some 10,000 residents in Jilin City. The city of Harbin, 230 miles downstream, was cut off from water use for four days as the contamination passed by. More than 16,000 tons of drinking water was brought into Harbin. "Benzene levels were 108 times above national safety levels," according to SEPA. Benzene is a highly poisonous toxin and carcinogenic. Environmental officials in Russia monitored the Amur River, which is the main water source for the city of Khabarovsk.

In an interview with *China Business News* after this incident, Yang Chanofei, director of the Policies and Regulations Department of SEPA, admitted that,

> The total volume of contamination is huge and has an impact on the world environment; environmental frictions with neighboring countries are rising…It is true that contamination that China is responsible for has an increasingly serious impact on the rest of the world, in particular neighboring countries…The Songhua River incident showed us a few things: China is at a stage where enterprise lacks the necessary environmental protection capabilities; the types of pollution are also becoming more complicated; inherent problems continue to trouble certain regions; law enforcement and environmental protection monitoring functions are weak; our response mechanism is inadequate.[7]

The January 13, 2007 *China Daily* reported that excessive waste discharges and land reclamation are worsening pollution in China's shallow coastal waters. Li Chunxian, spokesman for the State Oceanic Administration, said, "The coastal marine ecosystem is getting worse, and the quality of offshore ocean water has not improved. Large amounts of pollutants are filtering from the land into the sea."

Approximately 30 percent of China's area is desert, and China's rapid industrialization could cause this area to drastically increase. The Gobi Desert in the north is currently expanding by 950 square miles a year. The vast plains of North China used to be regularly flooded by the Yellow River, but its exploitation by dams for industry and irrigation has all but halted its natural flow, threatening to dry up its valley. The frequency of cessations of river flow has increased since the 1980s due to increased water usage; in 1997, the lower Yellow River did not flow at all for 230 days out of the year. Severe water scarcity in North China is a serious threat to sustained economic growth and has forced the government to begin implementing a large-scale diversion of water from the Yangtze River to northern cities, including Beijing.

Efforts to control China's pollution problem have been a stated top priority of China's leadership since March 1998, when SEPA was upgraded to ministry level. In 2006, a series of new laws were passed and the government greatly expanded expenditures on environmental protection. During its 11th Five-Year Plan (2006-2010), it planned to reduce total emissions by 10 percent and increase China's energy efficiency 20 percent.[8]

In 2007, China embarked on an effort to expand renewable energy sources, with the Medium- and Long-Term Development Plan for Renewable Energy mandating that 10 percent of its energy be produced from renewable sources, like hydropower, wind power, and biomass, by 2010, and 15 percent by 2020. "By the end of 2009, the central government reported a 15.6 percent reduction in energy intensity from 2005 levels (although energy intensity worsened in the first quarter of 2010)."[9]

To reduce emissions, China launched its first voluntary carbon trade in August of 2008, when a Shanghai-based automobile insurance company purchased more than 8,000 tons of carbon credits through a green commuting campaign during the Beijing Olympics. In August 2010, China launched a low-carbon pilot program in select cities and provinces to test how to implement low-carbon growth. By the end of October 2010, China had achieved its energy-efficiency goal by phasing out inefficient production capacity of 87 million tons of steel, 60 million tons of iron, and 214 million tons of cement since 2006. However, Chinese industries still use 20 to 100 percent more energy per unit of output than their American, Japanese, and European counterparts. China's 12th Five Year Plan (2011- 2015) set objectives congruent with Beijing's aim of reducing carbon intensity by 40 to 45 percent by 2020, but the country needs to implement aggressive measures to reduce carbon emissions while its economy and demand for resources continue to grow.[10]

China's leaders are concerned that environmental problems could undermine economic development, public health, social stability, and China's international image. Pollution and deforestation in China have worldwide implications. In 2006, China's top environmental official, Zhou Shengxian, announced there had been 51,000 pollution-related protests in

2005 – almost 1,000 a week. On June 19, 2007, the Netherlands Environment Assessment Agency announced that China's carbon dioxide (CO_2) emissions had been seven percent higher than those of the United States in 2006. Many experts were skeptical, but on June 13, 2008, the same agency announced that China's emissions had been 14 percent higher than those of the U.S. in 2007. "The Chinese increase accounted for two-thirds of the growth in the year's global greenhouse gas emissions," it found.[11]

In an interview with Bob Woodruff on ABC News, former President Bill Clinton noted that China surpassed the United States this year as the world's biggest emitter of greenhouse gases and said, "If India and China and the other emerging economies don't join in some sort of limitation, then they can burn up the planet." He also noted that China and India have declined to join the G8 nations in agreeing to curb greenhouse emissions. He added: "[The Chinese] are coming up with a new coal-fired power plant every 10 days or so. They don't want to make a commitment."[12]

In addition, China is now the largest source of SO_2 emissions in the world (SO_2 causes acid rain), and Japan and South Korea suffer from acid rain produced by China's coal-fired power plants.[13] A World Bank report, "Cost of Pollution in China," released in February 2007, reached the following conclusions:

The combined health and non-health cost of outdoor air and water pollution on China's economy comes to around $100 billion a year (or about 5.8 percent of China's GDP). Air pollution, especially in large cities, is leading to high incidences of lung diseases, including cancer and respiratory system problems, and therefore higher levels of work and school absenteeism. Water pollution is also causing growing levels of cancer and disease, particularly in children under the age of five. It is also exacerbating China's water scarcity problems, bringing the overall cost of water scarcity to about one percent of GDP. Six of the 20 most polluted cities in the world are in China.

The report stated that China failed to meet the environmental goals of its 10th Five-Year Plan and emissions of SO_2 and soot had been 42 and 22 percent higher, respectively, than their targets. In the period between 2001 and 2005, on average, about 54 percent of the seven main rivers in China contained water deemed unsafe for human consumption – a nearly 12 percent increase since the early 1990s. Up to 750,000 premature deaths each year caused by air and water pollution is the figure that the Chinese government convinced the World Bank to remove from the above-referenced report, citing the danger of "social unrest." China's bloggers have been very vocal about this cover-up.

On August 11, 2008, Isabel Hilton, ChinaDialogue.net's editor, interviewed Alexandra Harney, the *Financial Times'* former South China correspondent and author of *The China Price: The True Cost of Chinese Competitive Advantage.*[14] Ms. Hilton asked, "How would you assess the environmental costs, to China, of the 'develop now, clean up later' approach?" Ms. Harney replied,

We all know the figures of half a million people dying each year of pollution-related diseases. The *Financial Times* has reported that it's more like three-quarters of a million people passing away every year. Then there are untold numbers of people who are suffering from environmentally related diseases in villages and cities across China who don't come into those figures. So I think that we are only beginning to scratch the surface of the public-health implications of China's environmentally related disaster.

She went on to add, "People were at least superficially aware of the problem, but the desire for economic advancement overpowered any desire for cleanup." Her answer to the question, "Do you think that remains true when people understand what the cost is?" was,

No. I think, for example, that when you visit one of these villages – the cancer villages, the villages where women are all widows because their husbands have died from injuries or illnesses contracted in manufacturing or the villages where crops have been decimated by polluted water – people are smart. It's perfectly clear to them how the environment is directly affecting them and their health. There is increasing amounts of activism around the issue by the NGOs, who are doing interesting work. And I was really struck by all the protests by people in Xiamen and Shanghai, middle-class people who were taking to the streets about environmental issues. That's massive. The numbers of environmental refuges are also interesting. [Deputy environment minister] Pan Yue himself says that there are tens of millions of environmental refugees – people pushed off their land, for instance, by environmental pollution. Those people are certainly aware of what is happening to them.

China's CO₂ Emissions

A 2007 study, "Forecasting the Path of China's CO_2 Emissions Using Province Level Information," forecasted China's CO_2 emissions based on a provincial-level dataset from 1985 to 2004 from SEPA. It showed that China's CO_2 emissions have dramatically increased over the last five years and presented econometric forecasts strongly suggesting that the "magnitude of the projected increase in Chinese emissions out to 2015 is several times larger than reductions embodied in the Kyoto Protocol."[15]

An article, "Scientists Track Asian Pollution," in the September 4, 2008 issue of *The News Tribune* of Tacoma, Washington reported that a fleet of specially equipped unmanned aerial vehicles had been launched through the projected paths of pollution just as China shut down factories and banned automobiles form Beijing for the Olympics. These took chemical samples and recorded temperatures, humidity levels, and sunlight intensities in clouds of smog. The article quoted a report from the *Journal of Geophysical Research* that stated, "East Asia pollution aerosols could impose far-reaching environmental impacts at continental, hemispheric and global scales because of long-range transport," and that "A warm conveyer belt lifts the pollutants into the upper troposphere over Asia, where winds can wing it to the United States in a week or less."Dan Jaffe, a professor of environmental science at the University of Washington and a member of the National Academies of Science panel studying the issue, said, "This pollution is distributed on average equally from Northern California to British Columbia." He added that "Up to 30 percent of the mercury deposited in the United

States from airborne sources comes from Asia, with the highest concentrations in Alaska and the Western states."

On February 18, 2008, Pan Yue announced that SEPA and the China Insurance Regulatory Commission had jointly issued "Guiding Opinions on Environment Pollution Liability Insurance," officially establishing an environmental pollution liability insurance system. The press release stated that "the country is entering a period with a high frequency of environmental pollution accidents. Of the 7,555 large-scale projects in heavy chemical industry, 81 percent are located in environmentally sensitive areas including river watersheds and populous areas...As there's no institutional guarantee for treatment of pollution accidents, the enterprises often fail to assume the responsibility of compensating and restoring the environment, and the victims of the pollution fail to be compensated timely, which trigger many social conflicts." The vice minister said, "Enterprises profit from illicit polluting behaviors and everybody pays for the environmental damages."[16]

On February 26, 2008, Pan Yue announced the first batch of countermeasures against high pollution and high environmental risk products for 2008, involving 141 products in six industries. He proposed cancellation of tax refunds on 39 products to the Ministry of Finance, the State Administration of Taxation, the Ministry of Commerce, and the General Administration of Customs. The list included cadmium-nickel cells, mercury, lead-acid storage batteries, benzene arsenic, several pesticides, and organic arsenic. He said, "This list was one of the basic elements of green trade policy... to show our concrete action to fulfill international environmental obligations."[17] This is the same Pan Yue who said, "We can't import water and we can't import air" when interviewed in the documentary "China Rises," a four-part television series produced by the Canadian Broadcasting Corporation, *The New York Times*, ZDF, and France 5 in 2006. According to this documentary, China uses one-third of the world's steel and nearly half of its cement. Government enterprises still produce one-half of China's GDP and 100 million peasants have migrated to the cities from the farms.

China closed 10,412 coalmines between mid-2005 and mid-2008 in an effort to improve workplace safety and reduce its use of natural resources, according to Li Yizhong, head of the State Administration of Work Safety.[18]ChinaMining.org reported that China is likely to accelerate shutting down 2,500 small coalmines in 2009 and 2010 to ease the coal oversupply in the Chinese market. China is the world's largest producer and consumer of coal, but it has the world's deadliest mines, with an average of more than 13 people dying each day in mining accidents like flooded shafts and tunnel collapses. (The true death toll, including mining-related illnesses, is believed to be much higher.) Zhao Tiechui, Vice Minister of the State Work Safety Authority, said "too many companies concentrated solely on profits." He cited outdated technology, a lack of safety awareness, and poor management as the key problems. He said, "We have to change the mindset that economic growth is more important than people's safety.... We should make it clear to every official that they will be measured not only on GDP growth, but also their record on work safety."[19]

America Helping Cleanup of Chinese Environment

After two decades of informal collaboration, the EPA and SEPA signed a Memorandum of Understanding in December 2003 to provide a strategic approach to extensive cooperation. This established a Working Group on Clean Air and Clean Energy to coordinate and facilitate implementation of the Strategy for Clean Air and Energy Cooperation. Cooperative projects include regional air-quality management and projects related to the transportation, power, and cement sectors.

The regional air-quality management project explored the feasibility of applying U.S. air-quality management methods and technologies to a large Chinese city, Shanghai. It also formed a U.S.-China Working Group with the Beijing Organizing Committee to assist Beijing with having healthy air for the 2008 Olympic Games.

Under the transportation-sector project, a work plan was signed in 2004 to undertake an integrated set of fuel and vehicle projects as members of the Partnership for Clean Fuels and Vehicles.

The power sector project included assisting China in developing market mechanisms to improve air quality by reducing sulfur dioxide and fine particle pollution by implementing emissions trading programs. Also, the Advance Reburn System pollution-control project provided technical assistance on cost-effective control of nitrogen oxides, organic pollutants, and other pollutants, like mercury, from combustion sources.

The cement-sector project provided assistance in reducing emissions of dioxins and furans from cement production. China produces and uses more than 40 percent of the world's cement, and cement plants rank among its top five sources of dioxins and furans emissions. These plants also account for more than 40 percent of total industrial particulate (dust) emissions, and sometimes also release mercury and heavy metals.[20]

Working Conditions in China

In 1995, China passed a comprehensive labor law, covering labor contracts, working hours, wages, worker safety, child labor, and labor disputes. The law mandates a maximum workweek of 40 hours and minimum wages are established locally. If workers must work more than 40 hours, overtime pay at fixed rates is mandatory. Workers are guaranteed at least one day off per week, and working conditions are required to be safe and sanitary.

In reality, however, the rights of Chinese workers are routinely violated. Workers work far more than 40 hours a week, are paid below the minimum wage, do not receive overtime pay, and have few days off. Physical abuse and dangerous working conditions are also common.

Factories owned by Hong Kong Chinese, Taiwanese, and South Korean companies tend to have the worst conditions, as do small, privately owned, and government factories. Large factories owned and operated by foreign companies, or with direct investment from, and management by, Western companies, tend to have the least violations.

If China has adequate labor laws, why are its working conditions so poor and violations so rampant? For one thing, its labor laws are poorly enforced, especially at the local level. Factory owners have a huge incentive to ignore them because compliance costs money. A large supply of migrant workers, most of whom are ignorant of their rights and willing to work under dismal conditions without protest, floods the labor market. And the government's ban on independent trade unions leaves workers without representatives who can protest violations to management.

In response to these problems, Western corporations are increasingly adopting their own codes of conduct for their Chinese factories and suppliers, setting standards for labor rights, human rights, and social, ethical, and environmental policies. According to a recent estimate by the World Bank, about 1,000 different such codes exist today. Companies, multi-stakeholder groups such as the China Working Group, nongovernmental organizations, and unions issue these codes.

Pollution in India

You wouldn't find it healthy to live in many of the industrial cities of India today, any more than in those of China. India is developing more slowly, but its growth is already taking a toll on the health of its people. India's population has more than tripled since independence in 1947, from 350 million people to 1.2 billion, severely straining the country's environment, infrastructure, and natural resources.

Consider Vapi, at the southern end of India's "Golden Corridor," a 400 km belt of industrial estates in the state of Gujarat. There are more than 50 industrial estates in the region, containing over 1,000 industries and extending over more than 1,000 acres. Many estates are chemical manufacturing centers, producing petrochemicals, pesticides, pharmaceuticals, textiles, dyes, fertilizers, leather products, paint, and chlor-alkali. Waste products discharged from these industries contain heavy metals (copper, chromium, cadmium, zinc, nickel, lead, and iron), cyanides, pesticides, aromatic compounds like PCBs (polychlorinated biphenyls), and other toxins.

The Indian Medical Association reports that most local drinking water is contaminated because of the absence of a proper system for disposing of industrial waste. Industrial waste instead drains directly into the Damaganga and Kolak rivers. Vapi's groundwater has levels of mercury 96 times higher than World Health Organization standards. Approximately 71,000 people have no choice but to drink contaminated well water, as clean water sources are more than a mile away. The water is so discolored by contaminants it looks like a bottle of orange soda. Local produce contains heavy metals up to 60 times the safe standard. There is a high incidence of respiratory diseases, chemical dermatitis, and skin, lung, and throat cancers. Women in the area report high incidences of spontaneous abortions, abnormal fetuses, and infertility. Children's ailments include respiratory and skin diseases and retarded growth.

It isn't any better off in Sukinda, in the state of Orissa, where 97 percent of India's chromite ore deposits are located. Twelve mines operate without any environmental management plans, and more than 30 million tons of waste rock is spread over the surrounding area and the banks of the Brahmani River. The mines discharge untreated water directly into the river. Approximately 70 percent of the surface water, and 60 percent of the drinking water, contains hexavalent chromium at more than double national and international standards. The polluted Brahmani River is the only water source for 2,600,000 people. Health problems include gastrointestinal bleeding, tuberculosis, asthma, infertility, birth defects, and still-births. A study by the Orissa Voluntary

Health Association found that 24.5 percent of the local inhabitants suffer from pollution-induced diseases.[21]

The Indian economy is growing rapidly, but pollution is quickly spiraling out of control and rivers are dying by the dozens. Fully 80 percent of urban waste, including industrial waste, winds up in the country's rivers. Much of this comes from untreated sewage. The Ganges River has levels of fecal coliform, a dangerous bacterium that comes from untreated sewage, 3,000 percent higher than what is considered safe for bathing. More than three billion liters of waste are pumped into Delhi's Yamuna River each day. "The river is dead, it just has not been officially cremated," said Sunita Narain, director of the New Delhi-based Centre for Science and Environment, one of India's top environmental watchdog groups, to Spiegel-Online.com in reference to the Yamuna.[22]

Air pollution is also a growing problem. There are four main sources: vehicles, power plants, industry, and refineries. India's air pollution is exacerbated by its heavy reliance on coal for power generation. Coal supplies more than half the country's energy needs and nearly three-quarters of its electricity. Reliance on coal has led to a 900 percent increase in carbon emissions over the past 40 years. India's coal plants are old and not outfitted with modern pollution controls. Also, Indian coal has a high ash content, which creates smog. Vehicle emissions are responsible for 70 percent of the country's air pollution. Exhaust from vehicles has increased 800 percent, and industrial pollution 400 percent, in the past 20 years.

The blanket of smog hanging over India means the country is getting less and less sunlight. This phenomenon, known as solar dimming, may even protect against global warming. India is getting about five percent less sunlight than it did 20 years ago, according to a study by Padma Kumari and colleagues at the Indian Institute of Tropical Meteorology in Pune. Rice yields are dropping as brown clouds block out sunlight, and solar dimming is reducing the increase in maximum and minimum temperatures. Preliminary data from China suggests that it, too, is getting less sun because of rising particle pollution linked to industrialization. Similar dimming was caused in Western nations in the 20th century by smog; when the West cleared up its smog in the 1980s and 1990s, clearer skies returned, which researchers described as "global brightening."

Working Conditions in India

You would think that as India is a democracy, working conditions there would be better than in China. Well, you would be wrong.

For one thing, child labor is rampant. According to an article, "The Hidden Factory: Child Labour in India," in *The South Asian*, May 7, 2005, many consumer goods, like trinkets, ornaments, jewelry, clothes, and even tea, are "the products of a hidden factory of countless children, many as young as five years old, toiling for tireless hours, under harsh, hazardous, exploitative, often life threatening conditions for extremely low wages." The article states "India has the largest number of working children in the world." Credible estimates range from 15 to 60 million child laborers. What is even more horrible to comprehend is that a large percentage of these child laborers are de facto slaves, bonded to their jobs, with no means of escape or freedom until they can repay their parents' loans. The major industries using child labor are as follows:

Carpets – An estimated 50,000 to 1,050,000 children, as young as six, are often chained to carpet looms in confined, dimly lit workshops, making the thousands of tiny wool knots that become expensive hand-knotted carpets for export. Recruiters or organized gangs pay landless peasants cash advances to "bond" their children to their jobs. The children suffer from spinal deformities, retarded growth, respiratory illnesses, and poor eyesight.

Brassware – An estimated 40,000 to 45,000 children, as young as six, are involved in brassware production, including jobs like removing molten metal from molds and furnaces, electroplating, polishing, and applying chemicals. If they survive being injured from molten metal and exposure to furnaces operating as high as 2,000 degrees Fahrenheit, they often suffer from tuberculosis and other respiratory diseases due to inhalation of fumes from the furnaces and metal dust.

Leather – As many as 25,000 children, from 10 to 15, are involved in the manufacture of shoes. They suffer from respiratory problems, lung diseases, and skin infections from continuous skin contact with industrial adhesives and breathing the vapors from glues.

Gemstones – Children are commonly engaged as "apprentices" in the gem polishing industry. The learning process takes five to seven years and they work an average of 10 hours a day. Major health issues include tuberculosis and respiratory diseases.

Glass – This industry employs an estimated 8,000 to 50,000 children as young as eight. They work in an inferno due to the intense heat of glass furnaces (1,400-1,600° C) and suffer from skin burns, tuberculosis, respiratory diseases, mental retardation, and genetic cell damage.

Silk – An estimated 5,000 children, mostly girls from five to 16, are employed in silk manufacturing, which includes sericulture, dyeing, and weaving the silk. Chemicals and boiling water in the dyeing process are common health hazards; skin burns from the boiling water and respiratory diseases from the chemicals often result.

Agriculture –Parents pledge children as young as six to landlords as bonded laborers. The number of bonded laborers is not categorized by adults and children, but the total is estimated to range from 2.6 to 15 million. Children are involved in all types of agriculture, including rice growing, cattle grazing, and tea farming. They are at the complete disposal of their masters and receive in return a bare minimum of food and lodging. More than 90 percent of bonded laborers in India, many of whom became bonded as children, have never had the opportunity to go to school.

Mining – A 2006 report, "Our Mining Children," prepared by a team of non-profit organizations, described the condition of hundreds of thousands of migrant workers in the mining industry.[23]

Karnataka, for example, is a state with vast mineral resources, of which the Bellary district has the most extensive range. Minerals found there include iron ore, manganese, quartz, gold, copper, granite, and decorative stones. (India is the fourth-largest iron-ore producer in the world.) As a result of new government economic policies, a shift to privatization, an open market economy, and wide-open markets in China,

South Korea, and Australia, mining companies have bought up thousands of acres of land in the district since 2000.

All of the mines visited by government teams had child laborers, some as young as five. It is estimated that as many as 200,000, or 50 percent, of the workers are children. The mining economy is only profitable because of large-scale child labor and the flouting of social and environmental laws. The mine owners say they only employ the adults, but as the families live at the mine site, the children join in the work. Owners say the parents force them to employ the children. The parents admit that it is very hard work for the children, but say they cannot survive otherwise.

The shift to mining was a result of desperation and the desire for a quick profit. Historically, the main occupation in the area was agriculture. But starting in 1994-1995, mining began to take on greater importance after five years of recurrent drought and the mechanization of agriculture. In many places, landowners experienced crop failures due to heavy dust pollution from neighboring mining lands, and were therefore forced to convert their fields into mines as well. Landless agricultural laborers were forced to find new work and the mines became their only option. Miles and miles of agricultural land in the foothills have been converted into iron ore mines.

Mining is undertaken for only about eight months in a year, as the mines close during the monsoon season. Lands are taken on lease from the Department of Mines of the Government of Karnataka through the State Pollution Control Board. The mining activity consists of extracting the ore, breaking the rocks into small stones and pebbles, and grinding them into fine powder. The mining area has vast stretches of extraction sites, stone crushers, stockyards, dump yards, weighing and permit yards, truck yards, and wagon loading points along the railway.

Children work alongside the adults with their bare hands, using hammers and sieves. They have no safety equipment, do not cover their heads or eyes, and work barefoot sitting on the burning ore. They work in the open, without any shelter, whether in the hot sun or torrential rains. Young boys under 10 work with their fathers. As they are paid on a piece rate, there are no set working hours – or limits. Children are forced to work all day in order to grind enough ore into powder to make a living. As the wages are paid to the entire family, it is the males who are given the money. Many of the men spend most of their wages on liquor, so women and children have to work extra hours just to purchase basic food.

The workplace is a vast expanse of open mine fields without any shelter. It is also the living quarters for the workers. The migrant workers are given only a small plastic sheet, which is made into a tent for the entire family to live in. Infants and babies are crawling and walking at the mine site and sometimes assisting their older siblings at work. Infants inhale dust from the ore and eat iron ore mud when playing. Babies are left to sleep in the open. The tents are too small for the entire family to take shelter in if it rains.

There are no toilets provided, so women and girls have to undergo the humiliation of ablutions in public as the entire mine sites are felled clear and do not have a single tree or shrub. No water is provided at the workplace, so women and children walk long distances after work hours, or early in the morning, to fetch it from neighboring villages and private wells. Some mine owners supply drinking water by truck, but the supply is not regular or adequate. The rest of the water requirements are met from the mine pits by collecting contaminated water. Workers do not have clean water for washing their hands, bathing, or washing their clothes. They eat food with iron-ore-contaminated hands in the open site, while dust from the mines falls into the food as it is prepared. Many children suffer from skin allergies and intestinal and respiratory ailments as a result.

The workers live at the mine site, where they sleep in open pits surrounded by cesspools teeming with mosquitoes and other insects. They do not have electricity and cannot afford to purchase kerosene to provide lighting. Rations are purchased from nearby private traders at high rates for poor-quality food grains. Since they are constantly moving from one mine to another, the children have dropped out of school. As the mine workers are only casual laborers, they do not have health cards to give them access to the public health services set up by the Labor Ministry. They have to go to the private clinics that have mushroomed after the mines opened, and most of their disposable income goes towards purchasing medicines which provide only temporary relief. As they develop more serious and chronic illnesses like tuberculosis, silicosis, cancers, respiratory illnesses, disabilities due to accidents, and degenerative impairments, they are unable to work. As a result, they have to push their children to work earlier and earlier.

The coalition of non-profit organizations that prepared "Our Mining Children" made several demands for action by the Indian government. They said legal action against the employers should be taken by the Department of Labour under The Child Labour Act of 1986, The Mines Act of 1952 and the Bonded Labour System Abolition Act of 1976. Furthermore, mining leases should be cancelled for those who have employed child labor, and the government should take action toward the release and rehabilitation of the child laborers.

The report got little attention from the Indian government until charges of bribery and corruption were brought against the Chief Minister of Karnataka and several members of India's Parliament. In an article in Red-Orbit.com on August 18, 2006, it was revealed that six of the seven elected members of Parliament and State Assembly from the ore-producing region are mine owners. The article also stated "India is the third-largest supplier of iron ore to Chinese steelmakers."[24] The National Human Rights Commission asked for an explanation of the report. Finally enough pressure was put on the government to start an official inquiry into the irregularities in iron mining.

The Corruption Ombudsman of Karnataka State, Justice Santosh Hegde, finally submitted a 2,000-page report in December 2008. It examined how unplanned exploitation of mineral resources had been carried on for many years in violation of the Forest (Conservation) Act of 1980, the Mines and Minerals (Development and Regulation) Act of 1957, and the Karnataka Minor Mineral Concession Rules of 1994. The report found that illegal permits had been granted by the Chief Minister of Karnataka. China had bought most of the iron ore produced between 2004 and 2008. Illegal sales contracts had cost the government millions in lost tax revenue. None of the iron ore plants had any pollution-control equipment, such as electrostatic precipitating devices. The City of Bellary had extreme air pollution from coal dust. Thousands of acres of land had been deforested and ruined for agriculture. Ground water was being depleted by the ore plants at an alarming rate, causing water scarcity. As a result of the report, several bureaucrats were charged with serious misdemeanors and 150 mines were recommended for closure.

The Salesians, a Catholic charity, have been assisting the child laborers and providing them with a chance for an education through mobile schools at the mine sites. Karnataka is not the only place in India where children are put to work: the problem is great and complex, and the number of working children is in the millions. The Salesians run community centers in 72 towns throughout India to serve street and working children, and are also working to change the situation so children will be free to be children. Unfortunately, their efforts, and those of other non-governmental organizations, have not yet succeeded.

A 2010 study, "India's Childhood in the Pits," was conducted in eight states by Haq, a children's rights organization; Samata, a social-justice group; the group Mines, Minerals and People; and the Dhaatri Resource Centre for Women and Children. It revealed that while almost 50 percent of children in many Indian states were malnourished, children in mining areas were even more susceptible to malnutrition, hunger, and food insecurity. Displaced, homeless, or living in inadequate housing, they are forced to drop out of school and are vulnerable to abuse and exploitation. They are recruited for a number of illegal activities and are even trafficked by organized crime. Mining regions have large numbers of children engaged in hazardous activities, and the laws and policies related to mining and related industries do not address the specific rights and entitlements of children.

The Kyoto Protocol

The Kyoto Protocol is an amendment to the United Nations Framework Convention on Climate Change (UNFCCC) adopted in 1992. The UNFCCC was an international treaty intended to bring countries together to reduce global warming and cope with the effects of temperature increases that are unavoidable after 150 years of industrialization. But as greenhouse gases continued to rise around the world, it became evident that only a firm and binding commitment by developed countries to reduce emissions could send a signal strong enough to convince businesses, communities, and individuals to act. So the member countries of the UNFCCC began negotiations on a protocol, an international agreement linked to the existing treaty but standing on its own.

The Kyoto Protocol was negotiated in Kyoto, Japan in December 1997. It opened for signature on March 16, 1998 and closed a year later. It was written to not take effect until 90 days after ratification by at least 55 countries representing at least 55 percent of the world's carbon dioxide emissions in 1990. Iceland was the 55th country to ratify the Kyoto protocol, on May 23, 2002, and Russia satisfied the second condition when it ratified the agreement in November 2004. So the Protocol entered into force on February 16, 2005.

The goal of the Kyoto Protocol is to reduce worldwide greenhouse gas emissions by 5.2 percent below 1990 levels between 2008 and 2012. Countries signing it have specified targets that may be higher or lower than the worldwide target of 5.2 percent. The targets cover the six main greenhouse gases: carbon dioxide, methane, nitrous oxide, hydrofluorocarbons, perfluorocarbons, and sulfur hexafluoride. The protocol places a heavier burden on developed nations, under the principle of "common but differentiated responsibilities." This has two main reasons. First, developed countries can more easily afford the cost of cutting emissions. Second, they historically contributed more to the problem by emitting more greenhouse gases per person.

The Bush Administration received great criticism from other developed countries and environmentalists in the United States for not submitting the Protocol to Congress for ratification. However, prior to negotiating it in 1997, the U.S. Senate passed a resolution saying the U.S. should not sign any protocol that failed to include binding targets and timetables for both developing and industrialized nations or that "would result in serious harm to the economy of the United States."

The main reason for the refusal of the United States to ratify Kyoto is that it is supposedly unfair in making no demands on developing nations. (Under the Protocol, developing countries like China and India are exempt from reducing greenhouse gases.) Since China has now exceeded U.S. emissions of two of the six gases listed, this supposedly doesn't make sense. The U.S. could reduce its greenhouse gases by the seven percent target it was allotted in the Protocol and it wouldn't make a difference to achieving the worldwide target if developing countries are exempted.

Envoys from the world's top 20 greenhouse gas emitting countries met in Tokyo in March 2008 and agreed to draft a successor to the Kyoto Protocol, which expires at the end of

2012. They reconfirmed the principle of common but differentiated responsibilities. However, there were disagreements on how to achieve future reductions, and developing countries insisted that they not be held to the same targets as developed nations. A UN climate conference in December 2007 in Bali set a deadline of the end of 2009 for a post-Kyoto treaty.

A conference was then held in December 2009 in Copenhagen, Denmark, at which a treaty succeeding the Kyoto Protocol was expected to be adopted. In a meeting of the Group of Eight major industrialized nations, world leaders agreed to halve carbon emissions by 2050, but did not set specific targets because they could not agree on a base year. At this conference, delegates approved a motion to "take note of the Copenhagen Accord of December 18, 2009," though the motion was not unanimous and therefore not legally binding. The Copenhagen Accord recognizes the scientific case for keeping global temperature rises below 2°C.(Earlier proposals that would have aimed to limit temperature rises to 1.5°C and cut $CO2$ emissions by 80% by 2050 were dropped.)However, it does not contain the specific commitments for reduced emissions that are needed to achieve this aim. The agreement pledges $30 billion for the developing world over the next three years, rising to $100 billion per year by 2020, to help poor countries adapt to climate change. An agreement was also reached that would set up a deal to reduce deforestation in return for cash from developed countries.

The 2011 UN Climate Change Conference was held in Durban, South Africa to establish a new treaty to limit carbon emissions. It agreed to a legally binding deal comprising all countries, which will be prepared by 2015 and take effect in 2020.

Conclusion

The horrific effects of pollution in China and India, and its staggering cost in human life, are a graphic example of why Third World countries can outcompete American companies – not only because of their disparity in wages, but also because their governments do not enforce the same environmental and social standards. As Americans, who place a high value on human life and protecting our environment, we wouldn't have it any other way. But American manufacturing industries do pay a penalty competing against such countries. China and India have undergone rapid industrialization in the last 30 years, during which time the U.S. has spent billions on technologies and equipment to clean up and prevent pollution. These nations had a golden opportunity to benefit from all the hard lessons learned by developed countries during their own industrialization. If China and India had purchased the technologies developed in the U.S. and other Western nations, their industrialization would not have caused such horrendous pollution. Millions of lives would have been saved, and the U.S. trade deficit with China would not have grown so large. In the future, our trade deficit could be significantly reduced if industrializing nations would purchase this equipment and reduce further pollution.

6

Why Should We Save American Manufacturing?

The average American rarely thinks about manufacturing, and if he or she does, it is as "dying" or "dead." We've considered plenty of evidence that American manufacturing is indeed in serious trouble and may need to be on life support. Many may wonder why we should even *try* to save American manufacturing. So…what difference would it make if we lost virtually all our domestic manufacturing?

In reality, American manufacturing is far from dead. Our manufacturing output is actually at the highest level in our history and continues to rise. If American manufacturing were a country, it would be tied with Germany as the world's third largest economy, and it would be larger than India and Russia combined.

As recently as 2007, America was the world's number one manufacturer, accounting for 25 percent of global manufacturing output. China has since become number one: in 2010, it accounted for 19.8 percent of world manufacturing output, slightly ahead of our 19.4 percent.[1] But the U.S. still maintains a huge productivity advantage: in 2010, we produced only slightly less than China, but with only 11.5 million manufacturing workers, compared to 215 million over there.

In 2010, our manufacturing sector accounted for $1.7trillion, or 11.7 percent of GDP. While manufacturing's share of GDP declined from 28.3 percent in 1953 to a low of 11.2 percent in 2009, much of our money today is spent on business services, health care, and education, areas where inflation has been much higher than in manufactured goods. This difference in inflation rates explains much of why manufacturing has become a *relatively* smaller part of our economy.

The Importance of Manufacturing

Manufacturing is the key engine that drives American prosperity. Federal Reserve Chair Ben Bernanke said, on February 28, 2007, "I would say that our economy needs machines and new factories and new buildings and so forth in order for us to have a strong and growing economy." Similarly, in 2011 the Center for American Progress released a report entitled "The Importance and Promise of American Manufacturing: Why It Matters if We Make It in America and Where We Stand Today," by Michael Ettlinger and Kate Gordon.[2] It asserts that,

Manufacturing is critically important to the American economy. For generations, the strength of our country rested on the power of our factory floors—both the machines and the men and women who worked them.

We need manufacturing to continue to be bedrock of strength for generations to come.... The strength or weakness of American manufacturing carries implications for the entire economy, our national security, and the well-being of all Americans.

The report argues that supplying our own needs through a strong manufacturing sector protects us from foreign economic and political disruptions and protects our national security, where the risk of a weak manufacturing capability is obvious. Over-reliance on imports and high manufacturing trade deficits make us vulnerable to everything from exchange rate fluctuations to trade embargoes and natural disasters. The report notes that whether the U.S. still dominates world manufacturing, as it once did, is a different question than whether U.S. manufacturing can compete. American manufacturers still successfully make and sell goods on a massive scale. One reason is that we are the biggest-consuming country in the world, and "as a result, we cannot avoid being a large manufacturer. There are enough products that are expensive or difficult enough to ship that it's hard to avoid making them here. There's certainly truth to the story that some U.S. manufacturing succeeds because of this advantage."

The report observes that manufacturing in the U.S. covers a broad range of activities, but there are six large subsectors that account for the bulk of it. The top six subsectors by value added are these:

	Value Added	Shipments	Capital Expenditures	Exports	Compensation	Worker Hours
Chemicals	16%	14%	13%	15%	8%	5%
Transportation Equipment	11%	12%	10%	22%	14%	11%
Food	11%	12%	9%	5%	8%	13%
Computers & Electronics	10%	7%	13%	14%	11%	5%
Fabricated Metals	8%	7%	7%	5%	11%	13%
Machinery	7%	7%	6%	13%	9%	8%
	64%	58%	58%	73%	62%	56%

Source: Census Bureau Annual Survey of Manufactures, 2008

The report concludes that as "long as there is demand in the United States for manufactured goods as well as the innovators, manufacturing workers, and available capital necessary to remain competitive, manufacturing can continue to be important in the U.S. economy." The report concludes that American manufacturing is not too far gone to save, and that while manufacturing in the U.S. is under threat and faces serious challenges, it is by no means a mere relic of the past. It is a large, vibrant sector– even if sometimes it is hard to see this as manufacturing jobs are lost, factories close, and sections of the country deindustrialize.

However, a study commissioned by NAM's Council of Manufacturing Associations, "Securing America's Future: The Case for a Strong Manufacturing Base," prepared by the noted economist and former Council of Economic Advisors member Joel Popkin, warns that "if the U.S. manufacturing base continues to shrink at the present rate and the critical mass is lost, the manufacturing innovation process will shift to other global centers. If this happens, a decline in U.S. living standards in the future is virtually assured."[3]

I personally believe that while manufacturing is not likely to fall below critical mass in the short term, it may in the longer term. U.S. manufacturers produce 65 percent of the manufactured goods our country consumes, down from 80 percent three decades ago. Many goods that were once manufactured here are now imported. For example, in the 1960s U.S. manufacturers made 98 percent of America's shoes, but today 90 percent are imported.[4] American factories still provide much of the processed food that Americans buy, everything from fish sticks to beer. And U.S. companies make a considerable share of personal-hygiene products like soap and shampoo, cleaning supplies, and prescription drugs that are sold in pharmacies. But many other consumer goods now come from overseas.

Manufacturing is Critical to Our National Defense

We need to be able to produce the goods that allow us to defend America. American manufacturers supply the military with essentials including tanks, fighter jets, submarines, and other high-tech equipment. The same advances in technology that consumers take for granted support our soldiers. Kerri Houston, senior vice president for policy at the Institute for Liberty and a member of the U.S.-China Economic and Security Review Commission, writes that,

> If we are to retain our military superiority at home and abroad, we must maintain the ability to manufacture original equipment and replacement parts in the U.S. Needlessly sending defense jobs overseas will do nothing to ensure our long-term national security, which history shows will require a robust research and development, technical and manufacturing base.[5]

In his keynote address, "Lessons for a Rapidly Changing World," at Computer Associates' CA World 2003 conference, former Secretary of State Henry Kissinger said, "The question really is whether America can remain a great power or a dominant power if it becomes primarily a service economy, and I doubt that. I think that a country has to have a major industrial base in order to play a significant role in the world. And I am concerned from that point of view." He added, "But if the outsourcing would continue to a point of stripping the U.S. of its industrial base and of the act of getting out its own technology, I think this requires some really careful thought and national policy probably can create incentives to prevent that from happening."[6]

The U.S. cannot rely on other countries to supply its military because their interests may run counter to ours. If we faced a military threat to our homeland, how could we assure access to the goods needed to defend our country when these items are being manufactured in China? We cannot risk being held hostage by foreign manufacturers, so it is crucial that the capacity to produce components and technologies critical to U.S. weapons be located within the United States.

Col. Joe Muckerman, former director of emergency planning and mobilization for the secretary of defense, wrote a guest editorial entitled "Without a Robust Industrial Base DOD Will Lose Future Wars" in the April 17, 2008 *Manufacturing & Technology News*. He opined:

Joe Stalin said that World War II was not won on the battlefields of Europe but in Detroit. Had Stalin lived until the end of the Cold War, he probably would have arrived at a similar conclusion. The U.S. won the Cold War because it maintained technologically superior strategic weapons at a level that deterred the Soviet Union from attacking our vital interests. The United States was able to sustain this force for half a century during which the U.S. economy prospered while that of the USSR collapsed...Today the U.S. industrial base is fast becoming global and the U.S. economy is in trouble.

Similarly, "The Case for a National Manufacturing Strategy," released in April 2011 by the Information Technology & Innovation Foundation, echoes the idea that manufacturing is critical to our national security:

If we lose our preeminence in manufacturing technology, then we lose our national security. This is because as the U.S. industrial base moves offshore, so does the defense industrial base. And reliance on foreign manufacturers increases vulnerability to counterfeit goods.[7]

This report quotes Joel Yudken, who explains in his book *Manufacturing Insecurity* that "Continued migration of manufacturing offshore is both undercutting U.S. technology leadership while enabling foreign countries to catch up to, if not leapfrog, U.S. capabilities in critical technologies important to national security." The report reveals that the U.S. has "diminishing or no capability in lithium-ion battery production, yttrium barium copper oxide high-temperature superconductors, and photovoltaic solar cell encapsulants, among others.... Additional examples of defense-critical technologies where domestic sourcing is endangered include propellant chemicals, space-qualified electronics, power sources for space and military applications (especially batteries and photovoltaics), specialty metals, hard disk drives, and flat panel displays (LCDs)."

The ITIF report shows that most manufacturing sectors actually shrank, in terms of real value-added, from 2000 to 2009. In fact, from 2000 to 2009, 15 of 19 U.S. manufacturing sectors saw absolute declines in output; they were producing less in 2009 than they were at the start of the decade. U.S. manufacturing declined noticeably over the last decade, and not just in the number of jobs. Data from the Bureau of Economic Analysis shows that from January 2000 to January 2010, manufacturing jobs fell by 6.17 million, or 34 percent. The report also presents convincing evidence that the government's official calculation that manufacturing accounts for an 11.2 percent share of U.S. GDP is too high because it overstates output from the computer and electronics industry.

Reliance on foreign manufacturers also increases our vulnerability to counterfeit goods. According to a recent study by the Bureau of Industry and Security, in 2008 there were 9,356 incidents of counterfeit foreign products making their way into Defense Department supply chains – a 142 percent increase since 2005. The U.S. cannot rely on other countries to supply its military because their interests may run counter to ours. If we faced a military threat to our homeland, how could we assure access to the goods needed to defend our country when these items are being manufactured in China? We cannot risk being held hostage by foreign manufacturers, so it is crucial that the capacity to produce components and tech-nologies critical to U.S. weapons be located within the United States.

Manufacturing Provides Millions of Jobs

Many people do not realize that, although the U.S. has lost millions of manufacturing jobs in the last 20 years, these jobs are still the foundation of the U.S. economy and a major basis of our middle class. Manufacturing provides high-paying jobs for nearly 12 million Americans and creates an additional eight million jobs in related sectors. The states with the largest manufacturing workforces are California, Texas, Ohio, Illinois, and Pennsylvania. (California's manufacturing workforce of more than 1.9 million is almost the size of the Texas and Illinois manufacturing workforces combined.)[8]

Manufacturing Jobs by State

Source: Census Bureau, 2010

Part of the loss of manufacturing jobs is simply due to automation and the increasing productivity of American workers. American workers have achieved high productivity growth year in and year out, increasing their productivity by more than 50 percent in the past decade alone. In the past 20 years, manufacturing productivity, measured in output per man-hour, has more than doubled, much faster growth than other economic sectors.[9] And in the decade ahead, productivity growth will be the major source of growth in manufacturing output as Baby Boomers leave the workforce to retire.

Automation has helped keep American manufacturers not only competitive, but the most productive in the world. The growing trend of training manufacturing workers in so-called "lean" manufacturing is accelerating this. For example, one metal stamping company we represented went through lean manufacturing training in 2001. As a result, its productivity per employee doubled and the time it took for a part to go through the shop, from the first workstation to the last, went down from an average of four weeks to one day.

Another trend is the *domestic* outsourcing of service jobs within manufacturers, like janitorial services, cafeteria and food services, accounting, payroll, and legal departments. Thus jobs that may have once been classified as manufacturing are now classified as service jobs. As companies get rid of business units and the people who used to work in them, they get smaller. And as they get smaller and more efficient, their revenues go down but their profits go up.

Manufacturing Jobs Pay Higher Wages than Service Jobs

Manufacturing wages and benefits average about 25 percent higher than in non-manufacturing jobs. According to the National Association of Manufacturers, "In 2010, the average U.S. manufacturing worker earned $77,186 annually, including pay and benefits. The average non-manufacturing worker earned $56,436." As manufacturing jobs have declined over the past 40 years, the difference between the lowest and highest income brackets has steadily grown, as shown in the chart on the next page.

This difference is projected to get even worse, according to the Department of Labor's Occupational *Outlook for 2006-2016*. Employment growth is projected to continue to be concentrated in service-providing sectors of the economy. Service industries will generate almost all employment gains, and more than three-quarters of all jobs, by 2016. Professional and business services, and health care and social assistance, the sectors with the largest employment growth, will add 8.1 million jobs, more than half of the total projected increase in employment. The 10 industries with the largest projected wage and salary employment growth – led by management, scientific, and technical consulting services; employment services; and general medical and surgical hospitals – all are in the service sector.

Within the goods-producing sector, construction is the only area projected to grow. Employment in manufacturing is expected to decline by 1.5 million jobs. This is half the three million manufacturing jobs lost in the previous decade (1996-2006). Employment in goods-producing industries is expected to decrease from 14.9 to 13.1 percent of total employment. Four of the 10 industries with the largest projected wage and employment declines are in manufacturing, including printing and related support activities and motor vehicle parts manufacturing.

Because of the recent recession, construction has lost millions of jobs, and the manufacturing sector has declined by 2.5 million jobs in the five years since 2006 – one million more than the Department of Labor had projected for the entire 2006-2016 decade. The outlook for 2008-2018 is even worse, as service industries are projected to add 14.6 million jobs, or 96 percent of the total increase.[10]

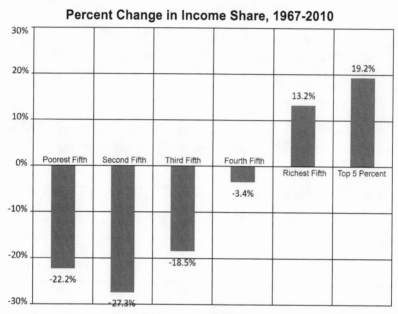

Percent Change in Income Share, 1967-2010

Source: Census Bureau

As the manufacturing percentage of our GDP has declined, the percentage of GDP produced by the financial sector has increased. The problem is that a large share of the finance industry consists of unproductive speculation and the expansion of debt. In an article in *Industry Week* magazine, John Madigan, a consultant with Madigan Associates, observes:

> Jobs paying $20 per hour that historically enabled wage earners to support a middle-class standard of living are leaving the U.S. Public sector aside; only 16 percent of today's workers earn the $20-per-hour baseline wage, down 60 percent since 1979. Service and transportation jobs, per se, cease to exist in the absence of wealth.

Rather, they exist and thrive as byproducts of middle-class incomes buying products and services.[11]

By contrast, the average salary for manufacturing management is $98,120, according to *Industry Week's* 2010 Salary Survey, down from $104,581 in 2008. By industry sector, salaries ranged from a low of $88,352 in the plastic and rubber products sector to a high of $133,077 in the chemicals sector. The survey noted that "More manufacturing managers work in the metals industry (13 percent) and industrial machinery producers (13 percent) than any other industries, followed by automobile and transportation manufacturers (11 percent)."

Manufacturing vs. Finance as % of U.S. GDP

Source: Bureau of Economic Analysis

The glass ceiling for women is still intact among companies that responded to the survey: 92 percent of managers are male, making an average of $31,300 more than female managers (up from $28,000 in 2008). While 92 percent of managers are white, it is interesting to note that their average salary is $97,998, while an African-American manager's average salary is $84,009 and a Native American manager's average salary is $82,444. (The average salary for a Hispanic is the lowest, at $80,684.) Sixty-eight percent of managers are between the ages of 40 to 59, and 65 percent of managers have more than 21 years of experience.[12]

Most outsiders have no idea of the variety of management jobs available at manufacturing companies. Besides the usual executive jobs, other management jobs available at medium and large manufacturers are in these areas: operations, plant and facilities, manufacturing and production, purchasing and procurement, sales and marketing, quality, supply chain, lean manufacturing and continuous improvement, human resources, R&D and product development, and safety and regulatory compliance. And, despite the challenges that the manufacturing industry has faced in the last several years, especially during the 2008-2009 recession, 80 percent of the people responding to the survey were either "satisfied' or "very satisfied" with manufacturing as a career path, and 70 percent were either "satisfied" or "very satisfied" with their current job.[13]

Inside modern manufacturing facilities in the U.S., you will see the most productive, skilled labor force in the world applying the latest in innovation and technology. And contrary to popular opinion, the industrial age is not over. In reality, we are on the edge of incredible advances in manufacturing, from nanotechnology to lasers to biotechnology.

Manufacturing also creates more secondary jobs, as there is a multiplier effect that reflects linkages running deep into the economy. For example, every 100 steel or automotive jobs create between 400 and 500 new jobs in the rest of the economy. This contrasts with the retail sector, where every 100 jobs generate 94 new jobs elsewhere, and the personal and service sectors, where 100 jobs create 147 new jobs. Each manufacturing dollar generates an additional $1.37 in economic activity, as manufacturers hire services like banking, finance, legal, and information technology.[14]

Another important point to consider is that the decline in high-paying jobs in manufacturing may be making the federal budget deficit worse. A high percentage of manufacturers are unincorporated small businesses. Thus, the owners of these businesses pay personal income tax, rather than corporate income tax. As the U.S. loses more and more manufacturers, tax receipts from these business owners are going down. In addition, their employees are paid an average of 25 percent more than employees in other sectors of the economy. When manufacturing employees lose their jobs due to plant closures, fewer than half return to manufacturing jobs. When they do find new full-time jobs, or are forced to take part-time jobs, they tend to take a pay cut. Thus their tax payments go down. The U.S. needs to keep as many manufacturing jobs as possible so that federal budget deficits don't go from bad to worse.

An Engine of Technology Development and Innovation

American manufacturers are responsible for more than two-thirds of private sector R&D, which ultimately benefits both manufacturing and non-manufacturing activities. More than 90 percent of new patents derive from the manufacturing sector and the closely related engineering and technology-intensive services sectors. Manufacturing R&D is conducted in a wide array of industries and businesses of all sizes. The heaviest R&D expenditures take place in computers and electronics, transportation equipment, and chemicals (primarily in pharmaceuticals).

Manufacturing innovation leads to investments in equipment and people, productivity gains, the spread of improved technology to other sectors, and new and better products and processes. It is an intricate process that begins with R&D for new products and improvements to existing ones. As products are improved in speed, accuracy, ease of use, and quality, new manufacturing processes are utilized. Education and training of employees is required to reap the benefits of these improvements in manufacturing processes.

The process through which R&D generates prosperity is complex and multifaceted. First, there are the direct benefits to firms from their own R&D. Second, other companies derive benefits from the R&D of the innovating company in a spillover effect. Third, the feedback from R&D improves other products and processes. Fourth, one industry's R&D has a beneficial effect on other industries and the economy as a whole. Spillover effects are increased through sales transactions and knowledge transfers when the parties involved are interdependent and in close geographic proximity.

Innovation in manufacturing requires a critical mass of interconnected activities. Innovation and production are intertwined because you need to know how to make a product in order to make it better. In his book *Great Again*, Hank Nothhaft, CEO of Tessera Technologies, writes that "In our arrogance and our own naiveté, we told ourselves that so long as America did the 'creative' work, the inventing, we could let other nations do the 'grunt' work – the manufacturing. We did not yet understand that a nation that no longer makes things will eventually forget how to invent them." Manufacturing is an incubator for technology and requires proximity to the facilities where innovative ideas can be tested and worker feedback can fuel product innovation. Without this proximity, technology jobs, like customer service jobs, eventually follow manufacturing jobs overseas.

Funding for R&D comes largely from the profits that companies invest back into their businesses. Thus the cash flow of manufacturing companies is closely linked to their ability to conduct R&D and make capital investments. The severe recession of 2008-2009 dramatically reduced corporate profits and resulted in a drop in corporate R&D. According to the 2011 Annual Survey by the Industrial Research Institute (IRI), 94 percent of R&D managers surveyed said they expected R&D spending to remain the same or increase in 2012. Managers expected this increase to be focused on new-business projects. While most expected that capital spending, support of existing businesses, and directed basic research would remain relatively flat, almost 70 percent thought that R&D budgets focused on new-business development would increase, while only 8 percent thought their spending in this area might decrease. (This will be the second year of increase since 2008, after a 30 percent drop during 2009-2010.) For 2012, this year's respondents project a change of plus 13 percent. External collaborations continue to be an area of increased emphasis. The overwhelming majority of companies continue to utilize these tools at the same or greater level than in previous years.[15] The most disturbing trend is that about 70 percent of companies surveyed now have R&D facilities overseas.

Maintaining an effective U.S. R&D network is essential for attracting domestic and foreign R&D funds and the manufacturing that results from the innovation process. This increases U.S.-based value added, producing economic growth. But today, with the offshoring of so much manufacturing, certain tiers in the high-tech supply chain are disappearing in the U.S. (This is the case, for example, with electronic components like capacitors and resistors.) When one tier in a supply chain has moved offshore, domestic research and supporting infrastructure are degraded. This can be a major problem for U.S. manufacturers transitioning to the next product life cycle. In the past, technology would flow from new domestic R&D-intensive industries into the remainder of the economy, boosting overall national productivity. Today, emerging technologies are flowing at least as rapidly to the innovators' foreign partners and suppliers.

In an article, "Rationales and Mechanisms for Revitalizing U.S. Manufacturing R&D Strategies," Gregory Tassey, senior economist at the National Institute of Standards and Technology, notes that U.S. R&D relative to GDP is the same as it was in 1960, while other counties have steadily increased their R&D intensity. In addition, American firms have shifted their R&D investments toward an increasingly global scope and shorter-term objectives, rather than radically new technologies with greater long-term potential.[16]

A related ITIF report, "The Case for a National Manufacturing Strategy," notes that "Manufacturing, R&D, and innovation go hand-in-hand." It quotes Susan Houseman, of the Institute for Employment Research, who writes, "The big debate is whether we can continue to be competitive in R&D when we are not making the stuff that we innovate. I think not; the two cannot be separated." It confirms that "the process of innovation and industrial loss becomes additive. Once one technological life cycle is lost to foreign competitors, subsequent technology life cycles are likely to be lost as well."

This report examples the U.S. losing leadership in rechargeable battery manufacturing years ago, largely because increasing demands in consumer electronics for more and more power in smaller packages drove most innovation in batteries. As a result, GM now has to source the advanced battery for its Chevy Volt from Korea. According to the report, "There is a deeply symbiotic, interdependent relationship between the health of a nation's manufacturing and services sectors: the health of one sector greatly shapes the health of the other. In particular, the technology-based services sector depends heavily on manufactured goods." It concludes that:

The U.S. economy's ability to remain competitive in services sectors, particularly high-technology ones, requires close interactions with the creators and suppliers of technologically advanced hardware and software. The message is clear: manufacturing and services are not separable — they are joined at the hip. The United States must discard the notion that it can give up its manufacturing industries but retain a robust set of services sectors capable of propelling the economy forward by themselves.

In my opinion, it doesn't matter whether American companies do R&D within their own facility or hire it to be done by outside consultants or product development firms. But it *does* matter whether the R&D is done in America. We need to keep innovation in our own country if we want to remain on the cutting edge of technology and maintain the critical mass of our manufacturing industry. Outsourcing R&D to China is like a mayor giving the key to his city to a would-be conqueror. We need to protect the key to our future security as a nation and keep R&D and manufacturing here. If the U.S. manufacturing base continues to shrink at its present rate, the critical mass will be lost. The manufacturing innovation process will shift to other global centers and a decline in U.S. living standards will result.

Manufacturing Generates Exports

The United States was the world's largest exporter until 1992, when Germany took over this title. The U.S. then maintained its position as second-largest until China surpassed us in 2008. Germany remained number one until 2009, when China surpassed it. The difference between the top three, however, has been small: Germany in 2009 exported $1.17 trillion, compared to $1.06 trillion for the U.S. and $1.2 trillion for China. The U. S. took back second place in 2010 when U.S. exports rose to $1.3 trillion, but China's exports went up also to $1.5 trillion.[17]

Manufactured goods make up just fewer than 70 percent of U.S. exports. While agricultural exports are about $150 billion a year, manufacturers export roughly eight times that. High-tech products are America's single largest export sector, at $287 billion, or 13.6 percent of total U.S. exports, in 2011. The European Union was the top importer of these goods, followed by Canada, Mexico, and China.

U.S. Manufactured Exports (in Billions)

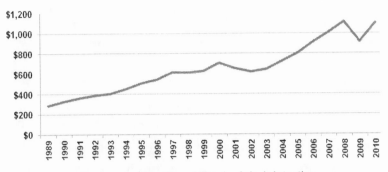

Source: International Trade Administration

According to the Small Business Administration, small-and medium-sized enterprises (SMEs) comprised 97.6 percent of all identified U.S. exporters, generated 64 percent of net new jobs between 1992 to 2009, and represented 31 percent of U.S. export value in 2008. The number of small-and medium-sized exporters more than doubled between 1992 and 2007, and nearly three-quarters of exporters have fewer than 20 employees.

On March 11, 2010, President Obama established the Export Promotion Cabinet by executive order, and tasked it with developing a plan to achieve the doubling U.S. exports in five years he had proposed in his 2010 State of the Union address. Sixteen representatives, from the secretary of state to the director of the U.S. Trade and Development Agency, were appointed to this cabinet. Its final report, released on September 15, 2010, was the product of an intensive six-month collaboration between this cabinet and the 20 federal agencies that make up the Trade Promotion Coordinating Committee.[18] The report states:

The National Export Initiative (NEI) is a key component of the President's plan to help the United States transition from the legacy of the most severe financial and economic crisis in generations to a sustained recovery…The NEI's goal of doubling exports over five years is ambitious. Exports need to grow from $1.57 trillion in 2009 to $3.14 trillion by 2015.

The NEI has five components: 1) improve advocacy and trade promotion, 2) increase access to export financing, 3) remove barriers to trade, 4) enforce current trade rules, and 5) promote strong, sustainable, and balanced growth. It has identified eight priorities, and the Export Promotion Cabinet has developed recommendations to address each of them. These recommendations cover all five components, cut across many federal agencies, and focus on areas where concerted governmental efforts can help.

One of the eight priorities promotes free trade agreements, which is unhelpful, but the other seven have merit and are worth pursuing. Although I'm skeptical about the ability of the plan to double exports in five years when we are fighting against the predatory mercantilism of countries like China, it is well worth pursuing these other priorities to improve the *ratio* of our exports to imports as much as possible, which helps to improve our all-important *net* exports.

The question is whether the plan will actually work. The biggest problem is that the U.S. is no longer the manufacturing source for consumer and household goods it once was. American brands like IBM, General Electric, and Ford were once known worldwide for their quality and innovation. But these products are now largely being made in Asia, mostly in China, and imported by the U.S., rather than being made here for export worldwide. It is no surprise that since the initiative was announced, America's monthly export figures have sometimes reached the needed trend of growth, but more often fallen short, and it unclear in 2012 whether the goal will be reached.

Manufacturing Supports State Economies

Manufacturing is a vital part of the economies of most states – even in those areas where manufacturing has declined as a portion of Gross State Product (GSP). And manufacturers are a significant component of state tax bases and the tax bases of manufacturing communities. As a share of GSP, manufacturing is among the three largest private-industry sectors in all but 10 states and the District of Columbia. It is the single largest sector in 10 states and in the Midwest as a whole. It is the second largest in nine states, and the third largest in 21 others. The states with the most manufacturing employees are California, Texas, Ohio, Illinois, Pennsylvania, and Michigan (Michigan dropped below Pennsylvania after the bankruptcy of General Motors in 2009).

Manufacturing as Percent of Gross State Product

Source: Census Bureau

Manufacturing Supports Our Infrastructure

"Infrastructure" refers to the assets that support an economy, like highways, streets, roads, bridges, dams, mass transit systems, airports, water supply systems, wastewater systems, electric power generation and transmission, telecommunications, flood management, and public recreational facilities. In the 1980s, the National Research Council adopted the term "public works infrastructure" because these various elements are *public* works, although they may sometimes be developed and operated as private sector enterprises.

Economically, infrastructure constitutes the structural elements of an economy that allow for the production of goods and services without themselves being part of the production process. For example, roads allow the transport of raw materials and finished products. Infrastructure in this sense also includes transmission systems for data, including telephone lines, cable television lines, satellites and antennas, and also routers, aggregators, repeaters, and other control devices.

These infrastructure networks are a vital link between the production of goods and services and their delivery to buyers. They are much more capital intensive than other service-producing industries, requiring much capital and manufactured goods to construct and maintain them. Manufacturers build the equipment used to construct, implement, and maintain this infrastructure. Thus the production of goods drives the demand for infrastructure, and the growth of infrastructure fuels the demand for manufacturers, creating synergies in both sectors.

Manufacturers also use public works infrastructure, either internally in their manufacturing processes (as in gas or electricity provided by a municipal power plant) or externally, as in the highways, streets, bridges, and airports used to transport their products. Most goods delivered by the major modes of transportation in the U.S. are tied to manufacturing. Manufactured products account for 87 percent of the value, and 70 percent of the ton-miles, of products carried by truck. (These percentages are even higher if one includes raw materials transported for use in manufacturing.) Manu-facturers' need for and use of infrastructure makes it profitable for infrastructure producers to make investments to improve the infrastructure, but these improvements then benefit everyone.

Manufacturing Matters to Americans

A July 2011 poll of 1,000 likely voters by the Alliance for American Manufacturing revealed that Americans want Washington to act on jobs, especially manufacturing jobs, which they believe will help restore America's status as the world's number one economy. "This poll is a stark reminder that while official Washington goes back and forth in our newest crisis, Americans still feel no one is focusing on the real problems that matter to them: losing jobs, losing our manufacturing base, and the decline of our position in the world," said Scott Paul, executive director of the Alliance.

Americans don't believe that Congress or the President have done enough to support manufacturing. Poll results showed that, by a more than two-to-one margin (67 to 29 percent), voters would prefer Washington focus on job creation, rather than deficit reduction. This was down from the 2010 poll, where 94 percent of voters wanted Washington to focus more on jobs, with 85 percent specifying creating manufacturing jobs and 88 percent wanting Congress and the President to strengthen manufacturing.

In the 2011 poll, voters gave the President and Congress even worse marks than in 2010 for taking action on jobs and manufacturing. In the 2011 poll, there was little difference between the opinions of independents, Democrats, and Republicans (64 percent, 67 percent, and 66 percent, respectively) on the viewpoint that "manufacturing is a critical part of the American economy and we need a manufacturing base here if this country and our children are to thrive in the future." A few of the key results:

- 90 percent had a favorable view of American manufacturing companies – up 22 percent from 2010.

- 97 percent had a favorable view of U.S.-made goods – up five percent from 2010.

- 72 percent had an unfavorable view of goods made in China.

- 83 percent had an unfavorable view of companies that go to China to manufacture.

- 90 percent supported Buy American policies "to ensure that taxpayer funded government projects use only U.S.-made goods and supplies wherever possible."

- 95 percent favored keeping "America's trade laws strong and strictly enforced to provide a level playing field for our workers and businesses."

Conclusion

Manufacturing is the foundation of the U.S. economy and our country's large middle class. Losing the critical mass of our manufacturing base would result in larger state and federal budget deficits and a decline in U.S. living standards. This, in turn, would result in the loss of the large portion of our middle class which depends on manufacturing jobs. America's national defense would be in danger and it would be impossible to maintain the country's position as a superpower. It will take cooperative efforts on the part of industry, government, and individual Americans to ensure that

American manufacturing survives and grows in the global economy.

7

Is Outsourcing Losing its Luster?

Moving operations to low-cost countries has offered a variety of advantages to companies, ranging from reduced wages for qualified workers to lower overall costs. But will these advantages continue indefinitely? The challenge for multinational companies in the next decade is to design an appropriate global footprint, determine which business processes and activities should be relocated, and survive and thrive in the offshore environment in a coherent and risk tolerant way. The question for smaller companies is whether the advantages of outsourcing manufacturing and other business processes will be worth the time, effort, and risk. This decision is often a balancing act, and the dynamics can often change rapidly and unexpectedly. They began to change in 2007 and will continue to change over the next several years.

India is Top Destination

India continues to lead the way as an offshoring destination, ranking at the top of the 2007 A.T. Kearney Global Services Location Index of 50 countries. China ranks second, based on 43 measurements grouped into three major categories: financial attractiveness, people and skills availability, and business environment. The other countries in the top 10 were Malaysia, Thailand, Brazil, Indonesia, Chile, Philippines, Bulgaria, and Mexico.[1] While Vietnam is number 20 on Kearney's list, it topped the Price-Waterhouse-Coopers list of "Emerging Markets 20 Index" in 2008.

The Kearny report found that the cost advantages of the leading offshore destinations have declined almost universally, while their people skills and business environment scores have improved. Although the report opines that the wage advantage of offshore locations will last for at least another 20 years, the key to their maintaining and enhancing their long-term competitiveness will lie in skills development, infrastructure investment, and regulatory-environment improvement.

Ongoing economic changes in these countries will drive global companies to constantly seek the next "hot" outsourcing location, according to KenRadio's IQ Report of May 22, 2007. Merger and acquisition activity will continue to increase as companies buy firms "that have local knowledge in the countries where their customers reside. Companies from developed countries will buy firms in countries like India, the Philippines, and Russia to gain access to lower-cost talent." The 2007 hot locations for outsourcing were India, China, Vietnam, Slovakia, Argentina, Poland, Sri Lanka, the United Arab Emirates, and Bulgaria.

In a 2007 research report for its clients, Gartner Inc. ranked India at the top of its list of 30 countries, based on such criteria as cost, language, government support, labor pool infrastructure, educational system, political and economic environment, cultural compatibility, global and legal maturity, and data and intellectual property security and privacy.[2]

According to XMG Global, a global IT research and advisory company, the global outsourcing market includes IT, business process outsourcing, call center services, and offshore delivery of outsourcing services. Total revenue for 2009 was US$373 billion, up from US$326 billion in 2008. India captured a 44.8 percent share of 2009 global outsourcing revenue and XMG Global senior analyst Vincent Altex wrote, "In an industry where double-digit growth is not ordinarily seen during a global recession, this proves that offshoring is part of a natural ongoing economic revolution notwithstanding a financial crisis."[3]

India's cost advantage has faded over the past couple of years as the dollar has dropped in relation to India's rupee. Significant wage increases – 20 percent per year – have further reduced the cost savings of outsourcing there. Wages for software engineers and IT managers have been soaring, and there is a high rate of turnover and competition for quality employees. Zinnov, a consulting firm that advises overseas firms on R&D issues, reported that engineers trained in basic research are getting harder to find, reducing India's appeal. Zinnov chief executive Pari Natarajan said, "If this trend continues, the cost advantage of doing R&D in India compared to the U.S. will go away."[4]

China Ranks Second

XMG ranked China second, with a 25.9 percent share of global outsourcing revenue, based on 2009 forecasted figures. However, XMG also reported that China's average wages rose by around 30 percent per year from 2007-2009 and predicted double digit wage increases of 15-20 percent for the next decade.

A 2008 article, "New Challenges for Foreign Producers: China's Manufacturing Competitiveness is at Risk," opined, "China is losing its luster as a location for low-cost production, as rising costs, inflation, and the steady appreciation of the renminbi (RMB/yuan) have increased factory operating expenses." From 2000 to 2006, China's inflation rate ranged from two to four percent, but it started rising in 2007, peaking in 2008 at 8.7 percent. It dropped down to zero in 2009 during the recession, but surged back up in 2010 and 2011 to a peak of 6.5 percent.

China's exports to the United States started dropping in the second quarter of 2007 because of the slowdown in the U.S. economy. Year-on-year growth in exports fell 15.6 percent in the second quarter 2007 and 12.4 percent in the third quarter. When the U.S. economy slows by one percent, China's exports decline by six percent.[5] China's exports to the U.S. grew by only 5 percent in 2008, dropped 12.3 percent in 2009, but increased by 23.1 percent in 2010.American investment advisor Gary Shilling said in 2008, "If you still own Chinese shares, sell." He saw China taking the brunt of the U.S. slowdown from the collapse of the U.S. housing market, to be followed by a similar collapse of home prices in Japan and

Europe. He contended that China's economy is heavily export-oriented (38 percent of GDP), and commented, "Without export growth and the foreign investment it brings, China's economy is in trouble." Only eight percent of Chinese earn enough to affect the domestic economy positively, and the Chinese save nearly a third of their pay.[6]

There have been a series of changes in the past few years that are weakening China's advantage as a low-cost producer of manufactured goods, particularly for low-value-added items. There has been a rise in the value of the yuan – 10 percent in 2008, no increase in 2009, a 9.8 percent increase in 2010, and a 4.9 percent increase in 2011. There has been an increase in the cost of fuel: crude oil was up as high as $135 per barrel in May 2008, dropped to as low as $40 per barrel in 2009, then ranged up to $109 in 2012. Wages have also gone up: 10 percent in 2008 after China raised its minimum wage, another 20 percent in 2009, and another 30 percent in 2010 after suicides and strikes at some major plants. China's minimum wage rose 19.6% in May 2011. And there has been an increase in the cost of raw materials.

China has been trying to stem an ever-growing trade surplus, manage domestic inflation, move development from inland its coastal areas, and decrease its dependence on heavily-polluting industries. Because of these objectives, it is becoming more expensive to manufacture there. The top reasons manufacturing costs will probably continue to rise there are:

A Reduction in the Value Added Tax (VAT) refund – China changed its refund formula as of July 1, 2007. Many products have had their VAT refund eliminated, while others have been reduced.

The Appreciation of the Yuan vs. the Dollar – China pegged the yuan to the U.S. Dollar at 8.27 until mid-2005, but it has been appreciating since an average of 7 percent per year since then.

Increased Costs for Importing Raw Materials – A guarantee deposit at the Bank of China for half the amount of the cost is now required for 1,853 designated raw materials that are imported by companies producing for export.

Labor Costs Continue to Rise – The endless supply of new migrant labor from the countryside has been diminishing for several years. Labor costs rose 18.5 percent in the first half of 2007and have risen 15-20 percent year over year since then.

More than 200 new laws went into effect January 1, 2008 which added to the cost of labor. These included a Corporate Income Tax Law, a Labor Contract Law, and an Anti-Monopoly Law. High-tech companies saw their tax rates more than halve, from 33 to 15 percent, in 2008, while companies producing low value-added products like toys, garments, and shoes will see their rates rise from 15 to 25 percent by 2012. (These new tax rules are deliberately designed to encourage high-value, technology oriented companies.) One provision of the new Labor Contract Law is that employees who have been with a company for at least 10 years will be entitled to a contract protecting them from dismissal without cause. The law also sets pay standards for probation and overtime hours.

A 2008 study by the consulting firm Booz Allen Hamilton and the American Chamber of Commerce of Shanghai, "China Manufacturing Competitiveness 2007-2008," reported that many buyers, suppliers, and U.S. importers were caught off-guard by the double whammy of increased export trade tariffs and the reduction or elimination of VAT rebates. These moves, it said, were part of the government's deliberate plan to promote higher-value products and reduce the export economy's reliance on industries that pollute the environment and pay the lowest wages. A representative from Booz Allen said, "The era of China as a low-cost, manufacturing-for-export market has come to an end." The 2007-2008 report concluded that China is deliberately and strategically repositioning itself toward the higher-value products where the West has traditionally felt more secure.[7]Marc Chandler, global head of currency strategy at Brown Brothers Harriman, opines that Fordism may be coming to China. (Fordism is a concept of political economy that recognizes that workers need to earn wages high enough to buy the products they make, to complete the circuit of production.)

The result of skyrocketing oil prices, a weak dollar, and increased competition for workers in coastal regions is that many U.S. companies are looking for new sourcing locales. The Booz study revealed that 17 percent of 66 U.S. manufacturing companies surveyed had concrete plans to move manufacturing capacity to other countries. The top destinations, in order, were India, Vietnam, Thailand, Malaysia, and Brazil. The most-cited reasons for leaving China were rising costs, inflation, and the steady appreciation of the yuan. One American owner of a factory in Pudong said wages have risen 30 to 40 percent for skilled workers, and almost 50 percent for unskilled workers, since he began there in 2004.

A corroborating article in *Knowledge@Wharton* entitled "New Challenges for Foreign Producers: China's Manufacturing Competitiveness is at Risk," states that "China is losing its luster as a location for low-cost production, as rising costs, inflation, and the steady appreciation of the RMB have increased factory operating expenses. Many labor-dependent companies are already leaving China for India and Vietnam, especially those from Taiwan and Hong Kong, and more are considering the move."[8]

Moving to one of these other Asian countries may not be the best answer, however, because they suffer from growing shortage of managers and skilled professionals. In October 2008, the Association of Southeast Asian Nations (ASEAN), whose membership includes Malaysia, Singapore, Thailand, Cambodia, Indonesia, and Vietnam, warned "The shortages were no longer limited to multinational companies but were affecting an increasing number of local firms wanting to expand globally. If these skills shortages are not addressed, they will constrain enterprise competitiveness and ASEAN's future development."[9]

Thirty years of pro-market reforms and explosive growth made China a manufacturing superpower. But now China may be facing the inevitable consequence – labor unrest. In 2009, a wave of strikes in China hit Japanese companies and their suppliers. These affected more than 100 companies, including Honda and Toyota. They were concentrated in southern China, which produces many of the country's exports. The strikers mostly belonged to China's 150 million-strong migrant labor workforce, which flows from villages to cities and industrial regions looking for work. Foxconn Technology Group, the world's largest contract manufacturer of electronic goods like iPhones and iPads, more than doubled its basic pay to 2,000 yuan ($293) a month after 10 worker suicides. Foxconn plans to charge more for their products and will increase factory automation to cover these wage increases.[10]

The second force pushing wages higher is that the supply of migrant workers has reportedly fallen 20 percent from its peak. As a result, some companies are moving production to the interior of China, where many migrant workers come from, to secure lower-wage workers. In addition, the Chinese population of working age (15 to 64) peaked this year. This birth bulge was a major reason that China instituted its one-child policy 30 years ago. Thus, with every passing year, the number of workers in this age group will shrink.

The August 18, 2010 issue of *Today's Machining World* reported that Wham-O Corporation, maker of Frisbees, Hula Hoops, and Slip 'n Slide, decided to bring half its Frisbee production, and some production of its other products, back to the U.S. Wham-O's products take up a lot of container space per dollar of value. "Their products are not labor-intensive to produce, primarily using injection molding presses. They are cheap, light and bulky. A container of Frisbees may hold only $5000 worth of product, so a 50 percent increase in container costs is a substantial piece of the overall cost, according to Kyle Aguilar, President of Wham-O."

Higher labor and shipping costs aren't the only factors contributing to China losing its luster as an outsourcing location. Quality problems are also bringing some manufacturing back to the U.S. Quality control issues have the potential to cost companies millions in lost customers, litigation, and the logistics of shipping defective products back to where they came from (if the Chinese company will even take them back). General Electric, Caterpillar, NCR, and Diagnostic Devices have all moved some production back to the U.S. for one reason or another.

The quality problems with products made in China are demonstrated by the product recalls of the U.S. Consumer Product Safety Commission. For example, in the August 2010 list of product recalls, 71 percent – 17 of 24 – were for products made in China. (Only one product recall was for a product made in the U.S.) In October, there were 21 product recalls: 12 were made in China, two were made in Taiwan, two were made in Vietnam, two were made in Mexico, and three were made in the U.S. There were eight recalls in November, and seven of the eight products were made in China. The products ranged from glass bowls and toys to tents, battery packs, and baby strollers. This ratio of recalls of Made in China to Made in USA products is roughly the same, report after report.[11]

While China has built its industry on low-cost labor for low value-added products, it is preparing for the transition to higher tech products by building research and science parks like Research Triangle Park in North Carolina. Rick Weddle, president and CEO of the Research Triangle Foundation of North Carolina, says, "New entrants into the research park market, such as China, are developing research parks on such a huge scale that they are changing the market dramatically. China has taken our model to the nth degree and has expanded dramatically on it."

There are about 700 research parks in the world, 400 of which are outside of the United States. The average size of a research park in the U.S. is 500 acres, but Research Triangle Park of North Carolina is 7,000 acres. Compare this to the largest science park in China, in Beijing, at 24,710 acres. China has eight other research parks that range in size from 628 to 16,010acres. China's research parks are high-tech industrial zones that offer a variety of incentives for industry to locate R&D and production there. They provide tax holidays and other financial incentives to recruit home expatriates who have been trained in the schools and universities of the United States.[12]

By contrast, the U.S. government does not have a national program to attract industry and jobs, leaving this task up to the states, which do not have the resources to compete against entire foreign countries.

Higher Oil Prices

Higher oil prices have been undermining China's manufacturing cost advantage. The cost of shipping a 40-foot container from Shanghai to the North American East Coast tripled from 2000 to fall 2008. Costs will double again if oil prices resume their upward trend toward $200 per barrel (oil was $109 per barrel in February 2012). By the fall of 2008, it cost $8,000 to ship a container to the American East Coast, including inland transportation. "Unless that container is chock full of diamonds, its shipping costs have suddenly inflated the cost of whatever is inside. And those inflated costs get passed onto the consumer price index when you buy that good at your local retailer. As oil prices keep rising, pretty soon those transport costs start canceling out the East Asian wage advantage," said CIBC World Markets Chief Economist Jeff Rubin.

The rising cost of fuel has increased shipping costs 71 percent over the past four years. Delivery times have also increased because container shipping companies have reduced their routes and the number of ships per route. Ports in Asia are now filling up with decommissioned freighters. "Soaring transport costs, first on importing coal and iron to China and then on exporting finished steel overseas, have more than eroded the wage advantage and suddenly rendered Chinese-made steel uncompetitive in the U.S. market," Mr. Rubin added. He noted that China's steel exports to the U.S. have fallen by more than 20 percent year-over-year, while U.S. domestic steel production has risen by almost 10 percent.[13] "This is going to cause a major re-think for people who have re-jigged their supply lines to China....It's going to turn global cost curves on their head," Rubin said.[14]

Similarly, "As energy costs go up, transportation costs rise, and the distance that goods travel begins to matter," said Paul Bingham, a trade and transportation specialist at Global Insight, a financial analysis firm. "For low-value products that take up a lot of space, like furniture, for example, trans-portation costs can get quite high," said Bingham. "And if you're not saving enough money from using low-cost labor, it makes sense to bring your production lines closer to home.[15]

The industries most likely to be affected by the sharp rise in transportation costs are those producing heavy or bulky goods that are expensive to ship relative to their price. For example, motors, machinery of all types, car parts, industrial presses, refrigerators, television sets, and other home appliances could all be affected. Thomas Murphy, RSM McGladrey's executive vice president of manufacturing and distribution, said, "Manufacturing will be regionalized and the countries with the raw materials will drive a lot of manufacturing investment. Energy will be a key driver of what is located where."[16]

Tesla Motors, a pioneer in electric cars, planned to manufacture 1,000-pound battery packs in Thailand, ship them to Britain for installation, then bring the mostly assembled cars back to the United States. However, when it began production in the spring of 2008, the company decided to make the batteries and assemble the cars near its home base in California, cutting more than 5,000 miles from the shipping bill for each vehicle. Darryl Siry, senior vice president, said, "It was a kind of no-brain decision for us. A major reason was to avoid the transportation costs, which are terrible."[17] And in the San Diego border region, some electronics companies that left Mexico in recent years for the lower wages in China are now returning to Mexico because they can lower costs by trucking their products overland to American consumers.

High oil prices won't just affect outsourcing in China. They will affect manufacturing, especially of low-cost products, in every country that requires shipping products in containers by boat. The Wal-Mart model is incredibly fuel-intensive at every stage, and each stage is now seeing an increase in transportation costs. If transportation costs remain high or go higher, it could strengthen the "neighborhood" effect. Instead of sourcing materials, parts, and components wherever they can be bought the most cheaply, regardless of location, manufacturers will instead choose to perform those activities as close to markets as possible. Because the whole global trading system is now based on "just-in-time" delivery of materials, parts, components, and subassemblies, they will have to set up redundancies in their supply chains, like warehousing more inventories and having multiple sources of supply and even production.

However, oil prices started dropping unexpectedly in September 2008, soon after the Wall Street meltdown. They fell back below $40 a barrel by January 2009, from a high of $143 in September 2008, and shipping costs dropped commensurately. Some energy experts said this was a temporary reduction due to decreased demand, while others said that the high oil prices of the last five years were an anomaly and that prices would remain low for the foreseeable future. Oil rose from $66 to $92 during 2010, then, took a big jump higher when one regime after another started to topple in the Middle East in the winter of 2010 and spring of 2011. It reached a high of $130 in June 2011 before dropping down to $80 by the end of the summer, and then went back up to $100 in November 2011. It has stayed above $100 since then, and it will be interesting to see which experts are right over the long term.

The global trade slump from the U.S. downturn slowed trans-Pacific shipments in 2008, with the growth of container trade at its lowest level ever from Asia to the U.S., and at a 15-year low from Asia to Europe. In the London *Times* of December 10, 2008, Michel Deleurian, head of network and product at Maersk Line, the world's largest shipping company, said, "We are certainly seeing a dramatic slowdown. The decline we are seeing in recent weeks is faster and deeper than what most people had expected only a few months ago."

The container industry slowdown continued throughout 2009, but it rebounded in 2010 and 2011. However, the outlook for the future includes continued higher costs from factors other than fuel costs, according to the BSR's report, "Sustainability Trends in the Container Shipping Industry," of September 2010. "Environmentally motivated regulations are likely to become the most important cost driver in the coming years, as governments and corporations raise the bar on air emissions, ballast water discharge, ship design, and ship recycling. Similarly, regulator changes related to security, business ethics, health and safety, and labor standards will put additional pressure on international container shipping lines to increase sustainability performance." The report states that "In the next five to seven years, market, stakeholder, customer, and regulatory pressures related to sustainability will drive significant changes in the way international container shipping lines operate and do business."

Some Business Coming Back

In the past, my experience as a manufacturers' representative was that when manufacturing moved out of the U.S., it rarely came back. However, recently we have been hearing about more and more companies coming back from doing business in China. The main problems these companies encountered were:

- Substitution of materials
- Inconsistent quality
- Stretched out deliveries
- Communication problems

- Inability to modify designs easily and rapidly

- Unfavorable purchase order and credit terms

For example, in late 2007, SeaBotix, a San Diego-based manufacturer of miniature underwater vehicles, told me their Chinese molder was substituting 10 percent glass-filled ABS (a plastic material used in injection molding) for the specified 30 percent variety. The vendor claimed the parts were made of the specified material, but an independent lab confirmed they weren't. The 10 percent material caused the parts to shrink more in molding, so the parts were smaller, didn't fit mating parts properly, and were not as strong. After their Chinese vendor refused to take the defective parts back or give credit for them, SeaBotix decided to bring its tools back to the U.S. and sourced the parts at a molder in Southern California. Don Rodocker, president of SeaBotix, said, "The Chinese tooling was one-third the cost of tooling in the U.S., the delivery was one-third the time quoted by U.S. companies, and the piece price was one-third the U.S. price. But each time we reordered the parts, the Chinese molder increased the price until they were three times the price we could get the parts molded for in San Diego. We would probably go to a Chinese toolmaker in the future for the molds, but would bring the molds back to the States to be run."

Silk Road International, an international procurement and project management company that specializes in helping clients find the right factories in China, Hong Kong, Thailand, and the U.S., featured an article entitled "Returning Products to a Factory in China" on its blog. In the article, David Dayton, who leads SRI from its Shenzhen, China office, offered a client the following advice with regard to returning products to a Chinese vendor:

- "This will kill any good will you may have developed with your supplier. You will need to find a new supplier."

- "You may not get the product back into the country—especially if it's defective or already opened because of import restrictions."

- "You must decide who will pay and where the cash will come from before you take any unilateral action."

- "There is really no such thing as 'credit'—the cash for the redo has to come from somewhere."

- "You will see the returned product again, somewhere."

- "What will it really cost you in terms of time, shipping costs, lost clients due to the production flaw?"

In his opinion, the bottom line was that if you have received the product in your home country and paid for it, it's too late to be finding problems. His recommended solution is to not allow product to "ship before you (you personally or someone other than the factory) approve it." This is what is referred to as "source inspection," which means you the customer must pay for someone from your company to travel to the vendor and inspect the parts before shipping, or you have to hire an independent person or company to do it.[18]

It was interesting to find a commentary on this article on the China Law Blog written by Dan Harris of Harris and Moore, a boutique international law firm. Dan commented on the "you will see the returned product again, somewhere" item with the experience one of their clients had when they returned a product to their Chinese vendor with explicit instructions to destroy it. Sometime later, a Seattle retailer called the client to ask why a distributor was able to sell the client's normal $100 item (wholesale) for $35. After considering whether they would need to honor their warranty on "gray market" defective goods, the client chose to honor their warranty on the defective product.[19]

In 2002, Vaniman Manufacturing, which makes dental equipment in Fallbrook, California, shifted most of its sheet metal fabrication offshore to China to save money, with a 50 percent cost reduction in the piece price. However, it was then required to purchase significantly larger lots of parts, resulting in a higher inventory cost. In turn, the larger inventory required more storage space, and transportation costs were higher. These additional costs, including "soft" costs like long-distance communications and travel to visit distant vendors, are a non-trivial part of what is referred to as "total cost of ownership."

After realizing that these additional costs were eating up the cost savings of the piece price, the company brought its sheet metal work back to a local supplier in the fourth quarter of 2007. Don Vaniman, who heads the company, cited several reasons: shipping delays, security hassles, and poor quality control. "If you order a thousand widgets in four shipments, three shipments might be all right, but the fourth might be totally wrong," Vaniman said. "In the U.S., a supplier would jump through hoops to fix that kind of problem, but in China, it could take six months to work out the details."

Vaniman said the local supplier was able to nearly match the Chinese company's costs by developing more efficient and more creative production techniques, using recyclable packaging for parts delivery, and delivering smaller lot sizes on a just-in-time basis. Due to smaller lots being delivered just in time, Vaniman was able to significantly reduce both inventory and the space required to store it. In addition, rising costs in China erased much of the price gap. Vaniman said that six years ago, the cost of producing its parts in the U.S. was as much as 50 percent higher than in China. Now it's only five percent higher – a premium he's happy to pay.

DJO Global, based in Vista, California with manufacturing plants in the U.S. and Tijuana, Mexico, makes orthopedic products, including wrist braces, arm slings, back and abdominal supports, and rigid knee braces. Because it is a medical device company, nearly all its projects go through strict quality assurance. In 2005, DJO's Continuous Improvement Project Team completed 55 projects, saving the company more than $3 million. One project was a cooler that forms part of a cold-therapy unit to reduce pain and swelling. When the company first developed the product, the coolers were sourced in the United States, but they were eventually moved to China, for a total landed cost of around $10. However, the company had to buy the coolers by the container load and when the molds broke; the supplier stopped shipping product for two months.

The project team figured out how to economically manufacture the cooler in-house – making their own injection molding tools, sourcing the blow-molded components locally, and creating fixtures for the high-pressure foam injection machine. Vice President Jerry Wright said, "The cooler will cost $2 less than it did to buy it from China, when you factor in the freight, handling, and inventory costs. It's a nice enhancement to the product line, and we don't have to go through the horrible supply-chain frustration with China."

These stories from San Diego County are just a microcosm of what's happening nationwide. Exxel Outdoors, for example, is hiring workers, adding machines, and increasing output at its 250,000 sq. ft. plant in Haleyville, Alabama. Exxel makes sleeping bags, tents, and ski vests. Exxel's CEO Harry Kazazian said, "In 2005, China's cost advantage began to erode as the yuan appreciated. In the first half of 2008, wages in urban China jumped 18 percent from a year earlier, and new minimum-wage and overtime rules will add more to these costs." Costs in Haleyville run three percent less than those in China, and the company can deliver a sleeping bag within three days from its Haleyville plant, while shipping one from China could take as long as two months.

In 2007, 60 percent of Exxel's sleeping bags were made in Shanghai, while the Haleyville plant produced the rest. By 2009, only a third came from China, and by 2010, Haleyville accounted for 90 percent. Kazazian projected his company's revenue would rise as much as 20 percent, to $42 million from $35 million in 2007, helped by a Wal-Mart order for Disney-themed kids' sleeping bags. "Labor is China's advantage and our weakest link," Kazazian said. "But they can't compete with me on my just-in-time production cycle. Customers pay as much as 10 percent more to get deliveries as needed rather than incurring expenses to store inventory." Barbara Garrison, V.P.

of operations, said, "Now that we've become more competitive, more people are looking at us. We're getting more inquiries."[20]

At a time when company controllers and chief financial officers are under increased pressure to manage cash flow to create more cash for operations and investments and enhance companies' valuations, the unfavorable purchase order and credit terms of Chinese companies are another big factor. In the U.S., standard payment terms for customers with good credit are 30 days after the date of the invoice. For the last several years, the accounting departments of many U.S. companies have been preserving cash flow by utilizing their vendors as short-term lenders by taking 45 to 90 days. In contrast, payment terms from Chinese suppliers can be as high as 50 percent due at time of order and 50 percent payable when goods are shipped. In this case, a company would be paying for products up to six weeks before receiving them, due to shipping times from China to various parts of the U.S.

There is also an increasing wariness by upper management regarding sourcing in China, especially with regard to sourcing *all* the component parts or subassemblies for a given product, because China doesn't honor U.S. patents. American companies are hearing about firms that sourced a product in China only to have a product identical to theirs appear on the market, made by some Chinese company at a much lower price. Companies that haven't paid attention to this danger and sourced their whole product in China have suffered the consequences.

There is also a growing realization that when it comes to quality, location may be the best guarantee of all. It's very, very hard to outsource quality, particularly to a distant land many miles and time zones away. Many companies are returning their call centers to the U.S. because of customer complaints, and I believe that a growing number of manufacturers will realize that "you get what you pay for" from offshore suppliers. Applying good quality principles takes money, technical education, and experience, many of which are in short supply in the low-wage countries. This also applies to IT: in a 2005 article in *IT Professional* entitled "Offshoring: What Can Go Wrong," Prof. Norman Matloff of the University of California pointed out that "distance, cultural differences, inexperienced programmers, and other obstacles might make you wish you'd kept that IT project at home."

"Made-in-China" Becoming Undesirable

Toys, electronics, pharmaceuticals, and other goods made in China are being recalled month after month due to contamination and inferior or poisonous materials. The resulting loss of consumer confidence in Chinese-made products has served as a wake-up call to every company sourcing there. Tainted, defective, and poor-quality products have made many consumers leery of buying goods produced in China and have woken people up to the seriousness of the offshore manufacturing issue.

David Dayton of Silk Road International reported on his blog on May 21, 2008 that he had recently had three different companies ask for help in outsourcing manufacturing *outside* of China. Two were in the toy industry and the other was in the home decor industry. The main reason was that the lead paint scares of 2007 were not forgotten in the toy industry, so "high end toys can't have the 'made in China' label."

Secondly, labor costs were rising so rapidly that reorders were priced too high to keep up with a hot-selling toy. The third reason was that there were enough consumer groups targeting "made in China" products that it was too sensitive to risk the marketing consequences, particularly if children's items were involved.[21]

World Economic Crisis Affects China

In response to the global credit crunch, China's exports and imports shrank in the fourth quarter of 2008 as its economy abruptly slowed. Economists had expected China's exports to rise 15 percent and imports 12 percent, compared with the third quarter of 2007. Instead, exports fell 2.2 percent and imports fell 17.9 percent. Chinese leaders worried that the economic downturn would cause unemployment to soar, jeopardizing social stability. Construction projects were suspended, car sales crashed, property prices plummeted, and China's stock markets fell nearly 67 percent. Social Security Minister Yin Weimin warned, "The global economic crisis is picking up speed and spreading from developed to developing countries and the effects are becoming more and more pronounced here. Our economy is facing a serious challenge."[22]

The slump in demand from developed countries in 2008 and 2009 resulted in factory closures in China. According to China's National Development and Reform Commission, 67,000 small and medium-size enterprises had already stopped producing in the first half of 2008 – before the global economic crisis hit. China increased export rebates November 1,

2008 on a quarter of all the goods on the customs tariff list to shore up its exports, especially textiles, clothing, and toys. By the end of 2008, about 670,000 businesses had shut down because of the downturn. As of February 2009, the Chinese government said that because of the economic crisis, 20 million migrant workers had lost their jobs or couldn't find work, and 12 percent of recent college graduates could not find jobs. Demonstrations and riots occurred in Guangdong province, a leading area for manufacturing toys, shoes, and other basic consumer products. The official *China Daily* newspaper reported in November 2008 that more than 7,000 companies had gone out of business or moved elsewhere. One of the largest was a factory that made toys for Mattel and Hasbro, resulting in 7,000 people losing their jobs.[23] In 2008, 62,400 enterprises and branches of companies closed in Guangdong, 4,739 more than in 2007, and 600,000 migrant workers left the region.

In response to the slowdown, on November 9, 2008, the government launched a $586 billion-dollar stimulus plan to boost infrastructure and housing spending over the next two years. This package aided cement, iron, and steel producers, and encouraged growth by removing loan quotas on lenders and increasing credit for major projects that help rural areas and small businesses. Prior to this stimulus package, China had also set aside funds for infrastructure construction and instituted measures to boost real estate sales. It also announced greater rebates on taxes charged to exporters, loosened credit restrictions, and cut taxes. The central bank slashed interest rates by 1.08 percentage points, four times the usual margin and the steepest cut in 11 years.[24] China thus responded to the global recession in a similar way to the United States – with a stimulus package. The difference is that China did so out of billions of dollars of reserves, rather than billions of dollars of new debt.

In January 2009, China's migrant workers got an early start on the Lunar New Year festival scheduled to start January 26. This is the world's biggest annual migration of humans, in which 188 million people, more than the population of Russia, head home for the holiday. For most migrants, this 40-day holiday is the only time they can leave their factory jobs and go home to see their families. However, many that year had no job to return to, and were worried about hunting for jobs after the holiday. The government stayed on high alert, fearful of the consequences of a huge mass of jobless, disappointed, rootless young men. It encouraged unemployed people who return home to start their own businesses. Officials in the city of Chongqing and Henan Province, two big sources of migrants, pledged to lend seed money. It was also hoped that reconstruction work after the devastating earthquake in Sichuan in 2008 would absorb some of the migrant workers.

On January 8, 2009, the National Development and Reform Commission released a sweeping new plan for the Pearl River Delta bordering Hong Kong. This plan covers the next 12 years and its general goal is to transform the region into a base for advanced manufacturing, innovation, and heavy industry. Closures of low-end manufacturers will make room for more sophisticate industries, especially automakers, petrochemical companies, and companies specializing in technology and services. Equipment manufacturers will focus on nuclear power facilities, ocean engineering, wind power equipment, power plants, and high-tech machine tools.

China rebounded in 2009, achieving 8.7 percent growth in GDP despite the slump. By 2010, there were fears that China's economy was overheating as its GDP surged 11.9 percent in first quarter. Growth wound up being 10.3 percent for the year. GDP was $5.88 trillion, ahead of Japan's $5.45 trillion. Then Chinese GDP growth was 9.7 percent in the first quarter of 2011 and 9.5 percent in the second quarter.

Inshoring and Nearshoring Growing

"Inshoring" refers to a foreign company setting up a plant in the U.S., while "nearshoring" refers to setting up a plant in the nearby location of Mexico. For companies from India, the reasons for this reverse offshoring trend include the declining exchange rate of the Indian rupee versus the dollar, the decline in H1-B visa availability, and the desire to be closer to their U.S. customer base. Other factors are the tight labor market in India for technology professionals and the tremendous upward pressure on wages. For example, Wipro Technologies, India's third-largest outsourcing company, set up an inshore development center in Atlanta, where it will work with the University of Georgia to educate and train nearly 500 employees. The Bangalore-based firm also established a "nearshore" location in Monterrey, Mexico.

Offshore Outsourcing Will Continue

Offshoring will clearly continue for the next five to 10 years, especially for multinational companies that sell products in the countries where they set up overseas operations. Manufacturing products locally for consumption in foreign countries will be even more crucial to profitability as transportation costs continue to increase. Companies and vendors can expect to see some rebalancing as they determine what work can best be performed where. The U.S. will both gain and lose ground as companies make choices about the best place to do a given piece of work – be it offshore, onshore, or nearshore. The desirable locations for outsourcing will change over time, just as they have over the past 50 years. The purely financial benefits of lower costs will erode over time. The challenge for America is to keep as many manufacturers as possible growing and prospering *within* the United States.

8

Returning Manufacturing to America

In the increasingly competitive global marketplace, American manufacturers must continually strive to reduce costs to keep or increase their market share. Reducing costs is one of the key factors in the decision whether to make parts in-house, outsource to domestic suppliers, or outsource offshore. Unfortunately, after companies make the decision to out-source, most don't look beyond the quoted unit price in making the decision about which supplier to select. This is especially true when comparing offshore with domestic quotes. Some companies choose to outsource offshore because the "top line" piece price is cheaper than a domestic supplier. But they don't add in the cost of transportation, much less other hidden costs.

In order to make the correct decision on offshoring, manufacturing companies need to understand the concept of Total Cost of Ownership. This is an estimate of the direct *and* indirect costs related to the purchase of a part, sub-assembly, assembly, or product. The Gartner Group originated the concept of TCO analysis several years ago, and there are a number of different methodologies and software tools for calculating TCO for various industries, products, and services. TCO includes much more than the purchase price of the goods paid to the supplier. For the purchase of the types of manufactured products we are considering here, it should also include all of the other factors associated with the purchase of the goods, such as:

- Geographical location

- Transportation alternatives

- Inventory costs and control

- Quality control

- Reserve capacity

- Responsiveness

- Technological depth

In the last decade, offshore outsourcing has evolved from a little-used practice to a mature industry. Even conservative companies are now willing to experiment with going offshore to gain a competitive edge. The concept has become part of the fabric of today's business.

Moving Overseas or Sourcing Offshore

Many times, the decision to offshore is based on faulty assumptions and can have unpleasant consequences. In some cases, the basis for the decision is well intentioned, such as winning new business by being closer to a customer. But, as with every business decision, there are underlying assumptions, and more often than not, they are erroneous. Here's a list of common well intentioned but often faulty assumptions about offshoring:

"Longer lead times won't affect our cost calculations very much."

"Overseas suppliers have the same morals and work ethic as we do."

"Overseas laws will protect our proprietary information."

"We can teach our suppliers to reach our quality needs and to build our product reliably and efficiently."

"Communication will not be an issue given daily conference calls, the Internet, and the fact that the supplier speaks English."

"Assessment and travel costs won't change our cost calculations very much."

"The increase in delivery and quality costs won't be significantly different than our cost calculations."

"Missing manufacturing models, methods, and tools such as the theory of constraints, 5S, Flow, *kaizen*, visual work place, project management, change management, statistical tools, and Six Sigma can be taught to suppliers before our bottom line is affected."

In actuality, many case studies have shown that these assumptions are often far from reality. We'll look at some of these later.

Most businesses that move overseas follow roughly this step-by-step pattern:

1. Perform some sort of gross feasibility check, especially for labor cost savings.

2. Gather information on potential suppliers.

3. Evaluate those suppliers on paper and by visiting their plants.

4. Run a production test pilot, typically one lot or two.

5. Evaluate the results.

6. Turn on full production of that product while beginning to expand into other products.

7. After a few months, either completely shut down the U.S. business or retain some capability to manufacture when emergencies arise.

The problems with this scenario are manifold. For one thing, it doesn't capture a reasonable amount of variation. Suppose each shipment of product takes weeks more than anticipated to get to the U.S. or a customer site for evaluation? It also ignores that the production method for the product has now gotten more complex by being offshored – and in general, costs rise with complexity. Furthermore, the company doesn't know how many *hidden* costs exist, like those due to lower process stability, unstable process capability over time, and the potential for future deviations from the current process. Worse, the company loses the ability to make quick changes to react to hidden costs that turn up later. It's all like trying to control production via remote control!

Hidden Costs Grow Geometrically

Accountants usually deal with "hard" costs like materials, material overhead, labor, labor overhead, quality control, outside services, sales, general and accounting costs, and profits. What they often *don't* measure are the intangible costs associated with a business, like the costs of delays, defects, and deviations from standard or expected production processes (the three D's).

These costs are often called "hidden factories" because they keep employees busy generating no tangible or measured value. (Another way to understand them is that they produce results that no one would ever want to pay for.) In addition to the more obvious direct costs – like additional meetings, travel, and engineering time – hidden factories also indirectly produce many "soft" costs, like loss of good will, loss of competitiveness, extended warranty costs, and legal costs. In 1977, the quality guru Armand Feigenbaum estimated that within the hidden factory might be 15 percent to 40 percent of total company effort.[1] (Writing in 1977, he was not considering soft costs associated with overseas suppliers, but his insight is still valid.) The three rules that apply to hidden factories are:

Hidden Factory Rule # 1 – Business complexity correlates with hidden costs. Hidden factories expand as the processes they hide in become more complex, less standardized, and less well understood by management.

Hidden Factory Rule #2 – Soft costs grow at geometric rates. That is, as hidden factories grow, the costs they produce grow even faster. Waste itself intrinsically produces more waste. For example, as process waste grows, one's understanding of the process becomes confused, making it harder to improve that process. Improving a process that has waste in it means that you are wasting some of your effort trying to improve mere waste.

Hidden Factory Rule # 3 – There are 10 common categories of waste in a hidden factory, which apply to any type of process, be it product or service. To wit:[2]

1) Transportation Waste – Wasteful physical movement of people, products, or information.

2) Inventory Waste – Anything that is unnecessarily stored, like parts or documentation ahead of requirements, because it can become obsolete by the time of use while tying up resources that could otherwise be used to generate profit.

3) Motion Waste – Any form of motion within a task that is more than it needs to be, thus wasting energy and time, and risking injury. Examples include bending, reaching, jumping, lifting, and turning.

4) Waiting Waste – Waiting ties up resources, delays the product or service from reaching the customer, and delays payment being made. Examples include waiting for parts to arrive from a prior work station, waiting for instructions, waiting for equipment to perform its task, waiting for computers to process information, and waiting for communication equipment to transfer information.

5) Over-Production Waste – Any product or service produced in excess of immediate needs is waste. One example would be making a large pot of soup based on estimates of what will sell that day, as the ideal kitchen would be able to make a single bowl whenever ordered. While there is an optimum amount that should be made, given process constraints, anything more than immediately needed is still waste, as resources are required to hold it, keep it hot, stirred, and so on. (Soup left over at the end of the day becomes physical waste.)

6) Over-Processing Waste – Over processing is the most common form of "soft" waste in an office environment. Requiring excessive signatures on a form, too many forms, or unnecessary copies are examples. For manufactured products, having tolerances that are too tight or requirements for grades of materials that are higher than necessary are examples of this type of waste.

7) Defects Waste – Any form of scrap or rework. This applies to mis-documentation, mis-communication, unhappy customers due to a process that was poorly followed, and unusable parts in a manufacturing process.

8) Underutilization of Resources Waste – Any resource, including people, money, materials, or equipment that is not used efficiently, effectively, and safely, is an under-utilized resource. Examples include an idle piece of equipment, equipment used improperly, or delegating tasks without adequate training.

9) Overburdened-Workers Waste – Worker productivity rises as the workload is increased, but then it peaks and it drops off if too much additional work is added. Any drop-off in productivity due to overwork is overburdened-workers waste.

10) Unevenness Waste – Processes break down with uneven loading of their workers. When one worker is performing significantly more work than the others, the output of the production process falls to the rate of that one worker.

The above 10 forms of waste add up to something known as the Cost of Poor Quality (COPQ).

When it comes to outsourcing, there's usually more to consider than the quoted price. Some outsourcing costs are less visible – or downright hidden. Here are the top hidden costs:

Currency Fluctuations – Last year's invoice of $100,000 could be$140,000 next year.

Difficulty in Managing an Offshore Contract – Underestimating the people, process, and technology required to manage an outsourcing contract.

Design Changes – Language barriers make it difficult to get design changes understood and implemented.

Quality Problems – Substitution of lower grade or different materials than specified is a common problem, for example.

Legal Liabilities – Offshore vendors often refuse to participate in product warrantees or guarantees.

Travel Expenses – One or more expensive long-distance visits to an offshore vendor can dissipate all your cost savings.

Cost of Transition – It takes time and effort to do things in a new way – usually from three months to a year to complete the transition to an offshore vendor.

Poor Communication – Communication with offshore vendors can be complex and burdensome, especially when foreign languages are involved.

Intellectual Property – Foreign companies, particularly Chinese, are notorious for infringing on IP rights without legal recourse for American companies.

The Reshoring Initiative

An attempt to bring manufacturing back to the U.S. called "reshoring" has grown increasingly popular in recent years. Reshoring ends the wait for government to do something about the offshoring problem. It promises to reduce our imports, increase our net exports, and regain manufacturing jobs – all without resorting to protectionism.

Harry Moser, retired president of GF AgieCharmilles LLC, a leading machine tool supplier in Lincolnshire, Illinois, founded the Reshoring Initiative (ReshoreNow.org). The Initiative is supported by the Association for Manufacturing Excellence, the Association for Manufacturing Technology, Sescoi, GF AgieCharmilles, the National Tooling and Machining Association, the Swiss Machine Tool Society, Mazak, and Big Kaiser Precision Tooling.

The Initiative shows companies how outsourcing within the U.S. can reduce their total cost of ownership (TCO) for parts and tooling and offer a host of other benefits It documents the benefits of sourcing in the U.S. for large manufacturers and helps suppliers convince their U.S. customers to source local.

A 2009 survey by Archstone Consulting revealed that 60 percent of manufacturers use rudimentary total cost models and thus ignore 20 percent of their cost of offshoring. But if a manufacturer is not accounting for 20 percent of its cost, offshoring may not actually be its most economical decision. In tough economic times and with stiff global competition, no company can afford this mistake.

Reshoring enables manufacturing companies to accomplish a number of things. It reduces product "pipeline" problems and surge inventory impacts on just-in-time operations. It improves the quality and consistency of products. It helps cluster manufacturing near R&D facilities, making innovation easier. And it reduces intellectual-property theft risk and regulatory compliance risk.

To help companies make better sourcing decisions, the Reshoring Initiative provides a free TCO software program that helps manufacturers calculate the real impact offshoring has on their bottom line. It provides an online library of more than 100 articles about cases of successful reshoring. And it provides publicity to promote the reshoring trend. In cooperation with the Initiative, the Contract Manufacturing Purchasing Fairs staged by the National Tooling and Machining Association and the Precision Metalforming Association help manufacturers find competitive U.S. sources.

The initiative has achieved increasing visibility and influence, including the recognition of *Industry Week* inducting Harry Moser into its 2010 Manufacturing Hall of Fame. The TCO concept was included in Rep. Frank Wolf's (R-VA) "Bring Jobs Back to America Act" (H.R.516). There have been numerous webinars; dozens of industry articles; presentations at major industry and government policy conferences in Chicago and Washington; and coverage by CBS, CNBC, *The Wall Street Journal, USA Today* and the *Lean Nation* radio show.

The Initiative is succeeding in changing OEMs' behavior. A number of companies have committed to reshore after reading Initiative articles. Fifty-seven representatives from OEMs, and 113 U.S. custom manufacturers, attended the 2011 NTMA/PMA Contract Manufacturing Purchasing Fair. Here OEMs found competitive domestic suppliers to manufacture parts and tooling: 64 percent of the OEMs brought back to the U.S. at least some work that was previously offshored.

Reshoring Stories

Anticipating cost savings, in 2000, Bailey International built a 100,000-square-foot manufacturing plant in Chennai, India and fitted it with the latest equipment for Bailey Hydropower to produce hydraulic cylinders for heavy equipment. The plant produced cylinders in 1,000 different sizes and manufactured five of the company's flagship cylinder models.

But in October 2009, Bailey sold the plant, started moving production back to Knoxville, Tennessee, and consolidated all of its operations into a 60,000-square-foot facility after implementing lean manufacturing measures to shorten its cylinder production line from 6,100 to 550 feet. Kevin Bailey, one of the owners, said, "A lot of businesses are trapped in the allure of offshoring, but my experience has been that there are more to the costs than what you are quoted. I think so often we are quoted cheap prices overseas and we don't realize there are hidden costs." He added, "The cost savings of operating in countries like India and China have been shrinking because labor and transportation expenses there are on the increase, but there are other costs as well. There is a totally different set of laws, different culture, a different work ethic and even a moral culture that is different."

Much business for Bailey International is producing custom cylinders for customers on short notice, and having to depend on long supply and transportation chains worked against that. "When we had the factory in India, it was virtually impossible to accommodate an urgent request and turn things around on short notice when you had five weeks that the product was going to be on the water before it reached you," Bailey said.

Controlling quality from the other side of the globe was also a problem. On one occasion, the company received a shipment of cylinders with defects that had to be corrected at its Knoxville plant before sending them on to a customer. "But at the same time we were correcting the defects, there were two or three more containers on the water headed here with the exact same problem," Bailey said. So instead of a small number of cylinders being produced before the mistake was caught, a whole production run, with thousands of defective cylinders, was finished before anyone was the wiser. "There are lots of different factors as to why, but we have seen the costs in those places go up, and we are finding that with some of the manufacturing technology improvements we have been able to make here that it is more cost-competitive to assemble cylinders here than it is to assemble them in India or China," he said.[3]

In a 2010 article titled "The Case for Backshoring: Which manufacturing operations should return to the United States?" business journalist William Holstein wrote:

For years, the NCR Corporation simply followed the pack. Like many other large U.S. manufacturing companies in the past couple of decades, the maker of automated teller machines (ATMs) relied heavily on offshoring and outsourcing to trim factory costs. By making much of its equipment in cheaper offshore locations in the Asia/Pacific region, and by hiring Singapore's Flextronics International Ltd. to make other equipment, NCR could slash hundreds of millions of dollars in plant expenses and be reasonably certain that its ATMs met quality standards.

But recently, NCR has rejected this strategy, at least to a degree. In 2009, it decided to move production of its most sophisticated ATMs from its plants in China and India, and from a Flextronics facility in South Carolina, and instead manufacture them itself in Columbus, Georgia, not far from the innovation center where its new technology is developed. The company was concerned that outsourcing had distanced its designers, engineers, IT experts, and customers from the manufacturing of the equipment, creating a set of "silos" that hindered the company's ability to turn out new models with new features fast enough to satisfy its client banks. "I think you'll see more of this occurring," says Peter Dorsman, NCR's senior vice president in charge of global operations, who says he's been contacted by dozens of companies studying whether they should make similar moves. "You'll see a lot more people returning manufacturing to America."[4]

The Illinois Reshoring Initiative

On February 4, 2011, the Illinois Reshoring Initiative announced its program to apply the principles of the national Initiative to revitalizing Illinois manufacturing. This industry-led program utilizes an integrated, measurable, five-step program to help large manufacturers and their local suppliers recognize the total P&L impact of offshoring and the benefits both will obtain from reshoring.

The Initiative's first conference was held on March 16, 2011 at Harper College in Palatine, Illinois. It featured keynote speakers Peter M. Perez, deputy assistant secretary for manufacturing of the International Trade Administration, and Harry Moser, founder of the national Reshoring Initiative. Mr. Moser commented, "In the past, manufacturing conferences have presented good ideas but offered few tools and no follow-up. The Illinois Reshoring Initiative's year-long program provides the TCO Estimator free to attendees and has 5 integrated steps that will assure that the good ideas are implemented and the results measured."

A report by the Boston Consulting Group, "Made in America, Again – Why Manufacturing Will Return to the U.S.," reveals that "China's overwhelming manufacturing cost advantage over the U.S. is shrinking fast." The authors conclude that within five years, "rising Chinese wages, higher U.S. productivity, a weaker dollar, and other factors will virtually close the cost gap between the U.S. and China for many goods consumed in North America."[5]This report substantiates the calculations of the TCO worksheet the Initiative developed.

The BCG report makes the same recommendation as Moser: conduct a rigorous, part-by-part, product-by-product analysis to account for total costs, rather than just factory wages. In doing so, companies may discover that manufacturing in the U.S. is a more attractive option that they thought, especially for products sold in the U.S. For products with high labor content that are destined mainly for Asian markets, manufacturing in China will remain the best choice.

They key is to recognize that China is no longer the *default* option to lower costs and increase profitability.

BCG's report argues that manufacturing will return to the U.S. for a number of key reasons. For a start, wages and benefits have increased 15 to 20 percent per year at the average Chinese factory, which will slash China's cost advantage, adjusted for the higher productivity of U.S. workers, from 55 percent today down to 39 percent by 2015. Another factor is the increasing cost of land in China. For example, industrial land costs average $10.22 per square foot in Shenzhen, but ranges up to $21. By contrast, industrial land in Alabama ranges from $1.86 to $7.30 and $1.30 to $4.65 in Tennessee and North Carolina. When costs like transportation, duties, supply chain risks, inventory, and other things are factored in, the savings for manufacturing in China, rather than in some U.S. states, will become minimal within five years. This analysis has been disputed, but it is still a clear sign that change is afoot.

Automation and other productivity measures won't be enough to preserve China's cost advantage. Indeed, they will undercut the primary attraction of outsourcing to China: low-cost labor. Demand for goods in Asia will increase rapidly, due to rising income levels, so multinational companies are likely to devote more of their Chinese capacity to serving the Asian market. But they will bring some production back to the U.S. to service the U.S. market.

Manufacturing of some goods will shift from China to other cheap-labor nations like Vietnam, Indonesia, and Mexico. However, this will be limited by the supply of skilled workers, poor infrastructure, supplier networks, political and intellectual property risks, corruption, and the risks to personal safety in those countries. Other nations also won't be able to absorb all of the high labor-content manufacturing leaving China because China has the highest proportion of able-bodied adults in the workforce (84 percent), and 28 percent of them are employed in manufacturing. The 215 million industrial workers in China are 58 percent more than the entire industrial workforce of all of Southeast Asia and India *combined.*

The authors of the BCG report conclude that within five years, they "expect companies to begin building more capacity in the U.S. to supply North America." A few examples they cite:

NCR moved production of its ATMs to a plant in Columbus, Georgia that will employ 870 people by 2014.

Coleman is moving production of its 16-quart wheeled plastic cooler from China to Wichita, Kansas.

Sleek Audio has moved production of its high-end headphones from Chinese suppliers to its plant in Manatee County, Florida.

Peerless Industries will consolidate all manufacturing of audio-visual mounting systems in Illinois, moving work from China in order to achieve cost efficiencies, shorter lead times, and local control over manufacturing processes.

These examples corroborate what I've been seeing in the San Diego region. For example, at a TechAmerica Operations Roundtable event last April, Luke Faulstick, Chief Operating Officer of DJO Global, said that they have brought back the manufacturing of their cold therapy unit from China, their printed circuit boards to a supplier in South Dakota, their textile manufacturing to North Carolina, and their screw machined parts to Texas. He recommended that any company embarking on the lean manufacturing journey rethink its offshore outsourcing.[6]

Conclusion

U.S. manufacturers should undertake a thorough analysis of their global supply networks, factoring in worker productivity, transit costs, time-to-market considerations, logistical risks, energy costs, as well as other hidden costs of sourcing offshore.

9

What's Being Done To
Save American Manufacturing?

Is anything being done publicly or privately to save American manufacturing? Yes: there are many state and federal programs, as well as programs developed by non-profit organizations, geared to helping manufacturers and preparing the workforce of the future. Unfortunately, most of these are a well-kept secret. Very few companies are even aware of them, and even fewer have taken advantage of them to survive and grow. One of the reasons is that most business owners do not instinctively think of calling on the government to help solve their problems; they tend to look to themselves. And even if they *do* think of government helping them, instead of getting in their way, they don't know where to begin to look.

Federal Government Programs

SCORE

The government program most familiar to small business owners is the Small Business Administration's loan program.

Some may also be familiar with SCORE, formerly the Service Corps of Retired Executives but now incorporating volunteer working professionals. This is a resource partner of the Small Business Administration; it offers free one-on-one consulting by volunteer executives and managers, as well as workshops on subjects like writing business plans, accounting, business financing, and selecting the right legal structure.

When I started my own manufacturers' rep agency, I took advantage of SCORE consulting and attended a few workshops. I returned the favor later by conducting a workshop on "New Strategies for Business Success" for San Diego's SCORE organization. In addition to the personal consulting available through the local SBA, there is now online consulting available through the score.org website.

Small Business Development Centers

Some business owners may have heard of a Small Business Development Center (SBDC) in their community. Hosted by universities, colleges, and state or city economic development agencies, and funded in part through a partnership with the Small Business Administration, these approximately 1,000 service centers provide no-cost consulting and low-cost training. I took some workshops through the SDBC on writing a business plan, grant writing, and writing a Small Business Innovation Research (SBIR) proposal.

Department of Commerce

At the federal level, aid to manufacturing falls under the purview of the Commerce Department's Manufacturing

Extension Program (mepcenters.nist.gov) administered by the National Institute of Standards and Technologies (NIST). On the MEP website, there is a link to manufacturing.gov, a website showing the ideas and innovations the U.S. government is working on for the future of the American worker. This website brings together information on key issues for manufacturers, as well as resources available from the government to improve the business climate for manufacturing.

In 2003, then-Secretary of Commerce Donald L. Evans announced the Manufacturing Initiative, a program designed to ensure that government policies foster a healthy and competitive manufacturing sector. Subsequently, roundtable discussions were held with small, medium, and large manufacturers in a range of industries. The recommendations stemming from these hearings were the foundation for the 2004 report "Manufacturing in America: A Comprehensive Strategy to Address the Challenges to U.S. Manufacturers." This first-ever report laid out the manufacturing agenda the Department of Commerce is spearheading today in conjunction with other government agencies. During 2004, following up on the program outlined in this report, the Department made six organizational enhancements, creating or upgrading the following:

The Office of Manufacturing and Services– A new group within the International Trade Administration, headed by an assistant secretary of commerce, to serve as advocate for the manufacturing community, coordinate existing government programs across agencies, and carry out the recommendations of the Manufacturing Report. Reachable at 202-482-1461.

The Office of Industry Analysis– A new group, headed by a deputy assistant secretary, responsible for assessing the cost-competitiveness of American industry and evaluating the impact of domestic and international economic policy on U.S. competitiveness, particularly in the manufacturing sector. Reachable at 202-482-1461.

The Office of Competition and Economic Analysis– Headed by a new director and working closely with the deputy assistant secretary for industry analysis, OCEA performs in-depth analysis on the effects of both domestic and foreign policy developments on U.S. business competitiveness. Reachable at 202-482-1461.

The Office of Trade Promotion– A new group, headed by an assistant secretary of commerce, established to reorganize and strengthen the Department of Commerce's export promotion functions. Reachable at 800-USA-TRADE or export.gov.

The Manufacturing Council– Fifteen private-sector manufacturing executives, responsible for providing oversight of the Manufacturing Initiative, advising the secretary of commerce on government policies and programs that affect manufacturing, and providing a forum for proposing solutions to industry-related problems. Reachable at 800-MEP-4MFG.

The Interagency Working Groupon Manufacturing Competitiveness (IWG-MC) – Created to facilitate a coordinated federal approach to challenges facing the sector domestically and internationally. Reports to the National Science and Technology Council's Committee on Technology and currently chaired by the director of the Manufacturing Engineering Laboratory at NIST. Participating agencies include Commerce, Agriculture, Defense, Education, Transportation, Energy, Health and Human Services, Homeland Security, Labor, NASA, the National Science

Foundation, the Office of Management and Budget, the Office of Science and Technology Policy, and the Small Business Administration. Reachable at 800-MEP-4MFG.

The IWG-MC has set up a web portal to showcase what the Department of Commerce and other federal agencies are doing to support manufacturing. In March 2008, it released a report, "Manufacturing the Future – Federal Priorities for Manufacturing R&D," on the federal government's manufacturing research programs. This report named three key areas where the government should focus its limited resources: hydrogen, nanomanufacturing, and intelligent and integrated manufacturing. These areas of focus "were selected based on their current and future importance to the nation's economic and national security," it said.

Albert A. Frink, a manufacturer for 30 years, was appointed to head up the Office of Manufacturing and Services. In September 2005, he wrote,

This new office... gives the Commerce Department a domestic agenda for the first time, working with other government departments and agencies. Before, it was primarily a trade promotion facility. The new deputy assistant secretary for industry analysis and director for economic analysis are working closely on regulatory reform with the Office of Management and Budget. Together with OMB, they are evaluating 76 recommendations from the manufacturing community to simplify, eliminate or otherwise change various regulations.

He added, "With respect to China, our marching orders are to do everything possible to level the playing field and to hold people to the agreements they have signed. There are a large number of trade laws in place, so we don't need new laws as much as we need to enforce the existing ones." Drawing on his own manufacturing experience, he recommended that small companies diversify their customer base, learn how to market themselves, and develop an export strategy. His concluding comments in the interview were: "We are not a low-cost producer country, but we are the greatest innovators in the world. We should play to our strengths: innovation and differentiation."[1]

When I contacted the Office of Manufacturing and Services in July 2008 to interview Frink about the progress that had been made in carrying out the Manufacturing Initiative, I found out that William T. Sutton had replaced him in September 2007. I was graciously permitted an interview with Sutton in September 2008. Prior to his appointment, he had served as president of the Air Conditioning and Refrigeration Institute. He provided the following progress report:

Since being established in 2004, the Office of Manufacturing and Services (MAS) has worked with other agencies to implement many of the recommendations of the Manufacturing Initiative. A great deal of progress has been made by MAS to carry out the letter and spirit of the Manufacturing Initiative, the purpose of which is to address challenges to manufacturing. To date, 36 recommendations have been implemented.

To implement one recommendation, for example, MAS created the Office of Industry Assessment (OIA) staffed by economists and analysts. They work to assess the cost of proposed regulations to American industries and evaluate the impact of domestic and international economic policy on U.S. competitiveness. OIA and MAS industry experts have advised several regulatory agencies on the cost and impact of proposed regulations on U.S. competitiveness.

MAS input has helped save industry significant regulatory costs, while ensuring that the safety, health, and other goals of regulations are still met. In one case, a proposed regulation establishing the permissible level of worker exposure to the toxic chemical hexavalent chromium was amended, resulting in a final rule that made the U.S. standard the strictest in the world, while reducing the cost to U.S. businesses by $287 million.

The IWG-MC has worked on implementing those recommendations of the Manufacturing Initiative that require interagency cooperation. Of the 56 total recommendations, more than 20 are in progress or under debate. These include the recommendation to eliminate the estate tax and make various scheduled-to-expire tax cuts permanent.

The Manufacturing Council is composed of 15 members appointed by the secretary of commerce to advise on government policies and programs that affect U.S. manufacturing. The Council, which holds public meetings, also provides a forum for discussing and proposing solutions to industry-related problems. Currently, it is looking into how manufacturing can better face near- and long-term challenges, like the increasing cost of energy, sustainable manufacturing practices that will help protect the environment, and the challenges and opportunities that will arise as globalization evolves. The advice of the Council is being incorporated into the Sustainable Manufacturing Initiative, alternative energy policy, and Manufacturing 2040, a public-private partnership working to meet future challenges to U.S. manufacturing competitiveness.

The director of the Manufacturing Engineering Laboratory at NIST chairs the Interagency Working Group on Research and Development (IWG-RD). In 2008, the IWG-RD released a report on three R&D areas of critical importance to manufacturing: hydrogen energy technologies, nano-manufacturing, and intelligent and integrated manufacturing. This report, "Manufacturing the Future: Federal Priorities for Manufacturing R&D," is online at manufacturing.gov.

The Office of Management and Budget oversees the development of regulations, including reviews that might simplify or eliminate them. The OMB provided year end reports on recommendations by the Manufacturing Council through 2007. The President's Council on Jobs and Competitiveness replaced the Manufacturing Council in 2008, and year-end reports on the Council's recommendations are provided.

The Intellectual Property Rights Attaché program has enabled the U.S. Government and U.S. business to work with key trading partners to improve the global landscape for intellectual property rights. The program has resulted in more timely and detailed information for officials of the National Intellectual Property Law Enforcement Coordination Council. This, in turn, allows them to quickly adjust U.S. policies and practices to meet IP-related challenges in these important markets.

America COMPETES Act of 2007

In October 2005, the National Academies (the National Academy of Sciences, the National Academy of Engineering, and the Institute of Medicine), in response to a bipartisan request by members of the U.S. Senate and the House of Representatives, issued a report titled "Rising Above the Gathering Storm: Energizing and Employing America for a Brighter Economic Future." The report stated that, "America is in substantial danger of losing its economic leadership position and suffering a concomitant decline in the standard of living of its citizens because of a looming inability to compete in the global marketplace."[2]

President Bush incorporated a number of the Academies' recommendations into his 2006 State of the Union Address, and various bills were introduced in the Senate and House to implement many of their recommendations. In 2007, the Senate and House took steps to authorize many of the recommendations in the FY 2008 budget, and President Bush signed the America COMPETES Authorization Act on August 9, 2007. This ambitious act aimed to double, over time, the funding of the National Science Foundation, the laboratories of NIST, and the Energy Department's Office of Science. It also established ARPA-E, the Advanced Research Projects Agency – Energy.

Unfortunately, budgetary pressures since have reduced the growth in funding for these programs, and actual appropriations have not equaled the levels authorized. One fine program, NIST's Technology Innovation Program, received no funding at all in the FY 2012 budget and is in the process of shutting down. This three-year-old program funded academic and industry research for "high risk, high reward" technologies that private industry would not fund. Similarly, the FY2013 budget provides no funding for the proposed Advanced Manufacturing Technology Consortia (AMTech) program.

On the bright side, the Obama administration has made permanent the Office of Innovation and Entrepreneurship at the Department of Commerce, reauthorized the Advanced Research Projects Agency for Energy (ARPA-E), supported new Regional Innovation Clusters, and established Energy Innovation Hubs. And its FY 2013 budget submission proposes a new $1 billion private-public partnership program aimed at commercializing U.S.-developed technologies. This National Network for Manufacturing Innovation, modeled after Germany's famous Fraunhofer Institute, would involve the Departments of Defense and Energy, the National Science Foundation, and NIST.

National Export Initiative

On March 11, 2010, President Obama established the Export Promotion Cabinet by executive order and tasked it with developing a plan to achieve the goal of doubling U.S. exports in five years that he had stated in his 2010 State of the Union Address. Sixteen representatives, from the secretary of state to the director of the U.S. Trade and Development Agency, were appointed to this cabinet, and its final report, released on September 15, 2010, was the product of an intensive six-month collaboration between it and the 20 federal agencies that make up the Trade Promotion Coordinating Committee (TPCC). In addition, the TPCC reviewed more than 175 responses to a Federal Register notice requesting input from small, medium, and large businesses, trade associations, academia, labor unions, and state and local governments.[3]Its report stated, "The National Export Initiative is a key component of the President's plan to help the United States transition from the legacy of the most severe financial and economic crisis in generations to a sustained recovery...The NEI's goal of doubling exports over five years is ambitious. Exports need to grow from $1.57 trillion in 2009 to $3.14 trillion by 2015."

In 2008, U.S. exports represented records levels of GDP (12.7 percent) and supported more than 10 million jobs, or 6.9 percent of fully employed workers. This was the highest percentage of GDP since 1914 and marked the high point of a 70-year trend that began in the early 1930s. However, exports fell from $1.84 trillion in 2008 to $1.57 trillion in 2009 due to recession, before rebounding to $1.84 trillion in 2010 and $2.1 trillion in 2011.

The executive order that established the NEI identified eight priorities, and the Export Promotion Cabinet has developed recommendations to address each, cutting across many government agencies and focusing on areas where concerted federal efforts can help lift exports. Here are its recommendations:

Exports by Small- and Medium-Sized Enterprises (Advocacy and Trade Promotion Component and Export Financing Component)

Help identify SMEs that can begin or expand exporting through a national campaign to increase SME awareness of export opportunities and U.S. government resources.

Prepare SMEs to export successfully by increasing training opportunities for both SMEs and SME counselors.

Connect SMEs to export opportunities by expanding access to programs and events that can unite U.S. sellers and foreign buyers.

Once SMEs have export opportunities, support them with a number of initiatives, including improving awareness of export finance programs.

Federal Export Assistance (Trade Promotion Component)

Create more opportunities for U.S. sellers to meet directly with foreign buyers by bringing more foreign buyer delegations to U.S. trade shows and encouraging more U.S. companies to participate in major international trade shows.

Improve cooperation between TPCC agencies to encourage U.S. green technology companies to export by matching foreign buyers with U.S. producers.

Trade Missions (Trade Promotion Component)

Increase the number of trade and reverse trade missions, including missions led by senior U.S. government officials.

Improve coordination with state government trade offices and national trade associations.

Commercial Advocacy (Trade Promotion Component)

Leverage multiple agencies' assistance in the advocacy process and extend outreach efforts to make more U.S. companies aware of the federal government's advocacy programs.

Increasing Export Credit (Export Financing Component)

Make more credit available through existing credit platforms and new products.

Increase outreach to exporters, foreign buyers' bankers, and other entities in order to build awareness of government assistance.

Make it easier for exporters and other customers to use government credit programs by streamlining applications and internal processes.

Macroeconomic Rebalancing (Strong, Sustainable, and Balanced Growth Component)

In the short term, the U.S. and its G-20 partners must work to ensure that the global economy shifts smoothly to more diversified sources of economic growth.

Over the long term, shifts in the composition of economic growth in our trading partners will also be crucial to U.S. export growth.

Actions to reduce surpluses and stimulate domestic demand for imports will be required by a broad range of countries.

Reducing Barriers to Trade (Removing Trade Barriers Component and Enforcing Trade Obligations Component)

Conclude an ambitious, balanced, and successful WTO Doha Round that achieves meaningful new market access in agriculture, goods, and services.

Conclude the Trans-Pacific Partnership Agreement to expand access to key markets in the Asia-Pacific region.

Resolve remaining issues with pending FTAs, such as the United States – Korea FTA.

Address foreign trade barriers – especially significant non-tariff barriers – through use of a wide range of U.S. trade policy tools.

Use robust monitoring and enforcement of WTO trade rules and other U.S. trade agreements.

Export Promotion of Services (Advocacy Component and Trade Promotion Component)

Build on the activities and initiatives outlined in Priorities 1–7 with enhanced focus on the services sector, since it accounts for nearly 70 percent of U.S. GDP.

Ensure better data and measurement of the services economy to inform commercial decision-making and policy planning.

Continue to assess and focus on key growth sectors and emerging markets such as China, India, and Brazil; increase the number of foreign visitors to the U.S.

Better coordinate services export promotion efforts.

There are four general themes that apply to all of the priorities and recommendations in order to achieve the goal of doubling the U.S. exports in five years:

1. Strengthen interagency information sharing and coordination.

2. Leverage and enhance technology to reach potential exporters and provide U.S. businesses with the tools necessary to export successfully.

3. Leverage combined efforts of state and local governments and public-private partnerships.

4. Have united goals for TPCC member agencies to support the NEI's implementation

The plan admits that the federal government cannot succeed alone in this initiative; its ultimate success will be determined by the success of U.S. companies selling their goods and services internationally. A continued dialogue with the business community will be required to help ensure that the NEI is addressing their export challenges.

On December 7, 2010, Energy Secretary Steven Chu announced the Renewable Energy and Energy Efficiency Export Initiative. "Expanding U.S. clean technology exports is a crucial step to ensuring America's economic competitiveness in the years ahead," he said. "The initiatives we are announcing today will provide us with a better understanding of the global clean energy marketplace and help boost U.S. exports."[4] This initiative is divided into two parts. First is an assessment of the current competitiveness of U.S. renewable energy and energy-efficient goods and services. Second is an action plan for new commitments to facilitate private sector efforts to significantly increase U.S. renewable energy and energy-efficient exports within five years. As part of this initiative, the Administration created export.gov/reee, a web portal that consolidates information on government programs in this area.

The Manufacturing Extension Partnership

A federal-state-private partnership, the NIST Manufacturing Extension Partnership (MEP) program is a network of 59 centers, with about 350 locations, serving small- and medium-sized manufacturers (SMMs) that are unable to afford the consulting services utilized by larger firms. These not-for-profit centers employ roughly 1,000 professionals, who work with manufacturers to help them adopt and use the latest and most efficient technologies, processes, and business practices.

Since it was established in 1988, MEP has assisted more than 184,000 firms. The program's success is in large part due to its guiding principles of being industry driven, market defined, and customer focused, with an ability to meet the ever-changing needs of manufacturing industry. While part of a national network, each MEP center works directly with local manufacturers to provide expertise and services tailored to their most critical needs, like risk assessment, process improvement, and worker training.

The responsiveness of MEP can be seen in its continual evolution of products and services, ranging from technical point-solutions, to system-level solutions like quality and lean manufacturing, to enterprise-level solutions like strategic marketing. MEP also offers a technical-skills training program that can help a company transition to new businesses, and it helps SMMs establish business relationships with the Department of Defense. Solutions are offered through a combination of direct assistance from center staff and partnerships with organizations such as state development agencies, colleges and universities, and private-sector consultants.

In 2010, 7,786 companies reported on the payoff of MEP programs completed during 2009. MEP programs had led to creating or retaining more than 72,000 jobs and increasing or retaining sales by more than $8.4 billion. MEP had leveraged nearly $1.9 billion in new private sector investment and generated cost savings of more than $1.3 billion. On average, every dollar the federal government spent on MEP generated $32 in new sales– a 3,200 percent return, or $3.6 billion in new sales annually. What's more, an investment of $1,570 created or retained one job.

Besides its state partners, MEP works closely with the following non-profit organizations:

State Science and Technology Institute – A nationwide network of practitioners and policymakers dedicated to improving the economy through science and technology. Through its membership, this network has unique access to information, which it uses to assist states and communities as they build technology-based economies, conduct research on best practices and trends in technology-based economic development, and encourage cooperation among and between state and federal programs.

Council for Community and Economic Research – An organization of professionals employed by a variety of organizations, including chambers of commerce, economic development organizations, government agencies, universities, utility companies, workforce development boards, community development organizations, and consultants and data providers.

National Association of Manufacturers– The nation's largest industrial trade association, representing more than 100,000 small and large manufacturers in every sector and all 50 states. MEP and individual MEP centers have partnered with NAM and its affiliates in numerous ways, like jointly addressing workforce issues, supporting development of manufacturing competency models and skill standards, conducting research on manufacturing supply chains, and raising awareness of manufacturing careers.

National Council for Advanced Manufacturing (NACFAM) – An industry-led policy research organization, working collaboratively with leaders from industry, education, and government to shape public policies and programs to make U.S. manufacturing globally competitive and improve its productivity, innovation, and competitiveness. MEP collaborates with NACFAM on issues of mutual interest and many MEP centers have representatives who participate in NACFAM activities. These activities cover technology and innovation, workforce education and training, supply chain optimization, and green manufacturing.

National Governors Association– The voice of the nation's state governors. The NGA Center on Best Practices focuses on state innovations and best practices on issues ranging from education to technology. MEP works with CBP to align MEP center priorities and practices with state economic development agendas, particularly focusing on innovation, business retention and expansion, and technology deployment as it pertains to advanced manufacturing industries.

In the past, MEP has focused on workforce training, lean manufacturing, and ways to increase company productivity. Its strategy for the next generation will move its focus from the shop floor to the entire enterprise and its position in the marketplace. It will help companies grow their businesses and develop the flexibility to remain globally competitive. It will focus on industry supply-chain requirements as well as overall economic development trends. MEP will need additional resources, processes, and services to accomplish this strategy.

There are MEP programs in all 50 states and Puerto Rico. To find one near you, go to nist.gov/mep/about.cfm.

In California, two organizations administer MEP. There is California Manufacturing Technology Consulting (CMTC) serving Southern California from San Diego up to Fresno. And there is the Corporation for Manufacturing Excellence (Manex), serving Northern California. Both leverage MEP funds with California Employment Training Panel (ETP) funds to reduce the cost of training to employers. Companies qualify for ETP funding if they pay into the unemployment insurance fund, have a 20 percent turnover rate or less, have a manufacturing NAICS code, or can prove they face out-of-state competition. Their employees are eligible for training if they are residents of California, work full time, meet minimum wage requirements (which vary by county), and have been employed at least 90 days prior to the start of training.

Since 1997, CMTC has helped train 11,160 employees and helped employers earn $9,852,605 to offset the cost of the training. CMTC's quality and impact are audited every quarter by an independent firm. Survey results indicate that CMTC received a rating of 4.8 out of 5 in customer satisfaction, which ranks CMTC in the top five percent based on more than 1,000 companies surveyed nationally. CMTC's industrial services are divided into these practice areas:

- Strategic Business

- Lean Enterprise

- Information Technology

- Energy Services

- Quality

- Supply Chain Management

CMTC also has MEP funding for the Small Manufacturers Advantage program, in which a free assessment is conducted and written improvement recommendations are provided. The report includes the assessment, a roadmap, self-implementation tools, relevant articles, and a listing of other California business resources. The report is designed in a format for self-implementation, but a follow-on Jump Start program of consulting by CMTC professionals can be scheduled at no cost.

The main problem with ETP funding is that the paperwork can be burdensome, especially for small companies. Companies must also pay the fees up front to the consultants and wait to be reimbursed after the employees trained have completed 90 days of retention after training. CMTC and

Manex relieve this burden by handling the paperwork in return for a 20 percent share of ETP grant funding, and may only require a portion of the total fee to be paid in advance. I obtained my certificate in Total Quality Management in 1994 through an ETP grant to The High Technology Foundation when I was president of its board. It was a 100-hour course using a curriculum developed by contracted professional trainers and approved in advance by an ETP program manager.

Federal Small-Business R&D Programs

President Bush signed an executive order in 2004 making manufacturing-related R&D a high priority for the more than $2 billion distributed through SBIR and SBTT programs. (See sba.gov/sbir.)These are:

Small Business Innovation Research– Established under the Small Business Innovation Development Act of 1982 to provide funding to stimulate technological innovation in small businesses to meet federal agency research and development needs. Eleven federal agencies currently participate.

Small Business Technology Transfer–Established in the early 1990s, STTR projects must involve substantial (at least 30 percent) collaboration between a small business and a not-for-profit research institution.

See Appendix A for a list of other federal programs.

State-Level Programs

Following is a sampling of state programs, as space does not permit information on all 50 states.

California

In 2006, Governor Schwarzenegger identified workforce skills development, referred to as Career Technical Education (CTE), as a state priority. The passage of an education bond provided $500 million for CTE initially, and subsequent budgets have continued to fund the program. The plan was approved by the California State Board of Education on March 12, 2008 and approved by the U.S. Department of Education on July 1. CTE is delivered primarily through K-12 schools, adult-education programs, and community-college programs. CTE programs are closely linked with those of workforce and economic development agencies and industry and rely on the participation of community-based organizations. The programs are as follows:

California K-12/Adult Programs

Elementary school awareness and middle school introductory CTE programs.

High school CTE, offered through 1,165 high schools in single courses, in course sequences or through over 300 integrated "learning communities."

Career pathways and programs through 74 regional occupational centers and programs.

Adult education offered through 361 adult schools and more than 1,000 sites.

Apprenticeship offered through more than 200 apprenticeship program and adult schools

California Community College Programs

Occupational programs at 109 colleges, leading to certificates, associate degrees, and transfers to four-year universities.

Noncredit instruction for short-term CTE programs offered by 58 colleges.

More than 160 apprenticeship programs at 39 colleges.

Middle College High Schools (13) and Early College High Schools (19).

Tech Prep programs delivered through 80 Tech Prep consortia, comprising 109 colleges and their feeder high schools.

Workforce development activities implemented through 115 regional delivery centers and 10 initiatives in emerging industries.

Contract education provided to organizations for their employees.

In 1991, the California Community College Economic and Workforce Development Program was established by law, and in 1996 economic development was legislatively mandated as one of the primary missions of California's community colleges. The Applied Competitive Technology Initiative was part of this program, in which 11 centers were established to grow California's economy and improve its global competitiveness through education, training, and consulting. Four more centers were later added, for a total of 15, nine of which were in Southern California, two in central California, and four in Northern California. The centers were all located at community colleges. Due to California's budget deficits since 2009, the number of centers was reduced, and there are now six, strategically located across California, receiving funding from the California Community College's Chancellor's Office to develop innovative solutions to help advanced technology companies compete. Additionally, there are six affiliate sites included as part of the CACT network.

California CACTs collaborate with the previously mentioned CMTC to utilize ETP grants to reduce the cost of customized training programs. ETP grants are funded by the unemployment insurance fees paid by all employers in California. Training programs include, but are not limited to, lean office and lean manufacturing, blueprint reading, geometric tolerancing and dimensioning, soldering certification, and quality systems like ISO 9001.

In San Diego County, the local branch of CACT is on the campus of San Diego City College in collaboration with the Advanced Technology Center and the San Diego Technology Incubator. The San Diego CACT supports businesses through workshops, consulting, customized training, and interactive demonstrations of the latest technologies.

From November 2006 through September 2007, I had a part-time consulting contract with the CACT at San Diego City College as their industry liaison. I recruited a new advisory board composed of general or operations managers from 10 local manufacturers. I conducted onsite needs assessments for workforce training at 18 companies. The companies ranged from a low of 32 employees to a high of 700. One was in the building and contracting industry and the rest were in high-tech manufacturing. Ten of the 17 were already ISO 9000:2001 certified, and three more were preparing to become certified within the next 12-18 months. Only two companies had no plans to become certified in the foreseeable future.

Topics related to "lean" were by far the major area of interest for training. Only the four largest companies already had strong lean manufacturing programs. Only two were totally unfamiliar with lean concepts, one of these being the smallest company. Three had acquired employees with lean experience from other companies, but they were not qualified to be trainers. One company had plans to send one of its employees with lean manufacturing experience through the training to become a "black belt" trainer to train its other employees. The other companies had enough exposure to lean from being members of the American Electronics Association (now TechAmerica) to appreciate the value of lean training.

The TechAmerica Operations Roundtable planning group I have participated in for five years does periodic surveys on topics of interest for future meetings, and subtopics related to lean have consistently been in the top five of meeting topics requested. (Lean and Six Sigma both showed up in the recent survey for planning topics for the 2012 program year.)

The main problem has been the unaffordability of the lean training available. In San Diego County, the cost of onsite training by private consultants ranges from a low of $1,000/day to a high of $1,700/day. Some of these consultants conduct classes for employees from multiple firms, and these classes range from $1,200 for 24 hours of training to $1,700 for 40 hours. The University of California at San Diego, the University of San Diego, and San Diego State all have programs, providing training from beginner "green belt" up to intensive train-the-trainer "black belt" certification. These are all taught on campus and range from one to six weeks, costing from $2,500 to $6,000.

The other big problem is the time taken away from work for companies to send their employees through the training, even onsite. I believe this is why only the larger companies (more than 200 employees) I visited had fully implemented lean manufacturing.

Fewer than half of the companies I visited were aware of California's ETP funding to help pay for training. Two had been granted direct ETP funding for training programs. (The smaller of the two was not able to complete its contract and was not fully funded for the employees who had been trained because it was not able to meet the 90-day after-training retention requirement.) One of the other companies utilized ETP funding indirectly through its membership in the California Employers Group, and another utilized ETP funding through CMTC. This company, and one other, were the only companies that were even aware of CMTC.

Indiana

Economic Opportunities 2015 (EcO15) is an ambitious effort building upon southeastern Indiana's growth areas. These include advanced manufacturing, healthcare services, and hospitality and tourism. The objectives are to raise residents up one level in their education, training, or job placement, coordinate and align a regional system, and be a catalyst for regional leadership. The initiative impacts the counties of Bartholomew, Dearborn, Decatur, Franklin, Jackson, Jefferson, Jennings, Ripley, Ohio, and Switzerland. The Community Education Coalition, the Heritage Fund, and the Community Foundation of Bartholomew County have partnered to provide leadership, oversight, and management support services for the initiative. The Heritage Fund works with community foundations in the region to distribute grant funds in county. EcO15 is funded in part by the Lilly Endowment, which provides grants supporting a regional system of life-long learning. The Lilly grants are focused on coordinating services and these primary economic growth areas:

Advanced Manufacturing – As more than 28 percent of the region's workforce (38,000 people) is in advanced manufacturing, a substantial portion of the grant will be dedicated to developing an advanced manufacturing network of excellence, incorporating the regional "Dream It. Do It." initiative discussed later in this book.

Health Care Services – More than 10 percent of the region's workforce (15,000 people) is employed in health care services. Grant proceeds will be leveraged to create a regional network of stationary and mobile clinical simulation labs that can be used for accreditation and advanced degree certifications.

Hospitality/Tourism – (14,000 people) Revenue from the gambling industry helped spur tourism efforts in the region and created a heavy demand for service employees. A grant will help create training and career pathway development for meaningful careers in hospitality and tourism.

To coordinate and align the regional learning system, the grants fund an EcO15 coordinator in each of the 10 counties. Each coordinator has an understanding of process and programs to better guide students and acts as a liaison between industry and educational institutions. A 40-member advisory council guides the Initiative. The council is made up of representatives from each of the 10 counties and includes leaders from community foundations, education institutions, workforce partners, private employers, economic development organizations, and governments.[5]

The Advanced Manufacturing Network of Excellence

More than $24 million has been invested in the creation of a regional Advanced Manufacturing Network of Excellence. This network has established a comprehensive advanced-manufacturing education and training program, using a hub-and-node network, across the ten-county region. The hub is in Columbus, Indiana, in the form of a new Advanced Manufacturing Center of Excellence. The nodes consist of coordinators and integrated technology labs in each of the counties to provide advanced-manufacturing education, starting in middle school and continuing through post-secondary education, as well as adult education courses. Educational partners include Ivy Tech Community College of Indiana, IUPUC, and the Purdue University College of Technology.

The Advanced Manufacturing Center of Excellence is a shared, state-of-the-art facility. The building contains dedicated integrated technology labs, built around a curriculum of science, technology, engineering, and math. These labs are blended with education, workforce, and business development s to deliver hands-on, project-based learning and applied research for students and companies. The center coordinates and supports the network by developing career awareness programs and pathways, and collecting and disseminating best practices. It helps companies become high-tech and knowledge-intensive.

Another part of EcO15 is the "Dream it. Do It" program of the National Association of Manufacturers. This initiative impresses on students that they can have terrific careers in manufacturing in a variety of manufacturing areas. In one year (2007-2008), there was a 28 percent increase in students enrolled in advanced manufacturing programs.[6]

A 2011 article, "Manufacturing Makes 'Dramatic Recovery' in Indiana," in *Inside Indiana Business* reported that, "The newly released 2011 Indiana Manufacturing and Logistics Report Card contains largely good news for the state; authors credit the two industries for buoying the state's economic recovery and, looking forward, also predict a 'record year' in manufacturing. However, not surprising to industry leaders, the state earned a 'C' grade in human capital—only a slight improvement over last year's 'C-.'" Michael Hicks, director of Ball State University's Center for Business and Economic Research and author of the report, said, "Overall, I'm pretty happy about what's happened in Indiana last year and is likely to continue over the next year or two...This is a really important time for Indiana to be doing well in manufacturing, because there's so much slack in the economy and such pent up demand for new business expansion." Indiana earned an "A" in both manufacturing industry health and logistics industry health, reflecting the size and growth of the sectors. Indiana ranks second among all states in per capita manufacturing jobs and ninth in logistics employment.[7]

Wisconsin

In January 2008, Governor Jim Doyle announced his Next Generation Manufacturing Plan to propel Wisconsin manufacturers into the next generation by focusing on efficiency and lean manufacturing. The plan offered $85 million in new and existing tax credits, to be used to leverage $1.6 billion in private capital investment, create 5,000 new jobs, and train 4,000 workers for the jobs of tomorrow. This was all part of Governor Doyle's "Grow Wisconsin" agenda.[8]

The plan is intended to make Wisconsin manufacturers more competitive by, among other things, providing $1.2 million to help the Manufacturing Extension Partnership in Wisconsin expand the number of manufacturers working to get lean. It intends to expand lean manufacturing across the state by investing $750,000 to leverage $500,000 from the federal government to assist more than 100 small and mid-sized manufacturers that had never used lean techniques before. The plan creates tax credits by streamlining five different economic development programs into one consolidated tax credit to help manufacturers train workers, create jobs, and invest in the future.

As a result of flooding in June 2008, 30 Wisconsin counties were declared a natural disaster by the federal government. Compounding the economic damage from the flooding was the U.S. economic slowdown. In response, the Wisconsin Counties Association submitted a grant to the Economic Development Administration to determine the key economic driver industries in these 30 counties, in an attempt to catalyze additional entrepreneurship and investment. The objective of the resulting program, Opportunity Wisconsin is to showcase four of these regional clusters: value-added food processing, next-generation manufacturing, water technology, and bicycles.

Two other programs were launched later that year in Wisconsin:

Innovate Wisconsin – This will increase the state's focus on R&D by means of tax policy changes. It establishes an innovation tax credit, in which companies that increase R&D spending by 25 percent over their three-year average will receive a $1 tax credit for every $1 spent above this threshold. (This tax credit is capped at 50 percent of a company's tax liability and unused credits can be carried forward for up to five years.) It also expands a sales tax exemption that applied to machines used in manufacturing to cover equipment used in R&D.R&D equipment will also be exempt from property taxes, as manufacturing equipment now is.[9]

Accelerate Wisconsin – This program provides new funding and tax exemptions to support investment in new Wisconsin businesses. This builds on the success of Act 255, which offered tax credits, grants, and loans to support start-up companies, attract angel investors, and venture capital.[10]

Trade Organization Programs

In addition to state and federal programs, many trade organizations are working to help their member companies survive and grow their businesses in the U.S. Some of the larger organizations are:

- Aluminum Association
- ASM International (American Society for Materials)

- Consumer Electronics Manufacturing Association
- Fabricators and Manufacturers Association
- National Association of Manufacturers
- National Tooling and Machining Association
- Rubber Manufacturers Association
- Society of the Plastics Industry
- Technology Association of America (now TechAmerica)

In addition, many professional engineering and technical associations are working to advance the skills and training of their members. Some of the larger organizations are:

- American Society of Mechanical Engineers
- American Society of Quality
- Institute of Electrical and Electronic Engineers
- Institute of Industrial Engineers
- Society of Manufacturing Engineers

(See Appendix B for a more complete list and contact information for the organizations.)

The "Dream It. Do It" Manufacturing Careers Campaign

The National Association of Manufacturers heard from its members that, despite layoffs during the last recession, manufacturers were still having trouble attracting employees with the right mix of skills in certain job functions. To learn more, NAM and Deloitte & Touche conducted extensive quantitative and qualitative research across the U.S. They found that an estimated 80 percent of manufacturers reported a moderate-to-serious shortage of qualified job applicants during the recent recession, a problem growing increasingly urgent with the increase in global competition and retirement of Baby Boomers.

They also found that manufacturing has an outdated image, filled with stereotypes of assembly line jobs, that has kept young people from pursuing careers in it. The "Dream It. Do It" campaign was created because these perceptions are out-of-step with manufacturing's broad range of interesting and financially rewarding careers. Examples include an electrical engineer for a private jet manufacturer, a product developer for a candy manufacturing plant, or a designer at an MP3 manufacturing company.

NAM's Manufacturing Institute/Center for Workforce Success received almost $500,000 in November 2004 from Elaine Chao, Secretary of Labor, for this campaign. Over a period of 36 months, the campaign created, tested, and disseminated a growing set of creative materials. These include radio advertising spots, billboard designs, newspaper and magazine ads, student and parent brochures, and a style branding guide. The materials are ready to use and provide the national brand to local users.

The campaign has formed strong and committed coalitions with local civic, political, education, and business entities; launched a focused advertising campaign; created a world-class website on the array of highly paid manufacturing jobs; and formed local partnerships with community colleges, technical schools and universities for students pursuing manufacturing careers. Its national partners are:

The American Association of Community Colleges – The primary advocacy organization for the nation's community colleges. It is helping to connect U.S. community colleges to the "Dream It. Do It" campaign. It will advise the campaign on various issues and opportunities for adult students in the manufacturing sector.

The College Board – A not-for-profit association whose mission is to connect students to college success and opportunity with a commitment to equity and excellence. It provides the college search functionality of the dreamit-doit.com Web site.

Monster.com – The leading online global careers network. It provides "Dream It. Do It" campaign job and internship searches, "build a resume" services, a "job search agent," and employer "post-a-job" functionality.

NAM's "Dream It. Do It" Manufacturing Careers Campaign is currently operating in the following regions:

Phoenix, Arizona	Nebraska
Connecticut	Nevada
Will County, Illinois	Chautauqua County, NY
Indiana	Northeast Ohio
Southeast Indiana	Upstate South Carolina
Western Michigan	The Tennessee Valley
West Central	North Texas
Minnesota	South Central Texas
Kansas City,	Virginia
Missouri	Southwest Virginia
Mississippi	Washington State

Initially, there is a membership fee paid to the Manufacturing Institute. This fee depends upon the size the campaign will cover geographically and ranges from $20,000 to $35,000, with annual renewal fees of $3,000 to $5,000. A smaller region, such as a county, will contract for less than a large area, such as an entire state. This fee provides access to the services and tools of the campaign and to the use of the "Dream It. Do It." brand, along with a partnership with the Manufacturing Institute. A second set of costs applies to the running of the campaign, as funds are required for staff, advertising, outreach activities, etc. For further information, visit DreamIt-DoIt.com.

National Institute for Metalworking Skills

In 1994, the National Tooling and Manufacturing Association and five other associations founded the National Institute for Metalworking Skills. NIMS has developed standards for 24 operational areas covering the breadth of metalworking operations, including stamping; press brake operation; roll forming; laser cutting; machining; tool and die making; mold making; screw machining; machine building; and machine maintenance, service, and repair. Standards range from Entry (Level I) to Master (Level III).

NIMS certifies individuals based on its standards. It requires that candidates meet both performance and theory requirements. Both the performance and theory examinations are industry-designed and industry-piloted. There are 52 distinct NIMS skill certifications, and companies use them to recruit, hire, place, and promote individual workers. NIMS also accredits training programs. Requirements include an onsite audit and evaluation by a NIMS industry team of administrative support; curriculum; plant, equipment and tooling; student and trainee progress; industry involvement; instructor qualifications; and safety. As of February 2012, NIMS has issued over 34,000 credentials and there are more than 160 accredited programs in operation.

Fabricators and Manufacturers Association

The FMA champions the success of the metal processing, forming, and fabricating industry. It educates the industry through the following programs:

Conferences – Developed in cooperation with volunteer Technology Council members, these are scheduled at regularly occurring intervals. They typically consist of multiple high-level presentations on one or more subjects, exhibits, plant tours, and networking functions.

FabCast – This webinar platform utilizes the Internet and the telephone to deliver live interactive technical education directly to your shop on such topics as laser cutting, roll forming, and metal stamping. Companies can train their whole team at once, even from multiple locations. They can break up full days of instruction into modules and spread them out over a period of time (i.e. two hours four days a week or four hours once a week for a month).

Precision Sheet Metal Operator Certification – FMA's PSMO Certification is the industry's only comprehensive exam on fundamental precision sheet metal operations. Fabrication processes covered in the exam include shearing, sawing, press brake, turret punch press, laser cutting, and mechanical finishing.

On-Site – Live training conducted at a company on its own equipment. Rather than releasing a limited number of staff to attend off-site training, it can be more cost effective to bring the expert into a facility to work with all team members engaged in a particular process. Training can be offered modularly and when needed (i.e. for first, second, and third shifts and weekends).

E-Fab – Online training that lets a company get the training it needs, when it needs it. E-Fab courses combine a full day's worth of instruction by FMA's leading subject matter experts with the flexibility of online delivery. This training is available 24/7, 365 days a year.

FMA also sponsors the Nuts, Bolts and Thingamajigs Foundation, whose mission is to nurture the tinkering spirit. The Foundation's stated goals are that "NBT will be the recognized resource for career development information programs, outreach, training, and services to facilitate a skilled manufacturing work force. NBT will be the recognized voice for the general public awareness of the challenge and solutions for renewing the future manufacturing work force."

NBT and the National Association for Community College Entrepreneurship have partnered to launch a unique summer camp that combines elements of manufacturing and entrepreneurship – how things are made and how businesses develop. Schools hosted a 2010 camp as part of a pilot program that will eventually develop into a national program with up to 300 locations across the U.S. Campers design and build a product, experiencing the start-to-finish satisfaction of creating something they can show off with pride. Throughout the process, they learn how to do CAD design and operate manufacturing machinery under the close supervision of expert manufacturing trainers. They also tour local manufacturing facilities, learning what kinds of jobs exist, what skills and training are required, and how those businesses developed. They have the opportunity to hear directly from local manufacturing company owners how they started their businesses, applying basic entrepreneurship principles to understand how a single product idea becomes a business.

FMA offers grants for manufacturing summer camps at numerous locations across the country. Each camp is aimed at changing the image of manufacturing for youth. Through partnerships with nonprofit organizations, such as the Boys and Girls Clubs of America, FMA provides guidelines on the basic structure of how a camp should be conducted. The organizations then use their community resources to develop the camps based on local manufacturing needs. The camps provide a positive hands-on experience so young people will consider manufacturing as a career option. They target youths at the critical level of early secondary education, exposing them to math, science, and engineering and giving them opportunities to see the technology being used in industry and the high level of skills required. See fmanet.org for more details.

Society of Manufacturing Engineers

The SME is the world's leading professional society advancing manufacturing knowledge, influencing more than half a million manufacturing practitioners annually. Through its local chapters, technical communities, publications, expositions, and professional development resources, it promotes an increased awareness of manufacturing engineering and keeps manufacturing professionals up to date on trends and technologies. Headquartered in Michigan, the Society has members in more than 70 countries and represents practitioners in all industries.

The SME Education Foundation aims to prepare the next generation of manufacturing engineers and technologists through outreach programs to encourage students to study science, technology, engineering, and mathematics as well as Computer Integrated Manufacturing education. Over its 30-year history, SME has invested $5.3 million in youth programs, helping more than 15,000 to explore career opportunities in STEM education. It has granted more than $4.7 million in scholarships to students pursuing manufacturing-related careers. And it has invested $17.3 million in grants to 35 colleges and universities to develop industry-driven curricula.

The Foundation is one of the major funders of Project Lead the Way, discussed below. It also sponsors the award winning "Manufacturing is Cool" interactive website, which engages students in basic engineering and science principles and provides interesting educational resources for teachers. SME has received positive feedback from teachers, parents, and students about its usefulness.

Another SME program is the SME Robotic Technology and Engineering Challenge (RTEC), created in 1986, which has developed into one of the premier student robotics competitions in the nation. In 2004, the competition established a permanent home in Marion, Ohio and was re-introduced as the National Robotics Challenge.

In 2010, SME acquired Tooling University LLC (ToolingU.) in Cleveland to provide online, onsite, and webinar train-ing for manufacturing companies and educational institutions. With more than 400 unique titles, Tooling U offers a full range of content to train machine operators, welders, assemblers, inspectors, and maintenance professionals. A free Workforce 2021 Readiness Assessment was introduced at the Tooling U. booth at the September, 2011 imX event in Las Vegas. This customized workforce assessment program gives manufacturers the opportunity to assess their own capabilities in the face of challenges they will need to solve before they are confronted with the severe skilled workforce shortages predicted by 2021. The first component of the assessment requires companies to answer questions about how they are preparing to meet the needs of the 2021 workforce. ToolingU. and SME professional development experts are available to explain solutions for readiness deficiencies identified in the assessments.

Non-Profit Organizations

CONNECT

If you have a technology-based company, CONNECT would be the best resource for you. CONNECT was originally launched 25 years ago by the University of California at San Diego (UCSD) as an "incubator without walls," and spun off as an independent non-profit organization a couple of years ago. CONNECT's Springboard program is a business creation and development program for innovators at all stages from lab to production, providing hands-on mentoring and coaching by more than 1,000 successful CEOs, CFOs, and CMOs in its Entrepreneurs-in-Residence Program. Companies that complete the Springboard program become eligible to present their pitch for funding to the Tech Coast Angels. CONNECT also manages the San Diego chapter of the MIT Enterprise Forum, where case studies of local companies are discussed and CEO presenters gain valuable advice to help their company set their course and meet challenges. And CONNECT gives awards in its annual Most Innovative Product competition. Some of its other programs are:

San Diego Sport Innovators is a program initiated in 2008 to accelerate the growth of San Diego's vibrant sports economy. SDSI provides mentoring, education, and capital funding opportunities for startups. Former basketball star and coach Bill Walton became executive chairman in 2010.

CommNexus San Diego, formerly the San Diego Telecom Council, is a network of communications industry companies, defense contractors, service providers, professional trade organizations, and local government. It facilitates new business relationships through its Marketlink program and helps early-stage high tech companies through its non-profit incubator EvoNexus, which provides mentoring, education, facilities, utilities, and other services. The San Diego region has become known as "Silicon Beach" in the telecommunications industry.

CleanTECH San Diego is a non-profit organization formed in 2008 through partnerships with private and public sector champions to accelerate San Diego's emergence as a world leader in the clean technology economy. Its mission is to stimulate innovation and advance the adoption of clean technologies and sustainable industry practices for the economic, environmental, and social benefit of the region. With more than 750 cleantech companies, San Diego ranks 7th in Sustainable World Capital's list of global cleantech regions.

The growing web of collaborative partnerships and networks includes Austrade, Biocom, the California Center for Sustainable Energy, the Carlsbad Chamber of Commerce, the Centre City Development Corporation, the City of Chula Vista, the City of San Diego, the California Clean Tech Open, Global CONNECT, the North County Economic Development Corporation, the San Diego Center for Algae Biotechnology, the San Diego Regional Chamber of Commerce, the San Diego Regional Economic Development Corporation, the San Diego Regional Sustainability Partnership, the San Diego Software Industry Council, San Diego State University, TechAmerica, The San Diego Foundation, the Scripps Institution of Oceanography, the Tijuana Economic Development Corporation, the UCSD Environment and Sustainability Initiative, and the UCSD Energy Policy Initiatives Center.

CleanTECH San Diego categorizes its members into two groups, Innovators and Facilitators.

Innovators are companies that create or invent new technologies, in areas such as advanced materials, air and environment, biomass energy and biofuels, energy efficiency, energy generation, solar, water, wind, energy infrastructure, energy storage, fuel cells and hydrogen technologies, green construction technology, recycling and waste, smart grid, transport technology, and wastewater.

Facilitators are companies that install or implement existing technologies, in architecture, construction, design and engineering, industrial products, lighting systems, energy audit, energy transportation, energy storage systems, recycling services, solar energy systems, sustainable building supplies, water, wave, wind, and ocean energy systems, and consulting in energy, environment, and green building.

In 2010, CleanTECH led a region-wide partnership to bring more than $150 million in Clean Renewable Energy Bonds (CREBs) to the San Diego region, launched a website and database showcasing the more than 750 companies that now call San Diego home, sponsored or co-sponsored more than 80 networking events, and received multiple awards honoring its collaborative initiatives on behalf of the region.

At a meeting of the San Diego Venture Group in April 2010, venture capitalist Ira Ehrenpreis commented that cleantech was now garnering 25 percent of venture funding, particularly in the area of renewable energy generation and energy storage. Enhanced water quality technologies and biofuels are also of great interest to venture capitalists.

Two cleantech companies that are "innovators" creating manufacturing jobs in San Diego are EcoDog and Hadronex. EcoDog's FIDO Home Energy Monitor provides a new level of visibility to electricity consumption and gives homeowners unprecedented power over their energy use with unique room-by-room views of where their energy dollars are spent and personalized GridSmart savings. Hadronex's award-winning Smart-Cover monitoring system is a completely self-contained, turnkey solution developed specifically for the water and wastewater industry. It is basically a high-tech manhole cover to prevent sewage spills by monitoring the level of sewer water in the system and providing an alarm when the sewer water is in danger of overflowing or spilling.

Greg Quist, co-founder and President of Hadronex, says,

> One of the important factors in our success here in San Diego is the confluence of environment and opportunity. Hadronex reflects the concern for the environment and the technological experience to do something about it. Our ideas and designs were catalyzed and supported by the water industry, and our products and business have been supported by the cluster of local manufacturers and technology companies.

David Drake, co-founder of EcoDog, says,

> The key for our fabrications process was to locate that very small sweet spot in contract manufacturing between capability, flexibility, and cost. We found the right partners who took responsible steps to improve the pro and who would allow direct engineering relationships to speed up closure. We also chose companies that were not too large or small in comparison with our own size. This has proven successful.

These companies are just two of many that are providing solutions to real problems while creating the higher-paying manufacturing jobs the region needs. With long-term limits on natural resource consumption, our nation needs sustainable economic development that provides high-paying manufacturing and service jobs. Cleantech manufacturing companies using innovative technologies provide a way to achieve both these goals.

Project Lead the Way (PLTW)

This organization has been working since 1997 to promote pre-engineering courses for middle and high school students. PLTW forms partnerships with public schools, higher education institutions, and the private sector to increase the quantity and quality of engineers and engineering technologists graduating from our educational system.

The PLTW curriculum was first introduced to 12 New York State high schools in the 1997-98 school year. A year later, PLTW field-tested its four-unit middle-school program in three middle schools. Today, the programs are offered in more than 1,300 schools in 45 states and the District of Columbia. PLTW seeks to prepare an increasing and more diverse group of students to be successful in engineering, engineering technology, and bio-medical science programs.

Currently, the courses in the PLTW High School Pre-engineering Program are:

- Foundation Course: Introduction to Engineering Design
- Principles of Engineering
- Digital Electronics
- Computer Integrated Manufacturing
- Civil Engineering and Architecture
- Biotechnical Engineering
- Aerospace Engineering
- Capstone Course: Engineering Design and Development

PLTW's middle-school program is called Gateway to Technology, and consists of nine-week stand-alone units which can be implemented in grades six through eight. The curriculum exposes students to a broad overview of the field of technology. The units are:

- Design and Modeling
- The Magic of Electrons
- The Science of Technology
- Automation and Robotics
- Flight and Space

Students receive training in current technology using the latest computer software and equipment in use in industry. They participate in a team-based, hands-on, activity-oriented program. They enroll in courses covering essential topics in technology, applying and reinforcing their study of math and science. The program allows them to explore a major career path and, if they wish to continue, will prepare them for further engineering education at a two- or four-year college. PLTW has articulation agreements with a number of colleges that accept specified courses for credit or advanced placement. Its graduates will be prepared to pursue a career in a field where the pay scales are among the highest for entry-level professionals or technicians.

Students who have done well in math and science and who like computers will find these courses intellectually stimulating and manageable. Each course has something special to offer because it is a daily hands-on experience in problem-solving skills, electronics, robotics, or manufacturing processes. Because PLTW believes that engineering, engineering technology, and biomedical science are exciting careers, instructors have been trained in a teaching approach that involves students in the same team-based problem-solving activities used in industry. These problem solving and analytical skills are applicable to any career field, so if a student decides engineering or biomedical science is not for him or her, that choice will take place in high school, saving later time and expense.

The summer camps began in 2007 and by the summer of 2008, 11 middle schools in San Diego County participated. Teacher training at San Diego State University began in 2007. The PLTW Design Challenge Series began in 2010 and provides a platform for the Introduction to Engineering Design and Principles of Engineering students to put their skills to the test by solving a design problem using specific materials in a short period of time. Each team of three students has the opportunity to showcase their extraordinary talents, in a variety of engineering fields, to a panel of engineering judges.

In 2006, a consortium comprising San Diego City College, the Center for Applied Competitive Technologies, San Diego State University, the El Cajon School District, and the San Diego Unified and Sweetwater School Districts received a grant of $450,000 to establish Project Lead the Way in San Diego County. (The Society of Manufacturing Engineers donated $125,000 in matching funds.) The grant supported a number of projects, like developing and operating middle school summer camps. It also introduced engineering course modules to middle schools using a Gateway to Technology curriculum. It trained teachers in how to teach the PLTW courses at San Diego State University. It introduced professional engineers into middle school and high school classrooms. It also offered identical engineering courses in high schools and community colleges and introduced evening engineering courses for college credit at selected high schools.

In January 2008, PLTW announced a partnership with Lockheed Martin for an innovative K-12 education outreach initiative, Engineers in the Classroom, to develop the next generation of engineers. Jim Knotts, Lockheed Martin's director of Corporate Citizenship, said, "Project Lead The Way's track record of preparing students for college engineering programs is unparalleled." He added, "Project Lead the Way students are five times more likely to major in engineering than the national average, their freshman to sophomore retention rate in the degree is over 80 percent, or double the national average, and their freshman GP in engineering study is greater than that of their peers."

In communities near Lockheed Martin's major business locations, the corporation works with schools that have, or will implement, the PLTW curriculum. Lockheed Martin supplements the curriculum with hands-on extracurricular activities which encourage teamwork and directly apply the principles learned in the classroom. In the first year, Lockheed Martin worked with PLTW schools in California, Colorado, Maryland, Minnesota, New York, and Texas. Starting mostly with high schools and expanding to their feeder middle schools, the initiative is creating a pipeline that offers the opportunity for seven continuous years of student involvement on the pathway to engineering. And competitive scholarships help bring the students from high school to college.

In February 2008, Northrop Grumman extended its partnership with PLTW through generous grants from the company's foundation. Two schools in Gloucester, Virginia joined the three public schools in San Diego that started the program in October 2007. In each school, a Northrop Grumman engineer is paired with a PLTW teacher to serve as a mentor and to guide students through real-life applications of the lessons learned in the classroom. Engineers share their knowledge and experiences to reinforce specific course assignments. They also support the program outside the classroom through presentations to interested parents and community groups.

In California, there are now over 235 middle and high schools enrolled in the program, and it is rapidly growing. In 2012, summer camp training will be held at the Cal Poly Pomona campus, the San Jose State campus, the San Diego State campus, and the Cal State East Bay campus. And a series of professional development workshops for PLTW teachers started in fall 2011. The list of sponsors of PLTW California now includes BAE Systems, Biogen Idec, Boeing, Chevron, General Atomics, the Girard Foundation, Intel, the McCarthy Family Foundation, Qualcomm, the San Diego Economic Development Corporation, the San Diego Foundation, Solar Turbines, and TechAmerica.

The San Diego Science Alliance

The San Diego Science Alliance, a non-profit consortium of leaders from business, K-12 education, higher education, and scientific institutions in San Diego County, was founded in 1994 to enhance science literacy in K-12 education by networking among organizations in the consortium, connecting needed resources with K-12 educators, and initiating, conducting, and supporting K-12 science education programs for San Diego County students and teachers. Its programs, projects, and resources include the following:

BE WISE (Better Education for Women in Science and Engineering) – A program that encourages middle-school girls to pursue careers in math, science, and engineering. Activities include girls' science overnights, alumnae follow-up Saturday symposia, and the distribution of science books to participating girls and school libraries.

High-Tech Fair – An annual event that introduces local companies to middle and high school students. Started in 1999, the fair has introduced more than 50 local companies to approximately 2,000 students. In addition to showcasing applications for mathematics, science, and technology, the event provides students with an opportunity to interact with local businesses that use science and engineering.

The Pisces Project – An award-winning project that brings university science graduate students into elementary-school classrooms to assist elementary educators with science instruction. 10 San Diego area school districts currently partner with the Pisces project.

Robotics – A program that enables students, teachers, and industry mentors to interact in the design, basic programming and building of robots. The students are in upper elementary through high school. Robotics expositions, competitions, workshops, and industry tours are offered in collaboration with other agencies.

Conclusion

These are just a few examples of the collaborative efforts, big and small, that are helping improve the economic and educational climate of states and regions in the U.S. Business, government, schools, and community leaders have found enough common ground to launch these innovative programs. However, these efforts won't be enough to ensure that the United States remains the world's leader in advanced manufacturing. American manufacturers must be willing to continuously invest in their products to improve performance, quality, and cost, as well as improve the skills of their workers to be more competitive in the global market. The next chapter will focus on what American manufacturers can do to save themselves.

10

What Can American Manufacturers Do To Save Themselves?

The U.S. today still leads the world in innovation, but American manufacturers must constantly do more with less to remain competitive in the global economy. They must achieve higher productivity with fewer people and lower profits. American companies need to get back to what made them great in the first place – unique, innovative products, made to high quality standards by a well-trained workforce. What can they do to survive, succeed, and thrive against the intense competition from China and other foreign countries? There are literally hundreds of books and articles with recommendations on how manufacturers can succeed and grow in the global economy. Their recommendations range from the ordinary – which apply to all types of businesses – to the more complex, which apply specifically to manufacturing.

Innovative strategies are the key to success. This chapter will focus on the following three: purpose, process, and promotion. These are:

Purpose – A vision of the reason for the existence of your company, your solution to fulfilling the desires of your customers, the Distinct Competitive Advantage (DCA) of your company's products or services, and your internal business model and guiding principles.

Process – How you use key tools like lean manufacturing and Six Sigma principles to eliminate waste and make your company as productive as it can be, delivering exactly what your customers want the way they want it.

Promotion – Use of the most cost-effective and productive marketing and sales methods and channels to market your product. Way of reaching new clients and getting existing ones to give you more business.

The white paper "Do More with Less: The Five Strategies Used by Successful SMB [Small and Medium Business] Manufacturers" by Infor ERP, the third-largest provider of business solution software, presents the following strategic guidelines:[1]

Vision – A clear understanding of the solution, the need you are looking to fulfill, the target audience you are serving, and the internal business model and guiding principles of the company.

Process – Adoption of lean manufacturing and Six Sigma principles that seek to eliminate waste through all aspects of the organization and process. These focus on the production and delivery of products directly associated with customer orders.

Metrics – Identification and application of business metrics and key performance indicators that can keep each aspect of the business on track. These help businesses meet or exceed established goals.

Automation – Use of automated technologies that can accelerate individual processes, such as design and engineering, production, quality control, product movement, inventory management, order fulfillment, and accounting.

Information Technology – Systematic integration and sharing of information for the efficient flow and management of work between internal and external functional areas of the company.

These are great recommendations and should be the basic foundation for building a successful manufacturing company. However, they don't go far enough in addressing the challenges of the serious offshore competition American manufacturers face today.

Of all the books and articles I have read over the past 25 years, the book that best addresses what small and midsize manufacturers can do to save themselves and compete in the global economy is *Saving American Manufacturing* by Michael Collins, published in 2006. Michael Collins has 30 years of experience in manufacturing. His book provides manufacturers with a framework for action and explains the complex problems facing manufacturers with clear concepts that offer a path to success.

In 2008, I arranged for him to come to San Diego to give a presentation on his book to the Operations Roundtable of the American Electronics Association and the Institute of Industrial Engineers. He presented his new method of growth and turnaround, leading to a process of strategic renewal. He trains companies to compete by being more innovative than their overseas competition. He recommends addressing the following:

New Services – Developing new services to offer existing customers.

Expanded Sales Coverage – Developing a new sales organization that expands sales territories and coverage.

Market Diversification – Prospecting and exploiting new market niches on a continuous basis.

Licensing – Licensing proprietary processes to other manufacturers or licensing technologies from other manufacturers.

Proprietary Processes – Developing a unique process that gives a definite competitive advantage over competitors.

New Products – Developing new products.

Vertical Integration – Bringing in-house most of the critical processes to increase quality, reduce cost, and shorten delivery times.

Quick Deliveries – delivering products more quickly, ranging from hours to days, depending on the type of products and services.

Certifications – Obtaining certifications can be a competitive advantage. Examples include ISO 9001, military specifications, nuclear certification, and FDA approvals.

New Sales Organizations and Sales Channels – Expanding the sales force by hiring outside sales persons or setting up a network of independent sales reps or distributors.

Lean Manufacturing – Adopting methods that reduce costs, waste, inventory and in-process time.

Cross Training of Employees – Providing more flexibility in the variety of applications and market niches that can be served.

Equipment Upgrade and Investment – Using the latest machines tools and other equipment can increase output, speed and other performance factors that affect delivery and/or cost.

For a complete description and information on how to utilize these strategies, along with examples of companies that have successfully implemented some of them, you can contact Michael Collins, or buy his book, at mpcmgt.com.

According to Michael Treacy's book *The Discipline of Market Leaders*, "no company can succeed today by trying to be all things to all people. It must instead find the unique value that it alone can deliver to a chosen market."[2]Treacy maintains that best-in-class companies must choose to be one of the three following types of company:

Operational Excellence Company – Companies that are not primarily product or service innovators, nor do they cultivate deep one-on-one customer relationships (Target, McDonalds).

Innovative Leader Company (product leadership) – Companies that push performance boundaries and innovate year after year, with not much attention to what consumers say they want. (Intel, 3M).

Customer Intimacy Company – Companies that focus on being flexible to cultivate long term relationships with their customers. (Airborne Express, Nordstrom).

Companies that fail to strategically define themselves are at severe risk of being out-competed by those that do.

Marketing and New Sales Channels

From my more than 25 years of marketing and sales experience as a manufacturers' representative, I know how important marketing is to the growth and success of companies. Businesses simply cannot succeed if they do not meet the needs of their market, and manufacturers often fail because they embrace a product driven, instead of a market driven, strategy.

So what is marketing? Marketing is creating customers for the products and services of a business. Marketing is everything a business does to move its product or service from seller to buyer. Everyone is in a marketing business, regardless of whatever else they do. Marketing begins in the mind of the customer. When does a business stop marketing? Never! There's an old story that if you build a better mousetrap, the world will beat a path to your door. This isn't true! You first have to let the world *know* you have a better mousetrap, through marketing, and then you have to make the mousetrap easily available to customers through the right sales channels.

Most small and medium-sized manufacturers do not put enough emphasis on marketing because they don't really understand what marketing is and don't have any marketing experience. Most can't afford a marketing manager, and many companies don't even have a sales manager. The owner of the company tries to do sales at the same time he or she is managing the day-to-day activities of the company. This is a recipe for disaster.

To successfully market your company's products or services, you need to master the marketing mindset. There are no rules that apply to every type of company, and there are no quick fixes or "magic pills" that will work for everyone. All marketing is a gamble, and no one can accurately predict the results. (And remember that if you are not doing what you love, all the tools in the world won't help.) But there are some basic principles that apply to all companies. "What's In It for Me" (WIIFM) is a universal law of marketing – tell the customer what's in it for him or her. These are three basic steps to effective marketing:

1. Know your market – who are your prospective customers?

2. Know each possible way to reach that market with a persuasive message.

3. Use methods that maximize your leverage – maximum result with minimum effort.

You need to be specific about what you want your marketing to do for you, like acquire more new customers or locate more qualified prospects. You and your sales team need to be able to describe your "business identity" in 25 words or less (also called an "elevator speech" because you can say it in the time it takes to get from one floor to another). For example, my business is ElectroFab Sales, a manufacturers' sales rep agency, and my business identity elevator speech is: "We help companies select the right manufacturing processes to make parts for their products from the companies we represent."

You and your sales team need to be able to describe what about your product or service is unique or different. This is called your Differential Competitive Advantage (DCA). In other words, give the reasons why customers would want to buy or use *your* product or service. We at ElectroFab have identified a DCA for each of the companies we represent. The key is to find a market in which your product or service can be a leader; an effective DCA always develops out of an under-filled or unfilled market need. Examples of DCA thrusts are:

- Lowest or highest price
- Wide selection
- Exclusive selection
- Customization
- Convenience
- Speed (of service or product delivery)
- Ongoing customer education
- Service follow-up
- Cutting edge
- Fills wide range of needs
- Specialized know-how

Because I represent only American companies, I can't use the lowest price DCA thrust when the companies I represent are competing against fabrication services in China. My companies have to compete on the basis of some of the other thrusts.

If you are having trouble determining the DCA for your business, ask your customers questions about what they like best about your company's products or services. Ask them what they look for in a supplier and how they decide which company to choose. Compare your products or services with those of your major competitors. It may be helpful to have a consultant or someone else outside of your company do a comparative matrix of your products or services.

As an example, the DCA of one plastic molding company we represent is that they have rapid prototyping equipment and a tool and die shop to make molds in-house. This provides shorter lead times in making the molds (tooling) and more rapid delivery of first articles and prototypes. They also have clean-room molding and assembly, which is critical for some medical parts and subassemblies.

If you can't determine your company's DCA, hire a marketing consultant to help you identify what is unique about your company and its products or services. You may even need help restructuring your company or redesigning your products to *create* a competitive advantage. If you do not have a competitive advantage that your sales people can easily describe, you are dead.

Once you have an accurate understanding of your target markets and DCA, you can choose the best marketing methods to use. The following are some of the best low-cost marketing methods:

Direct marketing – An interactive system of marketing using one or more means to affect a measurable response. Examples are brochures, catalogs, CDs and DVDs, fliers, letters, and special reports.

Distributors – Businesses that buy and resell your products in a specified territory and pay all their own business expenses and taxes out of their markup on your products.

Internet Marketing – Company websites, advertisements on search engines or other people's websites, email, e-newsletters, and press releases.

Sales Representatives – Independent Contractors that act as outside sales agents for more than one company for non-competing, compatible products or services.

Strategic Partnerships – This means joint use by contract of channels like sales reps and distributors. Non-competing companies promote each other for a percentage of revenue.

Telemarketing – This is marketing conducted by phone by in-house sales persons, sales reps, or telemarketing firms.

Out-Bound (proactive) – Pre-planned campaign to selected database of prospective customers

In-bound Marketing (reactive/proactive) – Pre-recorded message that plays when calls are received or put on hold

Most people don't understand the difference between a sales representative and a broker. A broker is an independent businessperson who handles a sales territory on an informal, non-contractual, and non-exclusive basis. Brokers pay all of their own business expenses, including taxes and insurance. They usually handle competing lines, so manufacturers are bidding against each other in the quoting stage, and the broker passes on the best price to his prospect or customer. Some brokers buy and resell like distributors, but without keeping an inventory. They are paid a commission on their sales.

Manufacturers' representatives are also independent contractors and pay their own expenses. But they usually work under a contract for a specific sales territory, specific accounts, or a target market sector, and do *not* represent competing lines. They are also paid a commission. The main reason manufacturers sell through reps are that they are the cheapest way to reach a mass market for products or services that cannot be sold through direct mail, mass media, or the Internet. It is often too expensive to hire salespeople to cover all of the territory in which they wish to sell. The costs of using sales reps are a fixed percentage of sales at a time when salaries and benefits are escalating and variable. And sales through reps benefit from the synergistic effects of selling multiple lines. Some of other advantages of using sales reps are the following:

Territory Competence – In-depth knowledge of customers and competition; investment in the territory.

Multiple-Line Selling – Product lines of multiple manufacturers have a synergistic effect where one line "rides" along with others as a package that a rep offers to customers.

Sales and Marketing Capabilities – Self-motivated, experienced in multiple-line selling, and self-managing.

Financial Advantages – No costs for commissions until shipment or payment by customer, so representative is financing cost of sales at a fixed commission vs. variable salary.

International Use of Sales Reps

Foreign companies from Japan, Korea, Taiwan, the European Union, and China have successfully used American sales reps to sell their products and services in the U.S. Obviously, it would have been prohibitively expensive for firms from these countries to sell into a country as large as the U.S. through direct factory reps.

Multinational American companies have been converting to independent sales reps, instead of direct sales employees, over the past 15 years. European rep firms are more like brokers/distributors, and often represent competing lines. In Japan, there are both trading companies (brokers/distributors) and American-style rep firms. In Hong Kong, Singapore, and Taiwan, you will find both trading companies and American-style rep firms. In Mexico and Latin American, there are both brokers/distributors and American-style rep firms, depending on the product. The same is true in Australia.

How to Find Sales Representatives

In the new paradigm of global competition, the role of sales representatives will continue to expand because companies cannot afford to sell their products internationally in the traditional manner of direct sales. The best ways to find sales reps for your products or services are referrals from other companies with non-competing products or services, trade shows, trade directories, trade associations, trade magazines, and sales rep search firms. If you are looking for international sales reps or distributors, U.S. Embassy Foreign Commercial Service offices will perform an agent/distributor search in a specific country for a reasonable fee. (See Appendix B for a partial list of sales representative associations provided by the Manufacturers' Representatives Educational Research Foundation (mrerf.org).)

(The following sections were written by Kim Niles, a quality management professional who also teaches Lean Six Sigma at the University of California at San Diego.)

Innovative Strategies are Key to Success

Business survival and success depend upon how any given company addresses its market needs. One of the ways is through innovation. Innovation is important to all companies in numerous different ways, but it is ultra-critical to some companies such as Apple, which must continue to produce more innovative iPods or lose market share.

The individual employee has four different ways to contribute to a company's success through innovation. He or she can address innovation at the design or development level, the business level, the operations level, or the process level, depending upon his or her circle of influence, as outlined below.

Focus on Innovation in Product or Service Design

During World War II, the Russian Navy acquired more than 50,000 German patents. In 1946, the patent clerk Genrich Altshuller was given 300 people and the responsibility of sifting through them to see if any of them would help Russia become more prosperous. Two years later, he reported that he had been given the wrong problem to solve and that the correct problem would be to develop ways to help Russia become more innovative. He was given the okay to continue, which became the beginnings of "TRIZ," a Russian acronym for the "Theory of Creative Problem Solving." During the 1980s, TRIZ began to spread worldwide, and today more than 3.1 million patents have been studied. TRIZ works best at a product's or service's design stage because there is an extremely good chance that no matter what you are trying to develop, the basic problem has already been solved and documented in a patent.

Dr. Ellen Domb, founder of *Triz Journal*, maintains that there are two underlying concepts to TRIZ. The first is that somebody someplace has already solved your problem, or one very similar. Creativity is finding that solution and adapting it to your own circumstances. The second concept is harder to understand, but relates to not compromising in your search for a solution. This doesn't mean that at any one time a compromise can't be made for practical reasons, but if your design isn't as perfect as it could be, it will be short lived, as your competition will soon improve upon it or your customer will demand something better. And patent searching is just one of 50 tools used to help structure creativity and assist in the development of solutions.

Innovation at the Operations Level

Innovation at the operations level takes the form of creatively translating what top management wants for the company into process-level changes that must happen in order to fulfill those desires. For example, if top management needs to free up cash to purchase capital equipment, innovation might be applied at the operations level to reduce dollars tied up by inventory. Here are a few different ways that this might be done:

- Some portion of the existing inventory might be handed over to another company to manage (Vendor Managed Inventory or VMI).

- Supply chain contracts might be renegotiated to have vendors deliver parts/assemblies just in time as needed.

- Processes might be combined or changed in ways to allow for more efficient use of raw materials so that less inventory is needed. Statistics may also be needed to find an optimum location to run within a process window.

Innovation at the Process Level

Innovation at the process level is the key to developing effective, safe, efficient, and consistent processes that maximize value-added and minimize waste at every process step. In order to improve anything, especially a process for accomplishing a task, a few key high-level steps are required:

Review existing process steps – Innovation at this stage takes the form of utilizing models, methods, and tools that capture what is being done in the process. For example, an innovative look at what it takes to create a can of soda may start at the mine where the aluminum ore is mined, because while it may only take three minutes of value-added time to produce a can of soda, the entire value stream actually takes three years. Innovative value-stream-mapping tools can easily show every step of the process. In addition, they show typical inventories held at each step and time wasted between those steps, which allow one to streamline bottlenecks and reduce inventory costs.

Identify areas for improvement – While some people are better at constructive criticism than others, the scope of areas for improvement is potentially huge. This requires an understanding of what is good and bad, how the process works, and how it can be improved. Innovation here may be found in understanding common forms of soft waste to the point of being able to recognize them at a glance. For example, an operator squatting to perform a task is motion-related waste. Over time, delay and safety costs will build if that task isn't improved.

Brainstorm improvement solutions – Brainstorming is an art form, but there are many different models, methods, and tools to assist a brainstorming group to reach an effective goal. For example, there are nominal group techniques (NGTs) that utilize sticky notes, affinity diagrams, and multi-voting so that all ideas can be brought to the table without putting anyone on the spot. Using affinity-diagram techniques, new ideas are generated from old ideas by putting the old ideas into categories. Using multi-voting techniques, the group's general understanding of, or feeling for, the importance of each idea can be measured and prioritized.

Implement the best solution – When a solution is implemented, innovation is needed to verify that the solution will work and implemented permanently, so the process doesn't just drift back to its old state. People naturally tend to resist change, so innovation here may be in the form of training, process documentation, or staff empowerment to "own" the new process.

Workforce Training

American manufacturers must be willing to invest in improving the skills of their workers to be more competitive in the global market. Germany and Switzerland lead the world in apprenticeship and workforce training. Apprenticeship programs have virtually disappeared from American industry, but we must rebuild them if we want to have the skilled workforce needed for the 21st century.

The Importance of Lean

As noted in Chapter One, in the past 20 years, a growing number of manufacturers have implemented lean manufacturing based on the Toyota Production System (TPS). The founders of TPS had to do more with less, so this became the guiding philosophy behind lean thinking the Toyota way. During the 1990s in the United States, TPS became known as "lean" manufacturing. There is no one best way, no 10-step model, and no implementation plan that will work for every company.

Lean manufacturing is based on the principle of continual improvement (*kaizen*). Lean manufacturing was developed to produce smaller batch sizes and just-in-time delivery, producing only the necessary units, in necessary quantities, at precisely the right time. This reduces inventory, increases productivity, and reduces costs. It has evolved into a system-wide management process that continually seeks to increase profits by stripping out wasted time, material, and manpower from the manufacturing process. These are called "non-value-added" steps in a "value-stream map" of the manufacturing process.

Value can best be described as the elements of the product or service that the customer is willing to pay for. The customer is the only reason why the business exists. Therefore an understanding of what the customer actually requires is an essential element of the strategy of a lean company. *Who* they are, *what* do they want, *when* do they want it, and *how* do they want it must be clearly defined.

These definitions will change over time, and companies that ignore this change will inevitably fail. This will require customer monitoring by the company's marketing and sales team, which could take the form of periodic customer surveys. In my business, for example, we contact new customers after the delivery of parts for several orders. If a customer becomes a regular customer, we keep in touch on a bi-monthly or monthly basis to make sure they are satisfied with the service of the company we represent. If the customer orders only periodically, we contact them every other month or once a quarter to keep abreast of their needs and make sure they remain a satisfied customer. It is important to contact a customer at least three to four times a year so they remember your company when they next require a product or service.

Lean manufacturing has expanded into "lean office" and "lean thinking" whose goal is to reduce the waste in the knowledge work of running a company. Because waste is harder to see in knowledge work, the focus is on increasing value-added work, improving flow, and achieving mastery. The basis for adding value is ultimately the belief that individuals and organizations exist to create value for society through their interaction with employees, suppliers, customers, stockholders, and communities. It encompasses an ongoing effort to align purpose, strategy, and people around serving others.

Lean manufacturing began at large companies because of the costs of training and the time involved to implement the process. But, as we saw in Chapter Seven, there is abundance of "lean" training available through state and federal programs today. Every small and medium-sized manufacturer should make such training a high priority in their company's strategic plan to survive and grow. In the automotive industry, the benefits of lean manufacturing are undisputed. Toyota has a greater market value than Ford, GM, Daimler, and Honda combined, and ranks in the top 10 of all companies worldwide. However, the benefits of lean manufacturing for a small company can be just as dramatic.

Pacific Metal Stampings, in Valencia, California, for example, is a short run metal-stamping company. To help offset the trend of moving manufacturing operations offshore, its management took a different approach: training employees. Within a year during 2000, more than 50 percent of its employees attended three separate classes of 140 hours each. These classes were production skills, lean manufacturing, and continuous improvement. Initially, the employees were not receptive to the lean manufacturing classes. Don Schlotfelt, president, said that the employees asked, "Why did they need to work harder, when they already work hard?" After the second class, a change in the culture was taking place. Schlotfelt said, "I was dumbfounded by the employees' positive attitude and their excitement about the changes." He added, "The results of the training were extraordinary. Average throughput went from five weeks to five days, on-time delivery improved by 70 percent, and work-in-process was reduced 40 percent." The long-term result was increased productivity, higher employee morale, improved company performance, additional business for the company, and greater profitability. Schlotfelt concluded, "Training alone will not stop the flow of manufacturing jobs offshore. Over-regulation, the second-highest taxes on manufacturing in the world, and unions pay a major role in American manufacturers losing their competitive edge."

Customer Service

Customer service is an area where American companies can outshine their Chinese and other foreign competitors. But this is possible only if they have a policy of providing their customers the best service, and train and motivate their employees to implement it. Customer service includes returning customer phone calls and addressing customer issues promptly and courteously. In short, you must treat your customers the way you would want to be treated.

While customer service may start with the employees who interface with customers, it doesn't end there. Workers on the shop floor carry out the commitments and promises of customer service personnel, so it is essential they realize their employment depends not only on pleasing their supervisor, but customers as well. Every employee has to understand that doing their job well, no matter how menial the job, is vital to pleasing customers, and by extension, ensuring their own job security. It isn't just about *doing a job*; it's about *pleasing customers*. If your employees are rude, argumentative, or indifferent to customers, you are late with your deliveries, or you have parts rejected due to poor quality, how long do you think it will be before your customers try another vendor?

Meeting delivery schedules is essential. Even if the parts are not immediately required for production, some customers track their vendor's performance in meeting delivery. Too many late deliveries, and you will be disqualified as a vendor. This actually happened to one of the companies we previously represented. Their customer purchased $300,000 worth of product annually, but the manufacturer we represented lost the business as a result of not meeting delivery schedules. While quality was also an issue with some customers, the major reason was late–frequently very late–deliveries, mostly caused by poor employee attendance and motivation.

An even worse situation is when a customer needs the parts for assembly on their own production line. When they have a production line down because they are missing a part, it means they have workers standing around with nothing to do. It also means they won't be meeting delivery commitment to their own customers. Causing a customer to have a production line down may subject your company to unwelcome scrutiny, not only from the buyer who placed the order and who is now getting all kinds of pressure, but also from your customer's production department, marketing department, and even upper management. If steps are not promptly taken to correct the problem permanently, you may receive notification from the purchasing department that you have been disqualified as a vendor because they finally lost patience and found a more reliable supplier.

Every effort should be made to comply with a customer's delivery schedule. Production personnel need to understand that the consequence of their missing work extends far beyond their losing a day's wages. It can also mean that their employer is unable to meet a scheduled delivery, which, in turn, could cause their employer to lose that customer. If enough customers are lost, that employee and others could be laid off.

Meeting customers' quality standards is also essential. Reworking or replacing rejected parts not only kills your profit, but delays delivery of acceptable parts. Parts that don't meet customers' standards, but are accepted anyway because they are badly needed, will alienate your customers. If a customer is constantly receiving parts from you that do not meet their standards, sooner or later they will lose confidence in you and turn to a competitor.

Cosmetic issues for exterior parts are especially problematic because cosmetics are so subjective. These issues are frequently not called out, or called out inadequately, on customers' drawings, so they require customer service above and beyond the minimum to ensure customer satisfaction. Exceeding a customer's quality standards for a particular part may gain you praise, but coming as close as possible to zero rejections will go even further toward keeping customers. Because quality starts on the production floor, employees must be *trained* and *motivated* to provide the level of quality your customers want.

During the various sales training sessions I have attended, the one thing emphasized repeatedly is that *the best prospect you have is the customer you already have.* Sometimes it becomes easy to take a good customer for granted, especially if they have been tolerant of your past transgressions. But even a loyal customer's patience can wear thin if it is tested too frequently. In addition, a "friend" in purchasing can be replaced by a stranger who sees only how you are now performing and has no experience with your past track record. If your current performance is lacking, this is all a new buyer has to measure you by. The absolute worst thing you can do, outside of falling down on the first order with a new customer, is to start taking an existing customer for granted.

American vendors who provide only passing levels of delivery, quality, or customer service will not survive, because customers can get that from Chinese vendors today for a far lower price. Only American companies whose delivery, quality, and customer service *exceed* their customers' expectations will prosper in the new global economy.

Going Green

Anyone who has shopped at their local grocery, drugstore, or hardware store lately has seen the variety of "green" products on the market. Are these products creating new manufacturing jobs? For the most part, no, because they are just eco-friendlier versions of existing products. "Being green is in their best interests not so much in making money as saving money," says Gary Yohe, an environmental economist at Wesleyan University. "Green companies are likely to be a permanent trend, as these vulnerabilities continue, but it's going to take a long time for all this to settle down."[6]

Pamela Gordon dispels the myth that environmental practices are bad for business in her book *Lean and Green: Profit for Your Workplace and the Environment*. She presents evidence from companies around the world that environmental protection and a profitable business can go together. Her book outlines four basic steps to creating a lean and green organization and presents stories of how 20 companies have enjoyed greater efficiencies and cost savings by using these steps to pursue environmental leadership. Many of these companies are leaders in their fields, like IBM, Agilent, ITT Cannon, Intel, and Apple. The stories show how they saved money and increased profitability with green technology and practices.

Since her book was written in 2001, everything related to green has become even more important because of concerns about global warming. Green has moved from the fringe to the mainstream. More consumers are choosing to buy green products, even when it means paying more. Major corporations are featuring their green technology and practices in their advertising campaigns. Some of the largest and most successful companies, like Coca-Cola, DuPont, General Electric, Ford, and General Motors, are now greening how they do business. For example, they are beginning to respond to increases in shipping and environmental costs with green policies meant to reduce both fuel consumption and carbon emissions. That pressure is only likely to increase as both manufacturers and retailers seek ways to tighten the global supply chain.

To take just one example, in August 2008 General Motors announced that it would add a 1.2-megawatt solar power installation to the roof of its transmission assembly plant in White Marsh, Maryland. The installation will generate about 1.4 million kWh of clean renewable solar energy, enough to serve the electricity needs of about 145 households. In addition, the plant reached landfill-free status in 2007 because it no longer sends any production waste to local landfills. All waste generated at the facility is recycled or reused.[3]

Dow Corning received the 2008 Global Specialty Chemicals Corporate Leadership Green Excellence award from the consulting firm Frost and Sullivan for its demonstrated commitment to renewable and sustainable energy resources. Dow has invested more than $35 million in new technology at its manufacturing site in Michigan, which will reduce carbon dioxide emissions by 20 percent. And at its Kentucky plant, a new manufacturing process has reduced carbon emissions by more than 1,200 tons.[4]

On November 19, 2008, Hewlett Packard announced three new imaging and printing solutions, and its Green IT Action plan, a step-by-step guide to help companies develop a plan to reduce the environmental impact of printing and imaging. The new imaging and printing solutions transform paper-based workflows into seamless electronic processes.[5]

In a 2008 opinion article for *Industry Week*, consultant John Madigan of Madigan Associates, with more than 25 years' experience in operations management at Continental Can and Storagetek, among other companies, wrote that "'Green' manufacturing technology offers more than a way to slow environmental destruction; it could be a powerful antidote for America's economic crises, mass job losses, and diminished international status."[6]

San Diego business consultant and author Glenn Croston advises companies large and small on green business strategy and the best practices for becoming eco-friendly. He says, "When people hear the word 'green,' they often think this means that something is expensive, hard to do, a luxury, impractical, and only for tree-huggers....In fact, going green often saves money, whether by cutting down on costly gasoline use or by wasting less paper." His book *Greening Your Business on a Budget* presents many low-cost ways to go green.

At a time when consumer confidence in made-in-China goods is at an all-time low, the opportunity is ripe for American manufacturers to feature how their products are made utilizing green manufacturing technologies. After the debacle of tainted and defective Chinese products, people are willing to pay more for products that are safe and made in an environmentally responsible manner. An August 7, 2007 Zogby poll revealed that one in three Americans would be willing to pay four times as much for American-made toys, and 63 percent were willing to join a general boycott of Chinese-made goods.[7]

Even when businesses are fighting for their survival in tough economic times, they are choosing to move forward by going green. "Indeed, companies would be foolish to abandon their green credentials at the first sign of difficulty," said Solitaire Townsend, chief executive of Futera Sustainability Communications, which advises companies on green strategies. "What is more, companies have much to gain from taking steps to improve their environmental performance. The guiding principles behind behaving in an environmentally sound manner are the same as the principles of thrift and economy. Using fewer resources is at the core of environmental sustainability and leads to cost savings. Thrift and being green go hand in hand," she said.[8]

More than 260,000 workers in California currently work in the green economy, according to the Employment Development Department. The Redwood Empire region, north of San Francisco, leads, with 5.1 percent of its workforce in green jobs, but Southern California leads in the actual number of jobs, with 106,350, or 1.6 percent of its workforce. The San Diego and Imperial county regions have slightly more than 21,000 jobs, or 1.8 percent. Traditional blue-collar jobs, such as carpenters, electricians, and heating and air-conditioning technicians, comprise the largest number of workers in the green economy. GreenJobs.org provides an on-line database of environment-related job postings, showing a growing demand for workers with "green" skills.

While it is good that that going green is saving money for manufacturers, benefiting some traditional blue-collar occupations and providing "green" products for consumers, the real question is whether it is creating new manufacturing jobs. In the last couple of years, the term "green technology" has evolved into the more encompassing term of "cleantech." The cleantech industry could be a powerful antidote for America's economic crisis and massive job losses in manufacturing. Cleantech manufacturing offers more than a way to slow environmental damage. It could create the higher-paying jobs needed to sustain a strong middle class while helping to solve our air, energy, water and food crises.

Conclusion

A manufacturer can apply all of the recommendations in this chapter and still fail because of circumstances and outside factors beyond its control. Very few American manufacturers can survive when their industry has been targeted by China for product dumping. The next chapter will consider some of the national policies that need to be implemented to save American manufacturing.

11

How Can We Save American Manufacturing?

There are many ideas and recommendations in circulation on how we can save U.S. manufacturing, ranging from extreme protectionism to more moderate measures. Unfortunately, most job-creation proposals from commentators, politicians, and economists involve either increased government spending, or reduced taxes, at a time of soaring budget deficits. Other recommendations would require legislation on taxes, regulation, or trade that would be difficult to accomplish. And many of these solutions involve borrowing money now, largely from China, or taking money from one group of citizens (or future generations) to give to another.

This chapter presents a broad spectrum of ideas and recommendations from studies, reports, and books by industry experts, committees, and organizations. It also includes my own viewpoint on what recommendations are the most critical, realistic, measurable, and achievable. Some of these ideas are new, while others have been recommended for years.

When my region was going through the recession of the early 1990s caused by the painful defense conversion at the end of the Cold War, Robert Caldwell, *San Diego Union-Tribune Insight* Senior Editor, commented that there was a consensus that the following measures were needed to bolster America's industrial competitiveness:[1]

- Reduce the cost of capital, needed to fuel industrial growth.

- Cut capital gains taxes, especially for long-term investments.

- Invest more in basic and applied research and development.

- Curb the soaring cost of health care.

- Measure any new environmental regulation against its impact on American corporations competing with foreign companies.

- Radically reform America's failing education system for grades K-12 and improve both adult education and retraining.

- Encourage corporate and management reforms.

However, we've seen little action on the above recommendations in the subsequent 20 years.

The capital gains tax was reduced from a high of 28 percent to 15 percent by President Bush in 2002, and extended for two more years at the end of 2010. But it will go back up to 20 percent in 2013 if not extended or made permanent.

A growing number of American manufacturers have made progress in embracing corporate and management reforms by adopting Total Quality Management, lean manufacturing, and Six Sigma (quality control) strategies.

By contrast, health care costs have continued to soar, research and development funding has been cut rather than increased, more environmental regulations have been imposed on American manufacturers, and our education system for grades K-12 is still failing.

If more of these recommendations had been adopted and implemented, American manufacturing would be in a better position today.

In 1991, Congressman Duncan Hunter (R-CA) held a series of meetings on the topic of "San Diego Aerospace, Defense and Manufacturing – Can We Keep It?" More than 100 leaders from business, local government, and non-government organizations participated. I attended these meetings as board president of The High Technology Foundation. At their conclusion, a conference report was released, recommending specific actions at the city, county, state, and federal government levels. A number of recommendations were implemented at the city and county level, but none of the recommendations for the state or federal levels were adopted.

The report made the following recommendations at the federal level, most of which related to taxes:

- Eliminate or sharply reduce the capital gains tax.

- Eliminate the luxury tax.

- Extend and increase the R&D tax credit.

- Extend and increase the net operating losses carryover.

- Eliminate Treasury Regulation 861-B, which encourages U.S. companies to conduct R&D overseas.

- Cancel the passive loss limitation.

- Require a balanced federal budget by a Constitutional amendment.

- Give the President a line-item veto.

- Reform impractical and outdated federal water policy laws.

- Relax federal banking regulation practices that unreasonably restrict financing for new housing construction.

- Reduce the time required to process Environmental Protection Agency and U.S. Fish and Wildlife Service permits and signoffs.

On the plus side, the capital gains tax was reduced, and the luxury tax eliminated, by President Bush's tax cuts in 2002– many years after the recommendation. The R&D tax credit was extended, but has been neither made permanent nor increased. The net operating loss carryover has been extended from 15 to 20 years. The carry-back of a net operating loss has been reduced from three years to two years. The 861-B rules were made more favorable for U.S. taxpayers conducting R&D both within and outside the U.S. in 1996, but the code section has not been eliminated. Passive loss limits have not been repealed. No progress has been achieved in adopting any of the other recommendations.

I have now read dozens of reports released by organizations, councils, and committees over the past four years. Some recommendations are similar, while others are diametrically opposed. Below are some of the most interesting proposals.

The Alliance for American Manufacturing is a unique non-partisan, non-profit partnership forged to strengthen manufacturing in the United States. It brings together a select group of America's leading manufacturers and the United Steelworkers. Its mission is to promote creative policy solutions on such priorities as international trade, energy security, health care, retirement security, currency manipulation, and other issues of mutual concern.[2] AAM believes that an innovative and growing manufacturing base is vital to America's economic and national security, as well as to providing good jobs for future generations. AAM achieves its mission through research, public education, advocacy, strategic communications, and coalition building around the issues that matter most to America's manufacturing sector. In September 2011, it made the following recommendations:

Establish a national infrastructure bank to leverage capital for large-scale transportation and energy projects.

Reshape the tax code in a revenue-neutral way to provide incentives for job creation and inward investment. R&D tax credits should help firms that not only innovate in America but also make their products here. Lower tax rates for manufacturing in America and eliminate tax shelters for hedge funds or financial transactions that have no real value.

Apply Buy American provisions to all federal spending to ensure that American workers and businesses get the first shot at procurement contracts.

Shift some education investment to rebuilding our vocational and technical skills program, which would address looming shortages in the manufacturing sector.

Refocus the trade agenda by giving American businesses new tools to counter China's currency manipulation, industrial subsidies, intellectual property theft, and barriers to market access.

Condition new federal loan guarantees for energy projects on the utilization of domestic supply chains for construction.

In addition, AAM recommended that the President immediately do the following:

Expedite small business loans through the Small Business Administration and Treasury Department to help firms expand, retool, and hire.

Convene a multilateral meeting to address global imbalances and in particular Chinese mercantilism. If China doesn't agree to participate, designate it a currency manipulator.

On the heels of the landmark agreement with automakers on fuel economy standards, **secure** an additional agreement from all foreign and domestic car companies to increase their levels of domestic content by at least 10 percent over the next three years.

Direct the Department of Defense to leverage existing procurement to contractors that commit to increasing the domestic content of our military equipment, technology, and supplies.

Approve additional applications for renewable and traditional energy projects, contingent on the use of American materials in construction.

Kick any CEO off of federal advisory boards or jobs councils who has not created net new American jobs over the past five years, or is expanding the company's foreign workforce at a faster rate than its domestic workforce. Replace them with CEOs who are committed to investing in America.

The **American Jobs Alliance** is an independent, non-partisan, non-profit organization whose mission is to encourage and facilitate a better understanding of the history and functioning of the American System of free enterprise and the activities necessary for its preservation so that American will once again, make, grow and invent all items that are vital for the survival of this and future generations. AJA's recommendations for strengthening manufacturing in the U.S.A. are:

Fix broken tax policies to encourage the domestic production of goods consumed in the United States and limit the tax deductibility of the offshore production of goods and services ultimately destined for the U.S. domestic market.

Expand the research and development tax credit to incentivize basic research and its commercialization and production in the United States.

Fix broken trade policies and enforce laws on the books to address China's currency manipulation, government subsidies, and import tariffs in the form of value added taxes to imports.

Renegotiate or terminate trade treaties and agreements that encourage the offshoring of American industries and services.

Enforce U.S. health, safety and production standards for imported manufactured goods and food products.

Identify key technologies and industries and fund research to nurture the commercialization and production of these technologies in the U.S.

Establish "buy American, hire American" policies that use taxpayer dollars for public works (infrastructure), defense projects and all government procurement contracts on the federal, state and local levels to put Americans to work.

Improve skills-based education and provide technical and vocational education programs in our schools to prepare the workforce need by U.S. manufacturers.

Economy In Crisis (EconomyInCrisis.org) is a non-profit organization dedicated to educating legislators and the American public on the destruction of our country's industrial base, the impact this has on our national and economic security, and how it affects our standard of living. EIC publishes critical-but-overlooked facts and figures, keeping its readers up-to-date with daily articles regarding the U.S. economy. It compares what led to American industrial and economic world leadership with current policies and the present crippling of our industries. EIC then extrapolates the near-term outlook and risks for our country, businesses and individuals. When possible, it offers solutions. AmericaWakeUp.net, EIC's sister organization, is dedicated to providing factual data on the current economic condition of the U.S. The data includes the number of U.S. companies being sold to foreign interests, the percentage of annual consumption spent on imports, the percentage of U.S. corporations owned by foreign entities, and foreign financing of U.S. government debt. EIC has identified six key policy failures which contributed to the economic crisis that started in 2008:

- One-way "free" trade (NAFTA, CAFTA, WTO, GATT) involving unfair tactics to put our industries out of business

- Failure to shield our key industries from foreign takeovers

- Insourcing, or production of goods and services in the U.S. by foreign corporations, providing very few jobs

- Offshore outsourcing

- Massive debt with foreign creditors

- Loss of leverage in foreign policy

EIC recommends solutions focused on the following:

Protection – Prevent the sale of strategic U.S.-owned domestic companies to foreign companies and eliminate offshore outsourcing except in extreme circumstances.

Fair Trade – Protect the U.S. from predatory foreign countries by treaties and tariffs where needed and practical.

Competitiveness – Ensure that it is once again profitable to produce most goods and services in America factories employing American workers.

The Coalition for a Prosperous America (CPA) is a nonprofit organization representing the interests of 2.7 million households through its agricultural, manufacturing, and labor members. It is working for a new and positive U.S. trade policy that delivers prosperity and security to America, its citizens, farms, factories and working people. It believes America can provide good jobs for workers, affordable goods for consumers, opportunity for farms and manufacturers, and a clean environment without compromising our national sovereignty and security.

In 2008, more than 300 organizations, companies, officials, candidates, and prominent individuals signed a document called *Fixing America's Economy*. The document was a joint effort crafted to describe the causes of the Great Recession and the solutions needed to restructure our economy to not only recover, but also grow jobs, wealth, and income. It also served as a template for many to speak with one voice, rather than sector by sector, when advocating to elected officials. In November 2009, this document was updated. The new document is called "Fixing America's Economy II: Rebuilding American Jobs, Wealth and Power." It is not a CPA document per se, but CPA is championing it in the hope that it will be useful. It reads:

America's economy faces an ongoing structural crisis that contributed directly to the 2008-9 financial meltdowns and limits the scope for a sustained recovery. The old means of economic growth – overconsumption, offshoring, and borrowing – have seriously undermined the national interest.

To resume sustainable growth, generate jobs, and pay down our spiraling debt, we need to make fundamental changes in the American economy. We also face a profound political crisis. Our governmental system currently lacks the ability to articulate and pursue ambitious national goals.

A bold national vision is needed to equip America to compete successfully in a global economy. America must reorganize its creative, financial, and governmental resources to meet a few fundamental challenges coherently, effectively, and urgently. A successful strategy will improve the standard of living for current and future American families, restore value to our currency, realign corporate with national interests, and reinforce the U.S. position as the paramount world leader.

To that end, we challenge all holders and seekers of public office to commit to the solutions presented here.

ESTABLISH a comprehensive national economic strategy centered on investment and production of agricultural and manufactured goods and services in the United States.

REBALANCE our international trade by achieving genuine reciprocity, especially with systems of state capitalism whose practices are beyond the reach of existing international rules and domestic law. This must include a review of all existing international agreements, as well as establishment by law of higher standards for future international agreements.

NULLIFY the subsidy effects of currency misalignments by the application of effective trade measures.

MODERNIZE the U.S. tax system to provide competitive incentives to invest in this country, ensure that imports pay their fair share of taxes, and remove government-imposed cost impediments to American exports.

DEVELOP AND IMPLEMENT a national infrastructure plan to convert our communications, transportation, and energy distribution systems into a national competitive asset. A principal objective must be to maximize the use of domestically produced goods on all projects funded with taxpayer revenues.

ACHIEVE energy independence by expanding domestic production and efficiency through investment and the development and application of new technologies.

REGULATE financial and goods markets effectively to deter excessive risk-taking and abuse of market power, while ensuring the safety of all goods sold in the U.S, whether produced domestically or abroad.

REVAMP the federal government's economic decision-making to facilitate the development, implementation, and continuous adaptation of a strategy to ensure that innovative technologies are applied in this country.

Conference for the Renaissance of American Manufacturing

This conference was held in Washington on September 28, 2010 and attended by more than 200 manufacturing executives, legislators, union leaders, trade policy experts, and state and federal officials. At this conference, Sen. Don Riegle Jr. of Michigan warned that the U.S. economy was on a "downhill trajectory" and "going at a velocity that is very dangerous.... The people are screaming to the elected officials that they think we are on the wrong path – because we *are* on the wrong path." Gilbert Kaplan, president of the Committee to Support U.S. Trade Laws, said, "The decline of American manufacturing happened not because of some inevitable shift to a post-manufacturing economy as some argue, but because the United States has picked the wrong policies and not paid attention to preserving and growing manufacturing. American urgently needs unequivocal and bipartisan policies in support of reviving manufacturing, with clear performance goals and timelines for action."[3]

After the conference, the Committee to Support U.S. Trade Laws, the Economic Strategy Institute, the New America's Foundation's U.S. Economy/Smart Globalization Initiative, and other groups released a Statement of Principles, recommendations for major reforms to the U.S. trade system, and recommendations for five specific legislative initiatives to revive American manufacturing. The Statement of Principles included the following:

> Changing tax policies so that manufacturing in the United States is encouraged, not discouraged, and making sure that imports pay their fair share of taxes.

Creating tax policies that foster manufacturing investment by strengthening R&D and capital investment, and allowing for accelerated depreciation.

Providing grants and low-interest loans to companies that manufacture in the U.S. (as long as other countries' governments are providing assistance to their industries.)

Encouraging a change in corporate culture so that manufacturing in the U.S. becomes a primary objective, and moving plants offshore is discouraged.

Some of its recommendations for reforms to the U.S. trade system were:

A "plus jobs and plus factories" requirement for all existing trade agreements and future agreements, in which it can be shown that the agreement on a net basis has created or will create jobs and factory builds in the U.S.

A commitment to balance trade in the U.S. by a certain date in the future.

Stronger, sustained trade action against foreign subsidization of manufacturing.

Creation of an unfair trade strike force within the U.S. government.

Addressing the fact that many imported products are not bearing environmental and health care costs.

The five specific legislative initiatives recommended were:

Legislation to countervail currency undervaluation and enhance enforcement of trade case orders.

Rewriting U.S. trade laws in the next session to bring them up to date, deal with the realities of the 21st century, and make sure they are effective in preserving and reviving U.S. manufacturing.

Rewriting tax laws to encourage manufacturing in the U.S. to ensure that imports pay their fair share of taxes and encourage R&D and capital formation for manufacturing.

Altering the governmental policy apparatus to provide a voice for manufacturing at senior levels.

Passage of a Manufacturing Education Act that will develop target vocational and technical training programs, at both the secondary and post-secondary level, in order to strengthen manufacturing education, and funding programs and institutions to improve the skills of career-changing adults interested in manufacturing jobs.

Small Business & Entrepreneurship Council

In contrast to some of the above more protectionist recommendations, the Small Business & Entrepreneurship Council, which strongly supports free trade, made the following recommendations:

Reduce U.S. Trade Barriers – Lower U.S. barriers to trade, thereby increasing competition, improving quality, and lowering prices for all consumers, including industries where the entrepreneur acts as a customer, such as with capital goods.

Open up Trade Opportunities Around the World – Enter free trade agreements with other nations, thus opening new markets and opportunities for U.S. entrepreneurs.

Restore Trade Promotion Authority to the President – Trade Promotion Authority, or TPA, is a critical tool for expanding trade and opportunity for U.S. entrepreneurs, businesses and employees. TPA allows for expedited consideration of trade agreements by Congress, but was allowed to expire at the end of June 2007.

Note that the SBEC is a 70,000-member organization that supports all small businesses, not just manufacturers. This includes farmers, wholesalers, distributors, importers, and exporters. One of their cited justifications for free trade is that total trade (imports plus exports) as a share of our GDP tripled from 9.5 percent in 1960 to 28.9 percent in 2007.[4] And the U.S. Trade Representative reports that more than 900,000 agricultural jobs are tied to exports, and that one out of every three agricultural acres planted in this country produces for export. But a Third World country exports raw materials and commodities, while a First World country exports manufactured goods. So while certain types of agribusiness may be benefiting from U.S. trade agreements, manufacturers are not.

John Madigan

Some innovative and unique recommendations were presented by consultant John Madigan in the online edition of *Industry Week*. His recommendations were:[5]

Create a government-sponsored program, similar to the Apollo Program, to create jobs based on solving environmental needs, focusing on self-sustaining and renewable solar, wind, water turbines; clean hydrogen energy; and desalination of ocean water. These would "jump-start a revival of U.S. manufacturing."

Use tax incentives to encourage companies to make environmentally friendly and sustainable finished products in the U.S.

Create prizes to reward innovation for environmentally friendly products manufactured in the U.S.

Utilize existing tax-supported agencies, such as the National Institute of Standards and Technology, to define and teach best practices to manufacturers through shared networks of knowledge resources.

Benchmark on successful companies – for example, Toyota, Wiremold, and Danaher Corporation – and employ proven lean executives on oversight boards.

Challenge economies-of-scale thinking and standard-cost accounting for more market-based accounting systems.

Focus on small businesses or start-up companies and nurture green manufacturing incubator zones.

Set up educational policies and programs in line with future needs – programs to encourage engineering, technical, and vocational education.

Define goals and metrics, with ambitious stretches for carbon emission reductions, water desalination, and energy production. These would meet targeted carbon footprint and job creation benchmarks. Measure and report on the results.

Launch a public relations campaign with a logo and motto to mobilize Americans behind the effort.

Publicize benefits to taxpayers for a program which, if conceived and funded correctly, will become self-sufficient and produce tax revenues from a revitalized, productive middle class with sustainable wages.

National Association of Manufacturers

In June 2010, NAM released a report entitled "Manufacturing Strategy for Jobs and a Competitive America."[6] In considering its recommendations, it is important to understand where they are coming from as an organization and what kind of companies comprise their membership. NAM is the largest, best-known trade association in the United States, headed by Jay Timmons, who succeeded former Michigan Governor John Engler in January 2011. Many Fortune 500 manufacturing companies are members, and the companies that comprise NAM's policy committees and subcommittees are mainly large, multinational companies. Many of these multinational companies have manufacturing operations in China and other foreign countries, which influences their position on trade issues.

NAM's report begins with what I consider absolute truths: "America's prosperity and strength are built on a foundation of manufacturing. Manufacturers create, innovate and employ millions of Americans in some of the best jobs our country has to offer." It states that the U.S. needs a comprehensive manufacturing strategy to compete against foreign governments that support their manufacturing industries. NAM's proposed strategy highlights the need for tax policies to bring America more closely into alignment with major manufacturing competitors, government investments in infrastructure and innovation, and trade initiatives to reduce barriers and open markets to U.S. exports. It emphasizes the need to create a national tax climate that allows U.S. manufacturers to be competitive in the global marketplace is unquestionably the highest priority. The report makes the following recommendations:

Promote fair rules for taxation of active foreign income of U.S. based businesses.

Institute permanent lower tax rates for individuals and small businesses. Capital gains, accelerated depreciation and expensing and estate taxes are also areas where long-term lower tax rates strengthen manufacturing and job creation.

Enact tax provisions that will stimulate investment and recovery, including strengthening and making permanent the R&D tax credit.

Support initiatives at the Occupational Safety and Health Administration and other oversight agencies that encourage employers and employees to join in cooperative efforts for safer working environments.

Implement a common sense, fair approach to legal reform. Direct tort costs account for almost 2 percent of GDP in the United States.

Create a regulatory environment that promotes economic growth.

Perform the bulk of a company's global R&D in the U.S.

Encourage the federal government's continued critical role in basic R&D.

Recognize intellectual property as one of America's competitive strengths that must be defended at all levels, domestically and globally.

Promote progressive international trade policy that opens global markets, reduces regulatory and tariff barriers and reduces distortions due to currency exchange rates, ownership restrictions and various other policies.

Promote a World Trade Organization Doha Round result that will slash tariffs and non-tariff barriers.

Modernize the United States' outdated export control system to encourage exports and strengthen national security.

Assist and energize exporting by small and medium-sized manufacturing through expanded export promotion programs as well as export credit assistance for both small and large firms.

Create a comprehensive energy strategy that embraces an "all of the above" approach to energy independence.

Promote policies that protect the environment, encourage additional investment and innovation, and recognize the global scope of many environmental issues.

Support innovations that include capital budgeting, private investment bonding, environmental permit streamlining and flexibility to the states as part of a comprehensive infrastructure strategy.

Encourage innovation through education reform, improvement and accountability.

Invest in science, technology, engineering and math education.

Improve the quality of education in early childhood, primary, secondary and post secondary school systems.

There is no question that the continuing expansion of federal mandates and labor regulations undermines employer flexibility, increases costs, and discourages hiring. We need to create a regulatory environment that promotes economic growth. U.S. manufacturers are forced to comply with scores of regulations that manufacturers don't have to face in other countries. As NAM's plan points out, "the Small Business Administration's Office of Advocacy has estimated that regulatory compliance costs amount to $1.1 trillion annually."

Implementing a common sense, fair approach to legal reform is also vital to bringing legal costs under control and eliminating the disadvantage they impose on American companies.

I share NAM's goal for the U.S. to be the best country in the world to innovate and perform the bulk of a company's R&D, but this goes against the trend of its own membership of large, multinational companies. More and more R&D is being conducted offshore in China and India each year.

I agree with NAM's recommendations for enacting tax provisions that stimulate investment and recovery, encourage the federal government's critical role in basic R&D, enhance efforts by the federal government to protect American intellectual property, and impede the trade in counterfeit products that costs hundreds of thousands of jobs.

I share NAM's goal to have the U.S. be a great place to manufacture for the American market and export to the world. America's outdated export-control system needs to be modernized to encourage exports and strengthen national security. Small and medium-sized manufacturers need more help with export promotion and export credit.

Thanks to environmental regulations, American manufacturers are already at a competitive disadvantage compared to China and other Asian countries. Until these countries start enacting similar laws and regulations, and start enforcing the existing ones, the United States should avoid signing environmental treaties that make it even harder for American companies.

Unfortunately, at a time when the federal budget deficit was approximately $1.3 trillion for 2011 and many cities and states are near bankruptcy, it is unlikely to be possible to invest in the infrastructure that will help American manufacturers move products and people more efficiently.

In conclusion, NAM's proposed manufacturing strategy has many admirable recommendations. But, it is really a codification of positions and recommendations promoted by NAM for the past 20 years – during which we have lost more than six million manufacturing jobs. NAM's strong emphasis on free trade will not save American manufacturing. Instead, continuation and expansion of free trade will lead to the destruction of more American industries and the loss of more American jobs.

U.S. Business and Industry Council

The U.S. Business and Industry Council has been fighting for American companies and jobs since 1933. It has a plan posted on its website called "To Save American Manufacturing: USBIC's Plan for American Industrial Renewal," by Kevin Kearns, Alan Tonelson, and William Hawkins. This plan includes four pages of recommendations and can be viewed at usbic.org. The first five of their key "emergency measures" are:

The President must declare that the United States faces a manufacturing, R&D, and outsourcing emergency no less threatening to America's long-term future than even the Great Depression. He must also make clear that the crisis stems mainly from the manipulation of world trading system by mercantilist countries and the encouragement of offshoring by U.S. trade policy.

The President should create an Apollo-type program task force in the federal government to oversee Washington's response to the manufacturing crisis. Its mission should be to restore domestic U.S. manufacturing to global preeminence and to boost domestic manufacturing employment and wages. The program should involve all agencies of U.S. government.

Federal R&D spending should be tripled and Washington should offer matching grants to industry. Special emphasis should be placed on tasking the national labs with helping to develop commercially viable high-tech products to be manufactured in the United States.

The U.S. trade deficit should be quickly and dramatically reduced by imposing a "variable trade equalization tariff" on imports from countries running a trade surplus 10 percent or greater of total bilateral trade. (Note: a tariff that is equal to the difference between the domestic price of a commodity, such as steel, to the price of the commodity from a foreign country.)

Companies manufacturing or assembling in the United States should be barred from treating service work performed overseas as a deductible business expense. Private companies that outsource overseas the processing of sensitive records, such as medical and financial records, must ensure that their subcontractors meet U.S. privacy standards or face stiff fines.

National Summit on Competitiveness

As a result of a national gathering of executives concerned about America's future competitiveness, a statement was released by the National Summit on Competitiveness on December 5, 2005. The key recommendations were:

Revitalize Fundamental Research

Increase the federal investment in long-term basic research by 10 percent a year over the next seven years with focused attention to the physical sciences, engineering and mathematics.

Allocate at least eight percent of the budgets of federal research agencies to discretionary funding focused on catalyzing high-risk, high-payoff research.

Expand the Innovation Talent Pool in the U.S.

By 2015, double the numbers of bachelor's degrees awarded annually to U.S. students in science, math and engineering, and increase the number of those students who become K-12 science and math teachers.

Provide incentives for the creation of public-private partnerships to encourage U.S. students at all levels to pursue studies and careers in science, math, technology, and engineering.

Lead the World in the Development and Deployment of Advanced Technologies.

Provide focused and sustained funding to address national technology challenges in areas that will ensure national security and continued U.S. economic leadership, including nanotechnology, high-performance computing, and energy technologies.[7]

Manufacturing Council

On September 27, 2005, Deputy Secretary of Commerce David Sampson tasked the Manufacturing Council to determine the "top action items" of the manufacturing industry for the year ahead. The Council suggested these actions:

Innovation and Workforce Development

Make permanent the federal R&D tax credit and enhance the level of credit for energy efficient and energy security R&D initiatives.

Provide enhanced incentives for new and ongoing investment in advanced technologies to improve U.S. based manufacturing's global competitiveness and strengthen our national security.

Improve and increase funding for displaced workers through retraining programs to provide them with the necessary skills for successful job transitions.

Trade Agenda

Implement aggressive tariff reductions through sectoral free trade agreements in chemicals and machinery.

Insist on reducing non-tariff barriers, focusing on customs clearances.

Improve intellectual property rights enforcement by increasing criminal prosecutions.

Enhance law enforcement cooperation between U.S. and Chinese authorities and reduce the export of goods that infringe those rights.

Tax Reform

Repeal or eliminate elements of the corporate and individual alternative minimum tax (AMT) that burden manufacturing.

Make permanent the current capital gains tax rate. Eliminate the death tax.[8]

TechAmerica

In 2007, the American Electronics Association (now Tech-America) released the report "We Are Still Losing the Competitive Advantage: Now is the Time to Act" as a follow up to its 2005 report "Losing the Competitive Advantage! The Challenge for Science and Technology in the United States." The follow-up report emphasized that improving American competitiveness requires more than just passing a few bills and appropriating funds. What is needed is an ongoing process, a new way of thinking that recognizes and adapts to the changing world. The report made the following recommendations:

Champion Dramatic Improvements in the U.S. Educational System

Improve K-12 math and science instruction to prepare the U.S. workforce for a 21st century knowledge economy.

Sustain, strengthen, and reauthorize the No Child Left Behind Act.

Promote undergraduate and graduate science, technology, engineering and mathematics education.

Create a human capital investment tax credit to promote continuous education.

Support and Increase R&D

Increase federal funding for basic research, specifically for physical science, engineering, math, and computer science research with the National Science Foundation, the National Institute of Standards and Technology, the

Department of Energy, and the Department of Commerce.

Strengthen the R&D tax credit and make it permanent.

Create a More Business-Friendly Environment in the U.S.

Reduce the onerous and disproportionate business tax levied on small and medium-sized companies by Sarbanes-Oxley section 404 compliance.

Address the rising costs of health care for U.S. business by enacting legislation to spur the deployment of health initiatives such as electronic medical records.

Fully fund the U.S. Patent and Trademark Office to help reduce lag times between patent filing and approval.

Engage Proactively in the Global Trade System

Advance free and fair trade policies and agreements and conclude the Doha Round of global trade talks.

Renew the President's Trade Promotion Authority.

Promote stronger enforcement of intellectual property protection worldwide.

Promote Broadband Diffusion

Provide industry the incentives necessary to promote broadband diffusion.

Ensure access to affordable broadband for every American by 2014.

While TechAmerica member companies are as small as 50 employees, its board of directors mainly derives from mid-size to large companies, many of them with offshore plants, so the organization's policy on free-trade issues is similar to that of NAM.

The National Academies

In August 2005, the National Academies (the National Academy of Sciences, the National Academy of Engineering, the Institute of Medicine, and the National Research Council) released a report, "Rising Above the Gathering Storm: Energizing and Employing America for a Brighter Economic Future." It made comprehensive, specific, and workable recommendations to address the United States' competitiveness challenge. Some of its key recommendations:

Increase America's talent pool by vastly improving K-12 science and math education.

Annually recruit 10,000 science and math teachers by awarding four-year scholarships.

Strengthen the skills of 250,000 teachers through training and education programs at summer institutes, master's programs, and Advanced Placement and International Baccalaureate training programs.

Sustain and strengthen the nations' traditional commitment to long-term basic research.

Increase investment in long-term basic research by 10 percent annually over the next 7 years.

Establish a program to provide 200 new research grants each year at $500,000, payable over five years to support the work of outstanding early-career researchers.

Establish a National Coordination Office for Research Infrastructure to manage a fund of $500 million per year over the next 5 years for construction of research facilities.

Set aside at least eight percent of budgets of federal research agencies for discretionary funding to catalyze high-risk, high-pay-off research.

Create a DARPA-like organization within the Department of Energy called the Advanced Research Projects Agency-Energy (ARPA-E).

Institute a Presidential Innovation Award to stimulate scientific and engineering advances in the national interest.

Make the United States the most attractive setting in which to study and perform research to develop, recruit, and retain the best and brightest students, scientists, and engineers.

Provide 25,000 new four-year sciences undergraduate scholarships each year to U.S. citizens attending U.S. institutions.

Federally fund Graduate Scholar or Awards in Science, Technology, Engineering or Math.

Provide tax credits up to $500 million each year to employers who help employees pursue continuing education.

Since the release of the National Academies' report in 2005, there has been legislation introduced to address competitiveness in both the House and the Senate, often based word-for-word on these recommendations. The America Competes Act (H.R. 2272) was signed into law on August 9, 2007 and focuses on basic research funding for physical sciences and on science, technology, engineering and math education priorities. (The bills introduced to address other recommendations had not become law as of June 2012.)

The Alliance for Science and Technology Research in America

In late 2007, ASTRA released a report, "Riding the Rising Tide: A 21st Century Strategy for U.S. Competitiveness and Prosperity," that presented a 14-point Innovation Action Agenda to reinvigorate the U.S. economy. "A dramatic change in our approach to innovation is required.... Doing so will require a transition to an innovation-driven economy capable of routinely developing and commercializing 'new-to-the-world' technologies, products, and services," it said. Some of its 14 points echoed the recommendation of the National Academies, TechAmerica, and other organizations to increase federal funding for the physical sciences, engineering, and applied research. But it went beyond that to recommend:

Provide direct R&D funding to the leading edge of science.

Create incentives to allow the benefits of federal R&D to be captured by U.S. companies; improve the education of scientists and engineers to attract smart foreigners to study and stay in the United States.

Create a business environment to support innovation and competitiveness by reviewing laws, regulations, and policies that inhibit innovation.

Develop a meaningful set of innovation indicators to guide U.S. innovation policy and strategy.

Create a better government system to analyze foreign innovation systems.

ASTRA's 50-page report can be downloaded at astra.org.

The American Manufacturing Trade Action Coalition

The mission of AMTAC is to preserve and create American manufacturing jobs through improved trade policy and other measures. The action steps it suggests are:

Block trade legislation detrimental to U.S. manufacturing jobs and investment.

Insist on vigorous enforcement of existing U.S. trade laws.

Develop proactive legislative and administrative remedies, including an examination of the value of existing trade laws to U.S. manufacturing.

Support a border-adjusted or Value-Added Tax (VAT).

Oppose extension of the Trade Promotion Authority (TPA).

Support legislation to reform currency manipulation and misalignment.

Support U.S. Department of Commerce's decision to apply U.S. countervailing duty (CVD) law to China.

Oppose the U.S.-Korea Free Trade Agreement (KORUS).

Support legislation extending the Berry Amendment and Buy American provisions to other government agencies.

Oppose duty-free access to the U.S. market for imports of all products from Least Developed Countries (LCDs) and African Growth and Opportunity Act (AGOA) countries.

For a complete description of the AMTAC agenda, see amtacdc.org.

The Information Technology and Innovation Foundation

In April 2011, ITIF released a report, "The Case for a National Manufacturing Strategy," that makes a strong case for such a strategy.[9] It presents information on some key reasons why manufacturing is important to the U.S. economy:

It will be extremely difficult for the United States to balance its trade account without a healthy manufacturing sector.

Manufacturing is a key driver of overall job growth and an important source of middle-class jobs for individuals at many skill levels.

Manufacturing is vital to U.S. national security.

Manufacturing is the principal source of R&D and innovation activity.

The manufacturing and services sectors are inseparable and complementary.

The authors argue that balancing U.S. trade through a revitalized manufacturing sector is crucial because:

The trade deficit represents a tax on future generations that compromises their economic well-being.

The United States is running substantial trade deficits across many categories of manufactured products.

Services and non-manufactured goods won't be enough to close the U.S. trade deficit. The trade deficit represents a tax on future generations.

The report reads, "The massive bill we run up every year by buying more imports than selling exports will have to be paid eventually when foreign nations demand payment in real goods and services, not in Treasury Bills."(Our average trade deficit each year of the previous decade was $458 billion, about $4,000 per household, for a total of $5.5 trillion.) The report concludes "without a robust manufacturing sector, it's simply impossible for almost any nation, unless it's endowed with oil or other natural resources, to balance its trade – and the United States is no exception." In the section "Why the United States Needs a Manufacturing Strategy," the authors present these primary reasons:

Other countries have strategies to support their manufacturers and by lacking similar strategies we are therefore forcing our manufacturers to compete at a disadvantage.

Systemic market failures mean that absent manufacturing policies, U.S. manufacturing will underperform in terms of innovation, productivity, job growth, and trade performance.

If a country loses complex, high-value-added manufacturing sectors, it's unlikely to get them back, even if the dollar were to decline dramatically.

The report notes that "A number of countries—including Brazil, Canada, China, Germany, India, Singapore, South Africa, Russia, and the United Kingdom, among others—have articulated national manufacturing strategies, and the United States needs one as well it if wants to stay competitive with these countries. Among other elements, foreign countries' manufacturing strategies include measures such as:

Offering competitive tax environments, including generous R&D tax credits.

Providing incentive packages, including tax breaks and credits, to attract internationally mobile capital investment.
Increasing government R&D funding.

Supporting programs designed to enhance the productive and innovative capabilities of their small to medium enterprise (SME) and large manufacturers.

Facilitating technology transfer between university and industry.

Producing a highly educated, highly skilled workforce, including by investing directly in workforce manufacturing skills.

Investing in physical and digital infrastructure such as wired and wireless broadband networks, smart electric grids, and intelligent transportation systems.

While acknowledging that these types of policies and incentives all represent legitimate competition between nations to win advantage in key manufacturing industries, they note that U.S. manufacturers aren't just competing against foreign manufacturers. They are increasingly competing against foreign manufacturers backed by the technology, economic, and political systems of their respective nations. And American manufacturing firms operating as independent entities will increasingly find themselves at a disadvantage in international markets against firms from countries backed by effective public-private partnerships.

The authors opine that a number of countries are supporting their manufacturers through unfair mercantilist strategies that manipulate or violate the mutually established rules of international trade. In contrast to the fair practices described above, these countries' goals are not to increase the global supply of jobs and innovative activity, but to induce their shift from one nation to another. These countries accomplish this goal by using a broad range of unfair mercantilist practices, including:

- Currency manipulation

- Standards manipulation

- Intellectual property theft

- Illegal mandates, including the forced transfer of intellectual property or location of manufacturing production as a condition of receiving market access

- Government procurement practices that exclude foreign competitors

- Abuse of regulatory, antitrust, or competition policies to the disadvantage of foreign competitors

In the "What Would a National Manufacturing Strategy Do?" section of the report, the authors state their "goal for a national manufacturing strategy would be to create the most competitive environment for U.S. manufacturing firms, of all sizes, to flourish." Their call is not for the re-creation of all the lost jobs from factories employing low-skill workers and producing commodity products. It's "a call to restore U.S. manufacturing to a competitive position in the global economy, even though the industries and jobs will look very different than they did a generation ago."

They don't mean "a de facto heavy-handed industrial policy that 'picks winners and losers.'" They "mean a process of designing our nation's tax, regulatory, and innovation policy environments to make the United States the world's most attractive location for advanced manufacturing (including both domestic and foreign direct investment)."They recognize that "most U.S. manufacturers, small or large, cannot thrive solely on their own; they need to operate in an environment grounded in smart economic and innovation-supporting policies with regard to taxes, talent, trade, technological development, and physical and digital infrastructures." They recommend the following:

Increase public investment in R&D in general and industrially relevant R&D in particular.

Support public-private partnerships that facilitate the transition of emerging technologies from universities and federal laboratories into commercial products.

Coordinate state, local, and federal programs in technology-based economic development to maximize their combined impact.

Provide export assistance to build upon the National Export Initiative, which seeks to double U.S. exports by 2015.

Increase export support for U.S. manufacturers through the Export-Import Bank loans.

The report acknowledges, "This will require a new understanding of the importance of U.S. manufacturing on the part of economists and policymakers alike and a deeper understanding of the forces affecting U.S. manufacturing industries." In conclusion, they state that "The American public gets it; it's time that economists and policymakers do so as well." They recommend that "Congress craft, pass, and fully fund, and the President sign and implement, a comprehensive national manufacturing renewal strategy for the United States."

The House of Representatives Committee on Small Business

In March 2006, Dr. Sheila Ronis, President of The University Group, a consulting firm, and director of the MBA/MSM program at Walsh College, submitted the 2006 Industrial Base Study she was commissioned to prepare for the Committee on Small Business of the U.S. House of Representatives. She made several recommendations for Congress, the Executive Branch, and industry. To wit:

Congress

Create a new super-committee populated with senior members from all committees of Congress to develop interagency mission funding mechanisms.

Establish a National Strategy Center to help policy makers plan for the future by integrating the economic, diplomatic, and military elements of national power.

Consistently fund programs in Commerce and Defense that will regain U.S. manufacturing prowess and leadership across the board.

Use funding within the national laboratory system to support the higher education system and U.S. industry in order to maximize U.S. knowledge and innovation advantages.

Provide incentives to America's most talented young people to become scientists, engineers, linguists, and diplomats.

Adequately fund alternative fuel research.

Rethink trade policy to encourage the creation and maintenance of high value-added jobs inside the country.

Reform the national pension and health care delivery systems.

Executive Branch

Work with Congress to ensure that requirements for a "grand strategy" are clearly developed, communicated, and properly resourced.

Demonstrate leadership in identifying and acknowledging the problems associated with the erosion of the U.S. industrial base.

Produce a statistical analysis of defense supply chains to ensure sufficiency and security of supply.

Be more aggressive with trade enforcement actions.

Reduce the national budget and trade deficits.

Industry

Stop reporting quarterly earnings estimates.

Aggressively pursue public-private partnerships.

More accurately calculate the risks associated with global operations in a world of transnational threats.

Initiate partnership programs with high schools, community colleges, and universities in order to shape industry-specific curricula and address the emerging skills deficiency in America's workforce.

(Excerpt reprinted with permission. For the complete report, contact Dr. Sheila Ronis at sronis@walshcollege.edu.)

National Defense

Col. Joe Muckerman, former Director, Emergency Planning and Mobilization, Office of the Secretary of Defense, 1986-1992, made several recommendations to respond to threats to our national security in a guest editorial in *Manufacturing & Technology News.*[10] He recommended the U.S. do the following:

> **Recognize the importance of the defense industrial base** – "During the Cold War... the country recognized that the foundation of its national security rested on a strong economy that could support and maintain technologically superior military forces."

> **Determine the technologies that must be monitored and supported with R&D funds** – "Estimate a range of wartime requirements and match them against an increasingly global industrial base."

> **Reconstitute the National Security Resources Board** – "The NRSB was responsible for assuring that the economy and industrial base were adequate to support that strategy."

He said that these actions "would go a long way toward assuring that the United States would remain a superpower and stand ready to fight and win a two-front war – defense of the homeland and vital overseas interests, not to mention the maintenance of a vibrant economy and high employment levels."

Tax Laws

Comprehensive tax reform is needed because under the current system, multinational corporations are favored over domestic companies. Taxes can foster economic growth or hinder it, and our domestic economic growth is being hindered by the current system.

On July 26, 2007, the Treasury Department hosted a conference, "Global Competitiveness and Business Tax Reform," that brought together distinguished leaders and experts to discuss how the U.S. business tax system could be improved to make U.S. businesses more competitive. As a follow-up, on December 20, 2007, the Treasury released a 121-page report, "Approaches to Improve the Competitiveness of the U.S. Business Tax System for the 21st century."[11]

The study acknowledges that "Globalization... has resulted in increased cross-border trade and the establishment of production facilities and distribution networks around the globe. Businesses now operate more freely across borders and business location and investment decisions are more sensitive to tax considerations than in the past." Furthermore, as globalization has increased, "nations' tax systems have become a greater factor in the success of global companies." The report notes that "Many of our major trading partners have lowered their corporate tax rates, some dramatically... As other nations modernize their business tax systems to recognize the realities of the global economy, U.S. companies increasingly suffer a competitive disadvantage. The U.S. business tax system imposes a burden on U.S. companies and U.S. workers by raising the cost of investment in the United States and burdening U.S. firms as they compete with other firms in foreign markets."

The study concludes that the current system of business taxation in the U.S. is making the country uncompetitive globally and needs to be overhauled. A new tax system aimed at improving the global competitiveness of U.S. companies could raise GDP by 2 to 2.5 percent. Rather than present particular recommendations, the report examines the strengths and weaknesses of the three major approaches presented:

1. Replacing the business income tax system with a Business Activity Tax (BAT).

2. Broadening the business tax base and lowering the statutory tax rate/providing expensing.

3. Lowering the top federal business tax rate to 28 percent. (If accelerated depreciation were retained, the rate would drop only to 31 percent.)

The BAT tax base would be gross receipts from sales of goods and services minus purchases of goods and services (including purchases of capital items) from other businesses. Wages and other forms of employee compensation (such as fringe benefits) would not be deductible. Interest would be removed from the tax base – it would neither be included as income nor deductible. Individual taxes on dividends and capital gains would be retained. Interest income received by individuals would be taxed at the current 15 percent dividends and capital gains rate.

The report suggested specific areas of our current business tax system that could be addressed, like the tax bias favoring debt finance, the tax treatment of losses, book-tax conformity, and the taxation of international income. The question is to what extent any of these approaches would markedly affect the competitiveness of U.S. businesses. The study says "Thus, it remains unclear whether a revenue neutral reform would provide a reduction in business taxes sufficient to enhance the competitiveness of U.S. businesses."

The study also comments on the importance of individual income tax rates. Roughly 30 percent of all business taxes are paid through the individual income tax on business income earned by owners of flow-through entities (sole proprietorships, partnerships, and S corporations). These businesses and their owners benefited from the 2001 and 2003 income tax rate reductions. This sector has more than doubled its share of business receipts since the early 1980s and plays an important role in the U.S. economy, accounting for one-third of salaries and wages. Moreover, flow-through income is concentrated in the top two tax brackets, with this group receiving more than 70 percent of flow-through income and paying more than 80 percent of taxes on this income.

I believe we also need to close a huge tax loophole that multinational corporations are enjoying at the expense of American workers and which is a big incentive for U. S. firms to invest abroad in countries with low tax rates. In June 2006, James Kvaal, who had been a policy adviser in the Clinton White House and was then a third-year student at Harvard Law School, published a paper "Shipping Jobs Overseas: How the Tax Code Subsidizes Foreign Investment and How to Fix It." In this paper, Kvaal points out that "American multi-nationals can defer U.S. taxes indefinitely as long as profits are held in a foreign subsidiary. Taxes are only due when the money is returned to the U.S. parent corporation. The result is like an IRA for multinationals' foreign investments: foreign profits accumulate tax-free. U.S. taxes are effectively voluntary on foreign investments."

In anticipation of the Council on Competitiveness's 25th anniversary celebration and the National Manufacturing Competitiveness Summit to be held in December 2011, Deborah Wince-Smith, President and CEO of the Council, commented, in an *Industry Week* article on November 13, 2011, that "U.S. manufacturers are at a tremendous disadvantage because the nation's capital-cost, tax, and regulatory system is very unfriendly to 21st century manufacturing in America. We're going to be recommending that we're much more in line with the rest of the OECD countries. The strategy also will call for eliminating the double taxation on repatriation of earnings from U.S. affiliates outside the United States."[12]

The importance of low tax rates to the success of start-up companies is emphasized by Henry Northhaft, CEO of Tessera Corporation, in his book *Great Again*, co-authored by David Kline. They wrote,

In other words, lower tax rates on the last dollar earned encourage individuals and businesses to work harder, take more entrepreneurial risks, and expand their operations because they can keep more of the fruits of that added labor or activity... a reduction in the marginal tax rate of 1 percentage point increases the rate of start-up formation by 1.5 percent and reduces the change of start-up failure by more than 8 percent...Tax rates don't just influence how much investment and growth a firm will choose to undertake. In an increasingly globalized economy, they also profoundly affect *where* a business will chose to invest or expand...the relative tax and regulatory burdens on U.S. start-ups have grown exponentially, whereas those on European and other foreign ventures have declined sharply.

Multinationals Use Tax Havens to Avoid Taxes

William Brittain-Catlin, author of "Offshore: The Dark Side of the Global Economy," writes that offshoring to tax havens like the Cayman Islands is "the way corporations move their money around to avoid and evade the scrutiny of regulators and government...It's offshore where the real world of international finance and business exists—and it's all hidden away under a cloak of secrecy, transfer pricing and tax dodging." He goes on to explain that the global financial market and the global corporation owe their origin directly to offshore tax havens. He points out, "Corporate profits will always move to where tax rates are lowest. That's the way the corporate economy works today...Every major company is engaged offshore at some level...To a certain extent, our modern world is offshore. Things are not fixed or attached to the nation-state."[13]

Some of the multinational companies that have reincorporated to the Cayman Islands or Bermuda are: New Hampshire-based Tyco International, Connecticut-based toolmaker Stanley Works, Ingersoll-Rand (a Stanley competitor), New Jersey manufacturer Foster Wheeler, and Cooper Industries of Texas. Enron, for example, had more than 880 subsidiaries in offshore tax havens, and paid no taxes in four of the last five years before it went bankrupt. It used the offshore tax havens to shuffle around loans and debt, saving a reported $1 billion in taxes. Stanley Works expected to cut its taxes from $110 million a year to $80 million by reincorporating in Bermuda. Tyco International said it saved more than $400 million in 2001 by doing the same. Foster Wheeler and Cooper Industries anticipated cutting their taxes by 40 percent.[14] Treasury Department officials estimate that between $70 and $155 billion a year disappears into the "Bermuda Triangle" of offshore tax havens.

The Government Accountability Office has released a report revealing that 83 of the nation's 100 largest corporations, including Citigroup, Bank of America, and Morgan Stanley, had subsidiaries in offshore tax havens in 2007. These three financial institutions were included in the $700 billion financial bailout approved by Congress in fall 2008. The GAO also said that 63 of the 100 largest federal contractors maintain subsidiaries in 50 tax havens. Senators Carl Levin (D-MI) and Byron Dorgan (D-ND), who requested the report, have pushed for tougher laws to fight offshore tax havens. Senator Levin, who heads the Senate Permanent Subcommittee on Investigations, has estimated that tax havens and offshore accounts cost the U.S. government at least $10 billion a year in taxes.[15]

Corporate tax rates as a share of GDP have declined dramatically over the past 50 years, from a high of 5.8 percent in 1953 to a low of 1.2 percent in 2003. While corporate revenues tend to decline during economic downturns as business profits falter, offshore tax avoidance has contributed to this trend. As U.S. corporate profits have decreased, profits abroad, particularly in low tax countries, have increased. The share of worldwide profits earned in tax-haven countries increased from 42 percent to 58 percent between 1999 and 2002.[16]

Since 1999, corporate tax revenues dropped $17.4 billion by 2004 because the 80 largest U.S. multinational corporations have been shifting profits out of the United States. From 1997-1999, their effective tax rate was 34.1 percent, while for 2004-2006 it was 30 percent. According to Martin Sullivan of Tax Analysts, Inc., the main reasons for this decline are as follows. First, an increasing share of U.S. multinational business activity is occurring outside the U.S. in low-tax jurisdictions. Second, U.S.-based multinationals are increasingly able to shift profits into low-tax countries. And third, the foreign countries where U.S. multinational corporations operate have lowered their corporate tax rates.

After the Enron scandal, 14 different bills were introduced into the House and Senate in 2002 to stop corporations from utilizing offshore tax havens. Two of the best known were the Corporate Patriot Enforcement Act of 2002, "to prevent corporations from avoiding the United States income tax by reincorporating in a foreign country" and the Patriotic Purchasing Act of 2002, "to prohibit certain expatriated corporations from being eligible for the award of Federal Contracts." Senate Bill 2119, the Reversing the Expatriation of Profits Offshore Act, was one of the most comprehensive; it was co-sponsored by Sen. Charles Grassley (R-IA) and Sen. Max Baucus (D-MT). While Democrats introduced most of these bills at a time when Republicans controlled the majority in both Houses, some had bipartisan sponsors. For example, Rep. Bill Thomas (R-CA) introduced H.R. 5095, the American Competitiveness and Corporate Accountability Act, which had provisions covering competitiveness, taxpayer provisions, and loophole closure. Unfortunately, none of these bills were voted into law. (For a summary of the bills, see citzenworks.org/enron/offshore-taxbills.php.)

The American Jobs Creation Act of 2004 did repeal the export tax incentive or FSC/ETI as it is called (foreign sales corporate/extraterritorial income), which the World Trade Organization had ruled illegal. In retaliation for the export tax incentive, the European Union had levied tariffs on more than 1,600 U.S. products, starting at five percent in March 2004 and increasing by one percentage point a month thereafter. (These tariffs were removed after the export tax was repealed.)[17] This Act also had the following provisions:

- It temporarily reduced tax rate on repatriated income to 5.25 percent for one year if income was permanently reinvested in the U.S.

- It created a new and more generous tax deduction for manufacturers to replace one that was eliminated.

- It extended enhanced Section 179 business expensing for two more years.

- It simplified international taxation.

- It boosted tax shelter penalties.

- It reduced double taxation on U.S. manufacturers that export and do business overseas.

- It provided Alternative Minimum Tax (AMT) relief for businesses and farmers.

The Act had a positive effect: Hewlett Packard alone repatriated $14.5 billion dollars in 2005. But some economists felt that the holiday for repatriation of foreign profits sent a confusing message about the intent of the U.S. international tax system. Instead, it provided greater incentives for firms to avoid annual repatriation of funds from abroad on a regular basis in hope of another holiday. And while taxes do play a role in the decisions of multinational companies about where to invest and create jobs, taxes are only one of many factors, and the effect may only be in the thousands of jobs, not the millions we have lost.[18]

Some economists and politicians want to close down all the tax havens. Some want the tax havens to be under more scrutiny, and some want them to be left alone. But it is unlikely that the Western industrial nations are going to crack down on these centers to eliminate them altogether, and there is no way that the U.S. would give up the offshore rights of its corporations unless other nations were to do so, too. It's time for experts in this field to come up with some realistic, reasonable limits on the use of offshore tax havens by corporations that were formed and originally incorporated in the United States.

Trade

As we saw in Chapter One, the United States was a protectionist country for the first 150 years of its history in order to protect its fledgling manufacturing industries at first and then gain preeminence as an industrial nation in the 20th century. As Ian Fletcher wrote in his book, *Free Trade Doesn't Work*, "Protectionism is, in fact, the *real* American

Way." But with the coming of the Cold War, we switched from protectionism to free trade in order to rebuild the economies of Europe and Japan through the Marshall Plan and bind the economies of the non-Communist world to the United States for geopolitical reasons.[19]

To accomplish these objectives, the General Agreement on Tariffs and Trade was negotiated during the UN Conference on Trade and Employment, reflecting the failure of negotiating governments to create a proposed International Trade Organization. Originally signed by 23 countries at Geneva in 1947, GATT became the most effective instrument in the massive expansion of world trade in the second half of the 20th century.

GATT's most important principle was trade without discrimination, in which member nations opened their markets equally to one another. Once a country and one of its trading partners agreed to reduce a tariff, that tariff cut was automatically extended to all GATT members. GATT also established uniform customs regulations and sought to eliminate import quotas. By 1995, when the World Trade Organization replaced GATT, 125 nations had signed its agreements, governing 90 percent of world trade.[20]

In 1994, GATT was updated to include new obligations upon its signatories. One of the most significant changes was the creation of the WTO. The 75 existing GATT members and the European Community became the founding members of the WTO on January 1, 1995. The other 52 GATT members rejoined the WTO in the following two years, the last being Congo in 1997. Since the founding of the WTO, a number of non-GATT members have joined, and there are now 157 members. The main countries still outside it are Iran, North Korea, and some nations in Central Asia and North Africa.

The reality now is that we can change the tax code and implement all of the other recommendations presented in this chapter, but if we don't change our trade policy, we will not be able to save American manufacturing. As noted in this chapter, some organizations favor free trade and some are against it. So the first logical question is: Do we even *have* free trade?

Brian Sullivan, Director of Sales, Marketing and Communications of the Tooling, Manufacturing & Technologies Association says, "We should rename 'free trade' because it isn't free and it isn't fair. Since it's trade that's regulated in favor of multinational special interest groups, why don't we call it for what it is: How about 'rigged market trade' or 'turn your back on your fellow countrymen trade' or 'throw American workers out on the street trade.'"[21] Sullivan urges trade reform and makes a number of recommendations. He thinks we should create a National Trade Commission. We should pass currency manipulation legislation, such as the Ryan-Hunter Bill of 2007. Also, we should pass a border equalization tax to address the unfair advantage caused by the rebate of VAT taxes. We should enact countervailing duty laws and laws that standardize Rules of Origin. Finally, he thinks we should pass laws that address infrastructure imbalances, including regulatory and enforcement standards.

At the present time, our largest trade imbalance is with China, but if we don't change our trade policies, we will eventually have trade imbalances with other developing countries to which manufacturing is being transferred. Why?

Because China copied the "monetary mercantilism" or "dollar mercantilism" that Japan invented, and other countries are joining them, with the United States as their primary target.

What is monetary mercantilism? Adam Smith coined the term "mercantile system" to describe the system of political economy that sought to enrich countries by restraining imports and encouraging exports. Mercantilism dominated economic policy in Europe from the 16th to the late 18th century. By building up their industries, England, France, and other mercantilist countries turned themselves into economic superpowers and brought down their military rival, Spain. Today, the efforts of the WTO to foster free trade have not prevented countries from pursuing neo-mercantilist policies.

In a working paper for the National Bureau of Economic Research, Joshua Aizeman and Jaewoo Lee comment that "the sizable hoarding of international reserves by several East Asian countries has been frequently attributed to a modern version of monetary mercantilism – hoarding international reserves in order to improve competitiveness." They opine that "the large hoarding of reserves in Japan and Korea occurred in the aftermath of the growth strategy that combined export promotion and credit subsidization (financial mercantilism)," and that "China's hoarding of reserves partly reflects the precaution against the financial fragility that is likely to follow the slowing of economic growth."[22]

In their book *Trading Away our Future*, Raymond, Jesse, and Howard Richman define "dollar mercantilism" as when "countries build up their dollar hoards as part of currency manipulations designed to encourage their exports and discourage their imports." These countries do this by borrowing their own currency and using "it to buy dollars so that they can drive up the price of the dollar compared to their own currency in currency markets...Instead of keeping the purchased dollars in their bank vaults, the mercantilist governments loan them back to us so that they can earn interest on them. In effect, the mercantilist countries are lending us money to buy their goods." They observe that "This new form of mercantilism intentionally produces trade deficits for the United States while allowing the practicing country to build up its manufacturing capacity at the expense of U.S. industry."[23]

Even though depreciation of the dollar caused the U.S. trade deficit to begin to fall in 2006, our deficit with China and Japan has continued to grow. As long as China, Japan, and other countries continue to manipulate their currency values in order to produce growing trade surpluses with the U.S., our trade deficits will continue to climb and our manufacturing workers will lose their jobs. The Richmans opine that "when it comes to government-driven trade deficits, *there ain't no free trade!* ... If we address the trade deficits now, then the United States, together with other advocates of democracy, will continue to dominate the world's economy. If not, then resolutely non-democratic China will dominate. The world's future is in the balance."[24]

The Buffet Plan

On November 10, 2003, a long article written by Warren Buffet and Carol J. Loomis appeared in *Fortune*. It was titled "America's Growing Trade Deficit is Selling the Nation Out From Under Us. Here's a Way to Fix the Problem – And We

Need to Do it Now." Buffet presented his plan to halt the trading of assets for consumables. He said,

My remedy may sound gimmicky, and in truth it is a tariff called by another name. But this is a tariff that retains most free-market virtues, neither protecting specific industries nor punishing specific countries nor encouraging trade wars. This plan would increase our exports and might well lead to increased overall world trade. And it would balance our books without there being a significant decline in the value of the dollar, which I believe is otherwise almost certain to occur.

Buffet's plan is for the Commerce Department to issue what he calls "Import Certificates" that would confer the right to import a certain dollar amount of goods into the United States. These certificates would be issued to U.S. exporters in an amount equal to the dollar value of the goods they exported, and could be sold to importers, who would need them to import goods. The price of an import certificate would be set by free-market forces, and therefore would depend on the balance between imports and exports. Market forces would keep the price of import certificates at exactly the amount required to achieve trade balance, eventually eliminating it.

Buffet envisions that ICs would be issued in huge quantities, possibly equal to a month's total of exports. He says, "Competition would then determine who among those parties wanting to sell to us would buy the certificates and how much they would pay. (I visualize that the certificates would be issued with a short life, possibly six months, so that speculators would be discouraged from accumulating them.)"

Buffett realizes that "there is no free lunch in the IC plan. It would have certain serious negative consequences for U.S.

citizens. Prices of most import products would increase, and so would the prices of certain competitive products manufactured domestically." But he feels that "the pain of higher prices on goods imported today dims beside the pain we will eventually suffer if we drift along and trade away our ever larger portions of our country's net worth."[25]

In September 2006, this idea was introduced legislatively by Senators Byron Dorgan (D-ND) and Russell Feingold (D-WI) in Senate Bill 3899, the Balanced Trade Restoration Act of 2006. The bill would have the Commerce Department issue import certificates, which they called "Balanced Trade Certificates," directly to exporters. It exempted oil and gas imports during the first five years, and then phased them in thereafter. The bill did not pass, and there has been no action on it since.

The Richman Plan

The Richmans are three generations of economists. Raymond Richman is professor emeritus of public and international affairs at the University of Pittsburgh and President of Ideal Taxes Association. Dr. Jesse Richman is assistant professor of political science at Old Dominion University. Dr. Howard Richman teaches economics on the Internet.

In 2008, in their book *Trading Away Our Future*, the Richmans proposed Import Certificates that would be auctioned by the Treasury Department, targeted to individual dollar-mercantilist countries, as evidenced by their excessive dollar reserves. The Richmans' plan would be for the Treasury to "announce to all the countries that have been accumulating dollar reserves in order to run a trade deficit with the U.S. that the following year their deficit on goods and services would have to be reduced twenty percent." A country "may respond by planning to increase their imports from us, reduce their exports to us, or some combination of both." If the annual goals weren't met, "the offending country would require an Import Certificate (IC) purchased from the U.S. Treasury Department or other designated agency of the federal government."

The Richmans envision that "over a period of five years, the U.S. Treasury Department would steadily reduce the amount of available Import Certificates so that the target country's trade exports to the United States would be no higher than five percent above their imports from the United States. The Treasury would publish the amount of IC's issued and the available amounts and the date of each auction. Each certificate would have to be utilized within a specified period." In addition, they "recommend the proceeds from selling the Import Certificates be placed in an off-budget fund that the U.S. Treasury would use to buy foreign currencies and foreign financial assets...These currency reserves could also be sold by the U.S. Treasury whenever the dollar is declining too rapidly in foreign exchange markets."[26]

This plan would balance our trade with the dollar-mercantilist countries, but it would not necessarily balance our trade overall. The advantage of the plan is that it could be instituted without violating World Trade Organization rules, since Article XII of the Uruguay Round GATT agreement specifically lets a country running a trade deficit restrict imports to protect its trade balance. (Article XII of the Uruguay Round of GATT can be found at wto.org/ English/docs_e/legal_e/article XII.)

The Fletcher Plan

Ian Fletcher is senior economist of the Coalition for a Prosperous America, a 2.7-million member organization dedicated to fixing America's trade policies and comprising representatives from business, agriculture, and labor. He was previously a research fellow with the U.S. Business and Industry Council, a Washington think tank, and before that, an economist in private practice, serving mostly hedge funds and private equity firms. Details about his book, *Free Trade Doesn't Work,* may be found at FreeTradeDoesntWork.com. Here is an adapted excerpt suggesting a solution to our trade situation:

America needs a broad-based tariff policy that can survive imperfect implementation and political meddling, a certain amount of which will be inevitable. We do *not* need an intricate, brittle, difficult policy that will only create work for bureaucrats, lawyers, and lobbyists. Among other things, a policy too complex for the public to understand will be beyond the reach of democratic accountability, the only ultimate guarantee that any tariff policy will remain aimed at the public good.

One of the great puzzles of American economic history is how the U.S. once succeeded so well under tariff regimes that were not particularly sophisticated. This is where the idea of a so-called natural strategic tariff comes in. This idea says that there may be some simple *rule* for imposing a tariff which will produce the complex *policy* we need. The simple rule will produce a complex policy by interacting with the existing complexity of the economy. All the complexity will be on the "economy" side, not the "policy" side, so all specific decisions about which industries get protection, how much, and when will be made by the free market. No intricate theory, difficult technocratic expertise, or corruptible political decision-making will be required.

There is obviously any number of possible natural strategic tariffs. The one we will look at here (probably the best) is actually the simplest: a flat tax on all imported goods and services.

Prima facie, this is strategically meaningless because it protects, and thus promotes, domestic production in all industries equally. And if a tariff is going to win the U.S. better jobs, it will do so by winning us more positions in good industries. While a flat tariff would help with the deficit, which is good, it would provide the same incentive for domestic production of computer and potato chips alike, so it would not push our economy towards good industries.

Or would it? The natural strategic tariff is a bet that it would. The key reason is this: *industries differ in their sensitivity and response to import competition.*

Although this is a complex issue, the fundamental dynamic is clear from the fairly obvious fact that a flat tariff would trigger the re-location back to the U.S. of some industries but not others.

For example, a flat 30 percent tariff (to pluck a not-unreasonable number out of thin air) would not cause the relocation of the apparel industry back to the U.S. from abroad. The difference between domestic and foreign labor costs is simply too large for a 30 percent premium to tip the balance in America's favor in an industry based on semi-skilled labor.

But a 30 percent tariff quite likely *would* cause the relocation of high-tech manufacturing like semi-conductors. This is key, as these industries are precisely the ones we should want to relocate. These are the high-tech, high-value, high wage industries with a future of many spinoff industries ahead of them.

Therefore a flat tariff would, in fact, be strategic.

I strongly urge that one of these plans be adopted as soon as possible. Otherwise, other experts should craft a new plan that would be equally beneficial. We can't continue to do nothing and allow the mercantilist countries to destroy our economy.

The Buy American Act

The Buy American Act was passed by Congress in 1933 and requires the U.S. government to prefer U.S.-made products in its purchases.[27] The Act restricts the purchase of supplies that are not domestic end products. For manufactured products, the Buy American Act uses a two-part test: first, the article must be manufactured in the U.S., and second, the cost of domestic components must exceed 50 percent of the cost of all its components. Other federal legislation passed since extends similar requirements to third-party purchases that utilize federal funds, such as highway and transit programs.

In certain government procurements, the requirement may be waived if purchasing the material domestically would burden the government with an unreasonable cost, as when the price differential between the domestic product and an identical foreign-sourced product exceeds a certain percentage, or the product is not available domestically in sufficient quantity or quality, or if doing so is not in the public interest. In recent years, the requirement has been increasingly waived to the point that we have lost domestic sources for some defense components and products.

In addition, the President has authority to waive the Act in response to the provision of reciprocal treatment to U.S. producers. Under the 1979 GATT Agreement on Government Procurement, the U.S.-Israel Free Trade Agreement, the U.S.-Canada Free Trade Agreement, the North American Free Trade Agreement, and the Central American Free Trade Agreement access to government procurement by certain U.S. agencies of goods from the other parties to these agreements is granted. However, the Buy American Act was excluded from the WTO's 1996 Agreement on Government procurement.

It's time to get back to enforcing the Buy American Act in the strictest interpretation, reducing the number of waivers. And the Act should not be waived in any future trade agreements.

What Industry Can Do

By industry, I mean trade and industry-specific organizations and professional societies. (A list of the major trade associations and professional societies is in Appendix B.) At the present time, there is very little coordination of efforts by trade organizations to influence public policy to save American manufacturing. At times, associations and organizations wind up working against each other as they lobby Congress on issues benefiting their particular group.

It is time for trade organizations to stop undercutting each other's efforts by lobbying on issues that just benefit their organization and their members. Trade organizations and professional societies should work together to save American manufacturing by selecting a few of the most critical issues on which they agree and devoting all their efforts to making sure these issues are addressed by public policy.

For example, the National Association of Manufacturers and the National Machine Tool Association are diametrically opposed on trade issues, but they agree on the need to improve math and engineering education, provide skills training to youth to prepare them for the workplace, and increase the federal budget for R&D spending. And there are several other issues, cited above, that are common among the major trade organizations. I have learned through experience that only by working together can we achieve mutually beneficial goals.

What Unions Can Do

While unions have already made concessions in negotiating new labor contracts and renegotiating old ones, they need be willing to make further concessions to save American manufacturing. I don't mean that we need to roll back wages and benefits to the low levels of developing countries. We would have to roll back wages and benefits to pre-World War II levels to be competitive. I mean that unions need to be realistic and reasonable in their demands.

For example, the United Auto Workers agreed to close its Jobs Bank program at General Motors on February 2, 2009 to comply with federal bailout mandates. Under this program, workers laid off from their jobs were initially paid upwards of 72 percent of their salaries through a combination of unemployment and supplemental GM wages and still received benefits. After approximately 48 weeks of unemployment, however, their benefits would expire and they would enter the Jobs Bank, in which they would be required to report to work and would receive 100 percent of their pay even if there was no work to be done.[28]

Unions also need to reconsider their unswerving allegiance to the Democrat Party. When their endorsements and financial support are taken for granted, their influence in the Democrat Party is diminished. Trade agreements, such as NAFTA, were approved by strong bipartisan support in Congress even though unions were strongly against them. American workers have been consistently sold down the river by legislators of *both* parties time after time with regard to trade issues. Unions would be better off supporting candidates from either party that support fair trade, instead of giving blanket endorsements to every Democrat. Candidates should have to *earn* the support of unions.

My Own Recommendations

I conducted a thorough review and analysis of the recommendations by various organizations for the first edition of this book. In the subsequent two and a half years, I have reviewed and analyzed even more articles, reports, and books. As a result, I have modified my opinion on the importance and urgency of some of my original recommendations. The following are my own immediate and long-term recommendations, in order of priority:

Immediate Recommendations

Enact legislation addressing foreign currency manipulation (S. 1619 and H. R. 639 pending at the time this chapter was last revised in June 2012).

Temporarily reduce the corporate tax rate on repatriated income if income is permanently reinvested in the United States.

Reduce corporate taxes to 25 percent and maintain low personal rates to benefit sole proprietors, partnerships, and "S" corporations.

Congress should not ratify any new Free Trade Agreements.

Make capital gains tax of 15 percent permanent.

Increase and make permanent the R&D tax credit.

Eliminate the estate tax (also called the death tax).

Improve intellectual property rights protection and increase criminal prosecution.

Prevent the sale of strategic U.S.-owned companies to foreign-owned companies.

Enact legislation to prevent corporations from avoiding U.S. income tax by reincorporating in a foreign country.

Change the tax code to a "partial exemption system" to eliminate incentives for companies to move offshore by taxing all corporate income at a reasonable rate once.

Enact legislation to establish a Natural Strategic Tariff Act or a Balanced Trade Restoration Act to authorize sale of Import Certificates, using either the Richman or Buffet plan.

If American voters and industry sufficiently pressured elected representatives to achieve bipartisan consensus, all of these immediate recommendations could be accomplished within one Congressional legislative year.

Long-term recommendations

Strengthen and tighten procurement regulations to enforce compliance with the Buy American Act of 1933 by all government agencies.

Establish a National Strategy Center to help policy makers plan for the future by integrating the economic, diplomatic, and military elements of national power to develop a national manufacturing strategy.

Analyze defense supply chains to ensure sufficiency and security of supply and if deemed necessary, reconstitute the National Security Resources Board.

Select and adopt best recommendations from the Treasury Department report "Approaches to Improve the Competitiveness of the U.S. Business Tax System for the 21st Century."

Increase federal R&D spending by 10 percent a year over the next seven years with focused attention to the physical sciences, engineering, and mathematics and offer matching grants to industry.

Lower health costs through association health plans, health savings accounts, medical liability reform, and electronic medical records.

Create a human capital investment tax credit to promote continuous education and workforce training.

Conduct a review of existing regulations to eliminate burdensome regulations and implement reforms, and review the impact of new regulations.

By 2015, double the numbers of bachelor's degrees awarded annually to U.S. students in science, math, and engineering, and increase the number of those students who become K-12 science and math teachers.

Establish a high school and technical education partnership initiative to ensure that students are being taught the necessary skills to make successful transitions to college and the workforce.

Based on my experience in industry and politics, I believe that implementing these recommendations would take a paradigm shift on the part of leaders in government and industry. But if this occurred, I believe these long-term recommendations could be achieved within four to eight years, if there were the national will to do so.

12

What Can I Do?

At this point, you may be feeling there is nothing you can do as an individual to stop the total destruction of American manufacturing and watch the United States go over the precipice. Don't think this way! The tide is gradually turning.

Even the major news media is waking up. On February 28, 2011, ABC News began a series with Diane Sawyer entitled "Made in America." John and Ana Ursy of Dallas agreed to accept the challenge of working with an ABC team to furnish three rooms of their home exclusively with products made in America. The questions posed by the team were: Is buying American-made more expensive? What staples are no longer manufactured in the U.S.? And what difference would it make if everyone promised to buy more American-made products?

When the team examined everything in these three rooms and removed all foreign-made products, the result was a virtually empty house – no beds, no tables, no chairs, no couches, and no lamps. Only the kitchen sink, a vase, a candle, and some pottery remained.

The kitchen was the most difficult room to furnish because there are only a couple of companies still making major appliances in America. But Viking Products provided the stove and Sub-Zero and Wolf the refrigerator, microwave, and oven. They couldn't find any coffee makers made in the U.S.; Bun-a-Matic assembles a coffee maker here out of parts made offshore. But there are no TVs made in America anymore and no light bulbs. (General Electric closed the last plant in the U.S. in July 2010.) But the team was able to furnish the bedroom with all American-made furniture, lamps, and bedding, and for less money — $1,699 compared to $1,758 — than the foreign alternatives.

All in all, the team found more than 100 manufacturers still making various consumer goods in America, and viewers submitted the names of many more. When one of the ABC reporters, Sharyn Alfonsi, examined the toy box of her own child, she didn't find any American-made toys in it. But she later found some U.S. toy makers, like Green Toys in San Francisco, which makes toys from recycled milk bottles. There are six other California companies shown on an interactive map on the ABC News website: Pure-Rest organic bedding in San Diego, Harveys Handbags in Santa Ana, Maglite Flashlights in Ontario, Danmer Custom Shutters in Los Angeles, Glass Darma handmade drinking straws in Ft. Bragg, and Sergio Lub Jewelry in Martinez.

You may be thinking, would what I do make any difference? Activist and author Sonia Johnson once said, "We must remember that one determined person can make a significant difference, and that a small group of determined people can change the course of history." Margaret Mead once said, "Never doubt that a small group of thoughtful, committed citizens can change the world; indeed, it's the only thing that ever has." Remember that our country was founded by a small group of people who did indeed change the world by forming the United States of America. So here below are some suggestions of what each one of us can do.

As a Consumer

First, look at the country-of-origin labels of goods when you go shopping. Most imported goods are required to have these labels. Many manufacturers have tried to get the Federal Trade Commission to relax the rules determining what is considered made-in-USA. But after two years of public hearings, studies, and reports, in December 1997 the FTC reaffirmed that a product will be considered made-in-USA if only when "all significant parts and processing that go into the product are of U.S. origin." Buy the made-in-USA item even if it costs more than the imported product. It is a small sacrifice to make to support the well being of your fellow Americans.[1]

If the product you are looking for is no longer made in America, then avoid countries, such as China, which have nuclear warheads aimed at American cities. It would not be an exaggeration to say that American consumers have paid for the bulk of China's military build-up; American soldiers could one day face weapons largely paid for by Americans. Instead, patronize impoverished countries, such as Bangladesh or Nicaragua, which have no military ambitions.

In addition, you will be reducing your "carbon footprint" by buying a product made in America instead of a product made offshore that will use a great deal of fossil fuel to ship to the United States.

If you have a made-in-USA appliance that needs repair and all the new ones are imported, have it repaired. If it can't be fixed, and it is a small appliance that you can live without, then don't buy a new one. We Americans buy many things that we really don't need just because they are so cheap. If a product that you are considering is an import, ask yourself, "Do I really need this?" If you don't, don't buy it.

If you are willing to step out of your comfort zone, ask to speak to the department or store manager of your favorite store. Tell them that you have been a regular customer for X amount of time, but if they want to keep you as a customer, they need to start carrying some more made-in-USA products. If you buy products online or from catalogs, contact these companies via email. Your communicating with a company does have an effect, because there is a rule of thumb in sales and marketing that one reported customer complaint equals 100 unreported complaints.

If you think Americans no longer care where goods are made or about the safety of foreign products, you may be surprised to learn that poll after poll shows the majority of Americans prefer to buy American. A nation-wide poll conducted by Sacred Heart University in September 2007 found that 69 percent of Americans check labels for information like manufacturer, national origin, and ingredients. And 86 percent of Americans would like to block Chinese imports until they raise their product and food safety standards to U.S. levels.[2] And a June 2007 *Consumer Reports* magazine poll found that 92 percent of Americans want country-of-origin labels on meat and produce.

Buying American has been made even easier by a book by Roger Simmermaker, *How Americans Can Buy American: The Power of Consumer Patriotism*, updated in 2010. Simmermaker says, "Supporting American companies leads to a more independent America. Ownership equals control, and control equals independence. We cannot claim to be an independent country or control our own destiny if our manufacturing base is under foreign ownership or foreign control. A nation that cannot supply its own needs is not an independent nation. If we are to claim independence from the rest of the world and truly be a sovereign nation, we must begin supplying our own needs once again."

According to Simmermaker, buying American is not just about buying made-in-USA goods. "Buying American, in the purest sense of the term, means we would buy an American-made product, made by an American-owned company, with as high domestic parts content within that product as possible... 'American-made' is good. 'Buying American' is much better!"[4] One of our greatest statesmen, Thomas Jefferson, stated, "I have come to a resolution myself, as I hope every good citizen will, never again to purchase any article of foreign manufacture which can be had of American make, be the difference of price what it may."[3]

Simmermaker has made it easy by listing companies and their nation of ownership. You can see his list at HowToBuyAmerican.com. And his website isn't the only one: you can also check many others:

BuyAmericanMart.com
IOnlyBuyAmerican.com
MadeInUSA.org
AmericansWorking.com
ShopUnionMade.org
MadeInUSAForever.com
StillMadeInUSA.com
AmericanMadeMatters.com
AmericasGotProduct.com

USALoveList.com

There are also brick-and-mortar stores springing up around the country that are stocking only made-in-America products, like the American Apparel stores, or primarily made-in-America products, like the Urban Outfitters stores.

As American consumers, we have many choices to live safely and enjoy more peace of mind with American products. It's high time to stop sending our American dollars to China while they send us their tainted, hazardous, and disposable products. If 300 million Americans refused to buy just $20 each of Chinese goods, that would be a *six billion dollar* trade balance resolved in our favor.

Some people say they are willing to stop buying Chinese products if they can find comparable "Made in USA products," but they would still rather buy Japanese cars because they are more fuel efficient and reliable. That may have been true from the 1970s through the early 1990s, but it hasn't been true for several years now. Chevrolet, Chrysler, and Ford cars are now just as fuel efficient and reliable as Japanese cars. In fact, the Motor Trend Car of the Year was an American car for 15 of the past 20 years. General Motors' Cadillac CTS was the Motor Trend Car of the Year in 2008, and the Chevrolet Malibu was a top finalist, beating out the Toyota Camry, which had been the Motor Trend Car of the Year in 2007. In 2010, the Motor Trend Car of the Year was the Ford Fusion, and the 2011 Car of the Year was the Chevy Volt.[4]

As an Entrepreneur

There is no lack of American know-how today. Each year, thousands of new products are invented and receive patents, but most are never produced. Knowing how to use technology to create a product doesn't mean you know how to create a business.

Most people think entrepreneurs start businesses, but in *The E Myth*, Michael Gerber shows that persons he refers to as "technicians" start most businesses. These are people who know how to do a particular job and create jobs for themselves by starting their own businesses. Thus, a machinist starts a machine shop or an accountant starts his own accounting firm. Although these would-be entrepreneurs may know how to do their specific job well, they may not know how to run a business. They do not know how to wear the many hats it takes to run a successful company, and they lack the money to hire the necessary personnel to do it for them. Fifty percent of all new businesses fail within a year, and 80 percent fail within five years. The main reasons are insufficient capital, lack of experience, and poor management.

New entrepreneurs need timely, user-friendly assistance in management training, resources for seed capital, access to government and economic development resources, and professional services that will sustain growth of their startup. At the present time, this kind of assistance is available in bits and pieces through a variety of programs and agencies, and it takes a great deal of time for entrepreneurs to locate and access the right sources of assistance.

In contrast, 65 percent to 80 percent of companies nurtured in small business incubators or innovation centers are still in operation five years later.[5]However, most of these companies are not technology-based manufacturers. As hard as it is to start any company, it is much more complex and difficult to start a technology-based company. In addition, the more complex the technology, the more time and money it takes to get the product ready for market. Business incubators and innovation centers usually concentrate on fostering companies based on already-developed technology. Start-up companies with long-term R&D projects, which absorb large amounts of money and time, are better served by venture capitalists.

If entrepreneurs have user-friendly assistance during the critical start-up phase on an ongoing basis, it greatly increases their chances of success and growth. Incubators provide a centralized source for this kind of assistance. An incubator provides a safe place for the "newborn" business to set up shop, in a controlled environment tailored to the needs of the entrepreneurs. Entrepreneurs are carefully watched over and groomed for success by the staff and network of consultants.

Depending on the type of company you are starting, you may want to seek guidance and counseling from one of the SBA-sponsored SCORE centers or Small Business Development Centers (SBDCs) mentioned in Chapter Seven. You can find SCORE at score.org and the SBDCs at sba.gov. In addition, you could see if there is a business incubator located near you by checking out the incubators that are members of the National Business Incubator Association at nbia.org. Universities and small business development corporations often sponsor business incubators.

The incubator's resident companies are given a package of services tailored and customized to the needs of entrepreneurial start-ups. The package usually includes a number of amenities. Affordable, flexible floor space that can accommodate a company's expansion as it grows is a common offering. Also popular are access to shared office and administrative support services, on-site one-on-one counseling by experts in various fields, and networking with other enterprise center resident companies. In addition to services and support, these centers provide valuable training and management experience to inventors and innovators. Some of these centers even provide funding or access to funding. (If you are interested in finding out about business incubators near you, contact the National Business Incubator Association at nbia.org.)

If you are considering starting a company to produce a new product, now is a good time. Find a niche item where consumers will be willing to pay more for a made-in-USA product. An acquaintance told me recently that he couldn't find a made-in-USA crib when he and his wife went to buy one for their expected baby. The best they could find was one made in Canada. I think new parents would be willing to pay more for a crib that would be lead-free and made in a safe, sturdy way by an American manufacturer. There are also military and defense products that are no longer made in the United States; it may be worthwhile to research which of these products could be manufactured again in the U.S.

As a Business Owner

Even if you are not a manufacturer, you can apply many of the guidelines and recommendations provided in Chapter Eight of this book. In addition, join a trade association that fits your industry (see Appendix B). The larger the trade association, the more influence it will have in changing policy. Better yet, be an active member – really get involved. If you can't find a trade association that fits your industry, join your local chamber of commerce or your state chamber of commerce. At the very least, you can join the National Federation of Independent businesses (NFIB) at nfib.org. NFIB has state chapters in many states. Now is the time for action! Don't sit on the sidelines while your industry and possibly your own business struggle to survive.

As an Employee

If you are an employee of a manufacturer, think of yourself as a soldier in an economic war – with China at the present time, but possibly Russia or Brazil in the future. We are in a battle for our industrial, technological, and support jobs. You can contribute to your company's success in the global economy by doing your job to the best of your ability. You can provide customer service that exceeds the expectations of your company's customers. And you can adopt the marketing mindset presented in Chapter Eight, where everyone in a company is part of the marketing team regardless of their job function.

If you are rude, argumentative, indifferent to customers, or contribute to late deliveries or poor quality work, how long do you think it will be before your employer's customers decide to try another vendor? Your employer's customers may not come back again if they are consistently getting poor quality parts and products and late deliveries. Customer service means treating customers like you want to be treated when you are the customer. It includes returning customer phone calls and addressing any customer issues, promptly and courteously. If you work on the shop floor, you play a vital role in carrying out the commitments and promises of the sales team. Doing your job well, no matter how menial the job, is vital to pleasing customers, and by extension, ensuring your own job security.

In the global supply chain of goods and services, *each worker is a value-added workstation*, so you need to be constantly thinking, "Am I adding value?" If you aren't, then your job will be at risk. If your company's products and services aren't providing value to their customers, then their success and survival as a company will be at risk. You can increase your value as an employee and improve your ability to fight this economic war by upgrading your knowledge and skills through continuous education. You can learn new skills, like those involved in lean manufacturing. You can also join a professional society or organization related to your job or profession. (See Appendix B. If you don't see one that fits your job or profession, you can check online.)

As a Voter

There's only one way for manufacturers to find relief from high taxes, bad trade laws, and burdensome regulation, and that is through Washington. Voter apathy is partially responsible for the state of our affairs as a country. Too many people have decided that there is nothing they can do on an individual basis and have even stopped voting.

Americans have been sold down the river by politicians on both sides of the aisle. Democrats profess to support blue-collar workers and unions, yet NAFTA and the WTO treaties were approved under the presidency of Democrat Bill Clinton. Republicans profess to support business, yet they primarily support large, multinational corporations, rather than the small businesses that are the engine of growth and the foundation of our middle class.

Some Democrats and Republicans in the House and Senate have had the courage and common sense to stand up for the American worker and small businesses. Senator Byron Dorgan (D-ND) has been outspoken on the subject of offshoring, and even wrote a book entitled *Take This Job and Ship It*. Former presidential candidate and Congressman Duncan Hunter (R-CA) has been very outspoken on the subject of saving American manufacturing and sponsored or co-sponsored many bills. Unfortunately, senators and congressmen with this mindset have been in the minority and their voices of reason have been ignored. In his 2008 book *Where Have all the Leaders Gone*, former Chrysler CEO Lee Iacocca wrote,

Am I the only guy in this country who's fed up with what's happening? Where is our outrage? We should be screaming bloody murder. We've got corporate gangsters stealing us blind. The most famous business leaders aren't the innovators, but the guys in handcuffs. And, don't tell me it's all the fault of right-wing Republicans or liberal Democrats. That's an intellectually lazy argument and it's part of the reason that we're in this stew. We're not just a nation of factions. We're a people and we rise and fall together. I have news for the gang in Congress. We didn't elect you to sit on your butts and do nothing and remain silent while our country is being hijacked and our greatness is being replaced with mediocrity. What is everybody so afraid of? Why don't you guys in Congress show some spine for a change?[6]

It's time we echoed the message of Howard Beale in the movie *Network*: "I'm mad as hell, and I'm not going to take this anymore!" Beale is an anchorman. Upon discovering that his employer will be bought out by a Saudi conglomerate, he stages an on-screen tirade, encouraging the audience to telegram the White House with the message "I'm mad as hell, and I'm not going to take this anymore" in hopes of stopping the takeover.

These campaigns do work sometimes. Americans became "mad as hell" in 2006 when they called, wrote, and emailed Congress about not allowing the Dubai Ports World company to take over management of six major U.S. seaports. The outrage of American voters caused such a furor in Washington that the bill was dropped and the Dubai company decided to fully transfer the U.S. operations of the company to a U.S. entity. Voter outrage doesn't always work in stopping legislation, as shown by the passage of the Health Care Reform Act (aka Obamacare) during the end-of-year season of 2009. But many of the legislators who ignored the will of voters by voting for it paid the price and lost office in the election of 2010.

In a poll asking Americans if they've ever contacted their elected representatives, eight out of 10 said that they never had. Yet it's never been easier to contact members of Congress. All you have to do is click on house.gov or senate.gov, type in your zip code, and you're automatically directed to your representative. A window automatically pops up where you can type a message to that representative. It takes less than two minutes.

Well, Americans now need to get as "mad as hell" about bad trade laws, bad tax laws, and over-burdensome regulations on manufacturers. It's time to become engaged in a grassroots fight to change the bad free-trade laws into better *fair*-trade laws that will reflect the interests of small manufacturers who've been absent from trade policy deliberations for far too long. If people whose lives are affected by manufacturing would write their legislators and tell them they want trade reform and tax reform and would follow up to watch how they voted, the results would be amazingly effective.

Trade agreements like NAFTA were sold on the threat that we dare not become isolationists. But should we throw away our own ability to exist and prosper as a country in order to offset the possibility of being called isolationist by such countries as China? No! We cannot export our wealth and remain a First World country. We cannot lose our manufacturing base and remain a superpower. In fact, we may not be able to maintain our freedom as a country, because it takes considerable wealth to protect that freedom. You can play a role as an individual in saving our country by following the suggestions in this chapter. The company or job you save may be your own.

NOTES

Preface & Introduction

[1] The National Association of Manufacturers, the Manufacturing Institute, and RSM McGladrey, "The Future Success of Small and Medium Manufacturers: Challenges and Policy Issues," The Manufacturing Institute, 2006.
[2] "Manufacture." *Merriam-Webster.com.*

Chapter 2

[1] David Montgomery, *Chapter 3: Labor in the Industrial Era*, Department of Labor, dol.gov/oasam/programs/history/chapter3.htm.
[2] Irving Bernstein, *Chapter 5: Americans in Depression and War, Department of Labor*, dol.gov/oasam/programs/history/chapter5.htm.
[3] Donald Fisk, "American Labor in the 20th Century," *Compensation and Working Conditions*, Fall 2001, January 30, 2003.

Chapter 3

[1] Robert Morley, "The Death of American Manufacturing," *The Trumpet*, Vol. 17, No. 2, February 2006.
[2] Scott Paul, "The Philadelphia Story: The Democratic Debate," *The Huffington Post*, October 29, 2007, huffingtonpost.com/scott-paul/the-philadelphia-story-th_b_70275.html.
[3] San Diego Regional Chamber of Commerce, "2004 Annual Manufacturing Study: Production in a Changing World," San Diego Regional Chamber of Commerce, May 2005.
[4] Robert E. Scott, "Growing U.S. trade deficit with China cost 2.8 million jobs between 2001 and 2010," Briefing Paper No. 323, Economic Policy Institute, September 20, 2011, June 1, 2012.
[5] Ann Belser, "Manufacturing Firms Holding Up Well Here," *Pittsburgh Post-Gazette*, December 9, 2008.
[6] Richard McCormack, "America's Oldest Industry is on the Brink of Extinction," *Manufacturing & Technology News,* Vol. 14. No. 13. July 17, 2007.
[7] Michael Webber, "Erosion of the Defense Industrial Support Base," Alliance for American Manufacturing, 2009, www.americanmanufacturing.org/files/Chapter7Webber_0.pdf,245-280.
[8] Richard McCormack, "U.S. Becomes A Bit Player in Global Semiconductor Industry: Only One New Fab Under Construction In

2009," *Manufacturing & Technology News*, Vol. 17. No. 3., February 12, 2010.

9 "U.S. Trade in Goods by Country," United States Census Bureau, www.census.gov/foreign-trade/balance/, .

10 Ibid.

11 Scott Sonner, "Buffet warns U.S. Trade deficit could cause 'political turmoil,'" *The Journal Star*, January 18, 2006.

12 Richard McCormack, "U.S. is world's biggest loser – by far – in WTO disputes," *Manufacturing & Technology News*, Vol. 14. No. 15, August 27, 2007.

13 Patrick J. Buchanan, "Death of Manufacturing," *The American Conservative*, August 11, 2003.

14 Paul Freedenberg, "That Blur in the Rearview Mirror is China," *The American Machinist,* September 19, 2006.

15 "Plants Closing," *Manufacturing & Technology News*, Vol. 14. No. 14. July 31, 2007. See also: PR Newswire, "Lennox International Opens New Manufacturing Operation in Mexico," July 20, 2008.

16 Usher C.V. Haley, "Shedding Light on Energy Subsidies in China: An Analysis of China's Steel Industry 2000-2007," Alliance for American Manufacturing, January 8, 2008, americanmanufacturing.org/content/shedding-light-energy-subsidies-china-analysis-china%E2%80%99s-steel-industry-2000-2007.

17 Larry West, "New EPA Air Quality Standards Please No One," About.com, September 22, 2006, environment.about.com/b/2006/09/22/epa-air-quality-standards-please-no-one.htm.

18 "New Law Increases Paperwork for Self-Employed Over a Thousand Percent," *National Association for the Self-Employed*, May 26, 2010, nase.org/LearningCenter/NASEPublications/WashingtonWatch/washingtonwatchlatest/Washington_Watch/2010-05-26/washington_watch_-may_26_2010.aspx.

19 "Losing the Competitive Advantage: Now is the Time to Act," American Economics Association, p. 15, 2005, techamerica.org/we-are-still-losing-the-competitive-advantage.

20 "We are Still Losing the Competitive Advantage: Now is the Time to Act," American Economics Association, p. 18, March 2007, www.techamerica.org/we-are-still-losing-the-competitive-advantage.

21 "Aerospace Manufacturing and Support Industries in California," Northern California Center of Excellence and the Center for Applied Competitive Technologies, 2010

22 "Small-to-Medium Manufacturers Report," National Association of Manufacturers

[23] "Manufacturing Can Become Newest Dream Job," Fabricators & Manufacturers Association International, White Paper 2007, media.thefabricator.com/assets/pdf/Skilled-Worker-Whitepaper.pdf p. 4.

[24] Richard McCormack, "Council On Competitiveness Says U.S. Has Little To Fear, But Fear Itself; By Most Measures, U.S. Is Way Ahead Of Global Competitors," *Manufacturing & Technology News*, Vol. 13. No. 21. November 30, 2006.

[25] Bruce Vernyi, "Where Are the Real Problems in Manufacturing?" *American Machinist*, September 21, 2007.

[26] Richard McCormack, "General Electric CEO Jeffrey Immelt: The U.S. No Longer Drives Global Economic Growth And Must Decide If It Wants To Be A Competitive Nation," *Manufacturing & Technology News*, Vol. 14 No. 21, November 30, 2007.

Chapter 4

[1] Robert E. Scott, "Growing U.S. trade deficit with China cost 2.8 million jobs between 2001 and 2010," Briefing Paper No. 323, Economic Policy Institute, September 20, 2011.

[2] Louis Uchitelle, "Goodbye, Production (and Maybe Innovation)," *The New York Times*, December 24, 2006.

[3] John Teresko, "Fighting the IP," *Industry Week*, p. 38, February 2008.

[4] U.S.-China and Economic Security Review Commission, "2007 Report to Congress," p. 62, November 2007.

[5] Richard McCormack, "Behind The Sound Bites Of Republican Presidential Hopeful Rep. Duncan Hunter: U.S. Multinationals Have Become Chinese Corporations," *Manufacturing & Technology News,* Vol. 14 No. 5, March 13, 2007.

[6] National Research Council, "Minerals, Critical Minerals, and the U.S. Economy," The National Academies Press, p. 7, Washington DC, 2007.

[7] See, Press Release, "U.S. Loses Capability to Equip Itself for Future Conflicts, new Forward Magazine Reports," Metal Service Center Institute, January 8, 2008 www.msci.org/news/archives/details.aspx?ArticleID=116.

[8] Richard McCormack, "U.S. Becomes A Bit Player in Global Semiconductor Industry: Only One New Fab Under Construction In 2009," Manufacturing & Technology News, Vol. 17. No. 3, February 12, 2010.

[9] "Bush Decision In Favor Of Chinese Imports Leads To Loss Of 500 Very Good American Job," *Manufacturing & Technology News*, March 29, 2007.

[10] "North Carolina Labor Department Studies Plight Of Laid Off Pillowtex Workers," *Manufacturing & Technology News*, December 21, 2007.

[11] Alan S. Blinder, "Free Trade's Great, but Offshoring Rattles Me," *The Washington Post*, May 6, 2007.

[12] "2006 Survey Report: Next Generation Offshoring, The Globalization of Innovation," Duke University's Fuqua School of Business and Booz Allen Hamilton, March 2007.

[13] "Trade Shows Are Impacted By Loss of Manufacturing," *Manufacturing & Technology News*, July 31, 2007 Vol. 14, No. 14.

[14] Ibid.

[15] William Raynor, "Outsourcing Jobs Off-Shore: Short and Long-Term Consequences," 2003; www.newwork.com/Pages/Opinion/Raynor/Outsourcing%20Consequen ces.html

[16] Ibid.

[17] Raymond Richman, Howard Richman and Jesse Richman, "How to stop China from stealing our jobs," *World Net Daily*, April 23, 2008.

[18] Paul Craig Roberts, "Offshoring Has Destroyed The U.S. Economy: Nobel Economist Michael Spence Says Globalization Is Costly For Americans," *Manufacturing & Technology News*, Vol. 18 No 10, June 20, 2011.

[19] Ralph E. Gomory and William J. Baumol, *Global Trade and Conflicting National Interests*, The MIT Press, p. 5, 2001.

[20] "Sloan Foundation President Ralph Gomory: Transferring Production Offshore Is Not Free Trade," *Manufacturing & Technology News*, Vol. 14, No. 16, September 17, 2007.

[21] Doug Hall, "Job growth retreats in some states, mirrors national trend," Economic Policy Institute, July 22, 2011: www.epi.org/publication/job-growth-retreats-in-some-states-mirrors-national-trend/.

[22] "Americans See China Crowding out U. S. as Economic Leader," Gallup.com, February 21, 2008www.gallup.com/poll/104479/americans-see-china-crowding-us-economic-leader.aspx

Chapter 5

[1] "40 Years of Achievements, 1970-2010," U.S. Environmental Protection Agency, epa.gov/40th/achieve.html

[2] "The World's Worst Polluted Places," A Project of the Blacksmith Institute, New York, September 2007, www.blacksmithinstitute.org/wwpp2007/finalReport2007.pdf

[3] "Forest countries seek carbon credits; World's most polluted places named," Finfacts Ireland, September 14, 2007, www.finfacts.com/irelandbusinessnews/publish/article_1011159.shtml.

[4] David Lynch, "Pollution Poisons China's Progress," USA Today, July 4, 2005.

[5] "The World's Worst Polluted Places," supra at 14.

[6] Antoaneta Bezlova, "Pollution Grows Along With China's Economy," *China Environmental News Digest*, November 30, 2005.

[7] "China Faces Increasing International Pressure on Environmental Issues," *China.org.cn*, June 14, 2006, www.china.org.cn/english/2006/Jun/171410.htm.

[8] "China Responds to Explosive Growth, Pollution, and Water Scarcity in Latest Five-Year Plan," Circle of Blue, March 15, 2011.

[9] "Identifying Near-Term Opportunities For Carbon Capture and Sequestration (CCS) in China," NRDC White Paper, Natural Resources Defense Council, December 2010.

[10] Amy Zeng, "China Plans for National Climate Emissions Trading in the Next Five Years," *Greening China*, January 13, 2011.

[11] Elisabeth Rosenthal, "China Increases Lead as Biggest Carbon Dioxide Emitter," *The New York Times*, June 14, 2008.

[12] Rick Pedraza, "Bill Clinton: China, India Can 'Burn Up the Planet,'" *NewsMax.com*, July 15, 2008.

[13] "Annual Report to Congress: Military Power of the People's Republic of China 2008," U.S. Department of Defense.

[14] Isabel Hilton, "Writer in the spotlight: Alexandra Harney," *Chinadialogue.net*, August 11, 2008, www.chinadialogue.net/article/show/single/en/2289-Writer-in-the-spotlight-Alexandra-Harney.

[15] Maximilian Auffhammer and Richard T. Carson, "Forecasting the Path of China's CO_2 Using Province Level Information," Department of Agricultural and Resource Economics, UCB, UC Berkeley, August 7, 2007.

[16] "The Second Environmental Economic Policy Introduced," Ministry of Environmental Protection, People's Republic of China, February 18, 2008.

[17] "China establishes liability insurance system for environmental pollution," Chinese Environmental Protection Agency (SEPA) Press Release, March 12, 2008, www.environmental-expert.com/news/china-establishes-liability-insurance-system-for-environmental-pollution-28860/view-comments.

[18] "More than 10,000 coal mines closed in last three years," China Daily, January 3, 2008

[19] Tania Branigan, "China to close 6,000 coal mines in safety push," *The Guardian*, November, 19 2008.

[20] "U.S. and China to Partner for a Better Global Environment," News Release, U.S. Environmental Protection Agency, April 7, 2006.

[21] "The World's World Toxic Pollution Problems 2011," Blacksmith Institute and Green Cross Switzerland, 2011,

[22] Daniel Pepper, "Choking on Pollution in India," *Spiegel Online International*, July 7, 2007.

[23] "Our Mining Children: A Report of the Fact Finding Team on the Child Labourers in the Iron Ore and Granite Mines in Bellary District of Karnataka," HAQ Centre for Child Rights, May 2007.

[24] Ann Ninan, "Mine-Field of Exploitation for Migrant Men, Women, Children," *Inter Press Service*, August 17, 2006.

Chapter 6

[1] Peter Marsh, "China Noses Ahead as Top Goods Producer," *Financial Times*, March 13, 2011.

[2] Michael Ettlinger and Kate Gordon ,"The Importance and Promise of American Manufacturing, Why It Matters if We Make It in America and Where We Stand Today," Center for American Progress, April 2011.

[3] Joel Popkin, "Securing America's Future: The Case for a Strong Manufacturing Base," NAM Council of Manufacturing Associations, June 2003.

[4] Stephen Manning, "Is anything made in the U.S.A. anymore? You'd be surprised," *The New York Times*, February 20, 2009.

[5] Kerri Houston," America's Fading Military-Industrial Base," *Investors Business Daily*, May 5, 2008.

[6] "Kissinger For US Offering Sops To Curb Outsourcing," The Financial Express, July 16, 2003.

[7] Stephen Ezell and Robert Atkinson, "The Case for a National Manufacturing Strategy," Information Technology & Innovation Foundation, April 2011.

[8] "The Facts About Modern Manufacturing," *The Manufacturing Institute*, 8th Edition, 2009.

[9] Ibid.

[10] "EMPLOYMENT PROJECTIONS – 2008-18", News Release, Bureau of Labor Statistics, U.S. Department of Labor, bls.gov/news.release/archives/ecopro_12102009.pdf.

[11] John Madigan, "Viewpoint -- More Than Just Earth-Friendly, Going 'Green' a Route To Jobs and Prosperity," *Industry Week*, July 2, 2008.

[12] "Industry Week's 2008 Salary Survey: Are You Worth What They're Paying You?" *Industry Week*, March 2008.

[13] Ibid.

[14] "The Facts About Modern Manufacturing," supra.

[15] "Industrial Research Institute's R&D Trends Forecast For 2011", Industrial Research Institute, 2011.

[16] Gregory Tassey, "Rationales and mechanisms for revitalizing US manufacturing R&D strategies," National Institute of Standards and Technology, Gaithersburg, MD, January 29, 2010.

[17] Floyd Norris, "As U.S. Exports Soar, It's Not All Soybeans," *New York Times*, February 11, 2011.

[18] "Factsheet: Exporting is Good For Your Bottom Line," U.S. International Trade Administration, www.trade.gov/cs/factsheet.asp.

Chapter 7

[1] "Corporate FDI Plans Constant Despite Credit Market Turmoil," News Release, AT Kearney, December 10, 2007, www.atkearney.com/index.php/News-media/global-executives-optimistic-about-developing-nations-and-plan-increased-foreign-direct-investment.html.

[2] "Gartner Identifies Top 30 Countries for Offshore Services in 2010-2011," Press Release, Gartner Research, December 20, 2010, www.gartner.com/it/page.jsp?id=1500514.

[3] "XMG Global Issues 2009 Outsourcing Year-end Revenue Forecast," News Release, XMG Global, September 23, 2009;xmg-global.com/research-and-insights/analyst-alert-3/2009-3/xmg-global-issues-2009-outsourcing-year-end-revenue-forecast/.

[4] "India losing sheen as offshore R & D hub," *The Economic Times*, February 20, 2008.

[5] "China fears exporters will be devastated by a US slowdown," *FinFacts*, November 16, 2007; finfacts.com/irelandbusinessnews/publish/printer_1000article_1011832.shtml

[6] A. Gary Shilling, "Chinese Chance," *Forbes*, May 29, 2008.

[7] Booz Allen Hamilton, "China Manufacturing Competitiveness 2007-2008," American Chamber of Commerce of Shanghai, Shanghai, March 2008.

[8] "New Challenges for Foreign Producers: 'China's Manufacturing Competitiveness Is at Risk'', Knowledge @ Wharton; www.knowledgeatwharton.com.cn/index.cfm?fa=printArticle&articleID=1812&languageid=1

[9] "Skilled Labor Shortages Could Hurt ASEAN Economies," *Industry Week*, October 22,2008.

[10] "Foxconn, iPhone Maker, To RAISE Prices To Cover Pay Increase For Chinese Workers," *The Huffington Post*, July 22, 2010.

[11] Lloyd Graf, "Frisbee Manufacturing Returns," *Today's Machining World*, August 18, 2010.

[12] "China Manufacturing Competitiveness 2007-2008," supra.

[13] "Get ready to pay more for everyday items, especially imported ones," *PR Newswire*, May 27, 2008.

[14] "High Oil Killing China Labor Advantage," *MoneyNews.com*, May 29, 2008.

[15] Dean Calbreath, "Rising costs affect China, plus firms that import," *The San Diego Union Tribune*, June 15, 2008.

[16] "Small Manufacturers Must Concentrate on Global Strategies," *The Manufacturing News*, May 28, 2008.

[17] Dean Calbreath, supra.

[18] David Dayton, "Returning Products to a Factory in China", *Silk Road International Blog*, January 9, 2008.

[19] Dan Harris, "Returning Substandard Products to your China Factor: In Another Lifetime, Brother," *China Law Blog*, March 25, 2008, www.chinalawblog.com/2008/03/returning_substandard_products.html

[20] Shobhana Chandra, "China Loss is Alabama Gain as Sleeping-Bag Firm Adds U.S. Jobs", *Bloomberg*, October 14, 2008.

[21] David Dayton, "Thailand vs. China, part II"; *Silk Road International Blog*, May 21, 2008.

[22] Langi Chiang and Zhou Xin, "China's exports, imports fall as economy hits wall", *Reuters*, December 10, 2008.

[23] Jim Hemerling, Hubert Hsu, Jeff Walters, and David Lee, "Sourcing Consumer Products in Asia: Managing Risk and Turning Crisis to Advantage," The Boston Consulting Group, March 2009.

[24] "Chinese economic stimulus program," *Wikipedia*.

Chapter 8

[1] Ed Marcum, "Some businesses learning value of bringing factories back to the U.S.," *Knoxville News Sentinel*, August 7, 2010.

[2] James H. Harrington, "Poor-Quality Cost", ASQC Quality Press, 1987.

[3] Ibid.

[4] William J. Holstein, "The Case for Backshoring, Which manufacturing operations should return to the United States?" *Strategy+Business*, January 25, 2010.

[5] Harold L. Sirkin, Michael Zinser, and Douglas Hohner, "Made in America, Again, Why Manufacturing Will Return to the U.S.," Boston Consulting Group, August 25, 2011.

[6] Ibid.

Chapter 9

[1] Excerpts from interview with Hal Davis, author of, "The Future Success of Small and Medium Manufacturers: Challenges and Policy Issues," National Association of Manufacturers, 2006.

[2] National Academy of Sciences, National Academy of Engineering, Institute of Medicine, "Is America Falling Off the Flat Earth?" The National Academies Press, 2007.

[3] "Report to the President on the National Export Initiative: The Export Promotion Cabinet's Plan for Doubling U.S. Exports in Five Years," National Export Initiative, September 2010.

[4] "Renewable Energy and Energy Efficiency Export Initiative Announced Today," News Release, Department of Commerce, December 7, 2010.

[5] "Economic Opportunities 2015 ($Ec0_{15}$))," Community Education Coalition; www.educationcoalition.com/initiatives/EcO15/

[6] The Ec015 website is www.EcO15.org.

[7] "Manufacturing Makes 'Dramatic Recovery," News Release, *Inside Indiana Business*, July 14, 2011.

[8] "Governor Doyle Launches Next Generation Manufacturing Plan," News Release, Wisconsin Department of Commerce, January 15, 2008.

[9] "Two New Initiatives Aim to 'Innovate' and 'Accelerate' Wisconsin," S*STI Weekly Digest*, January 9, 2008.

[10] Ibid.

Chapter 10

[1] "Do more with less: The five strategies used by successful SMB Manufacturers,"InfoR.com; infor.com/erpsmbguide/.

[2] Michael Treacy and Fred Wiersema, "The Discipline of Market Leaders," Soundelux Audio Pub, 1995.

[3] John Madigan, "Viewpoint – More than just Earth-Friendly, Going 'Green' a Route to Jobs and Prosperity," *Industry Week*, July 2, 2008.

[4] Jonathan Katz, "Dow Corning Wins Sustainability Award," *Industry Week*, November 10, 2008.

[5] Adrienne Selko, "HP Unveils 'Green IT Action Plan'," *Industry Week*, November 20, 2008.

[6] John Madigan, "Viewpoint -- More Than Just Earth-Friendly, Going 'Green' a Route To Jobs and Prosperity," *Industry Week*, July 2, 2008.

[7] Roger Simmermaker, "'Free trade' that isn't free': Neither tariffs nor trade protection is the problem', How Americans Can Buy American," March 26, 2008.

[8] Fiona Harvey, "Staying on Course in a Tougher Climate," *Financial Times*, October 9, 2008.

Chapter 11

[1] "Saving America's Threatened Industrial Base," *The San Diego Union-Tribune*, p. C-5, December 22, 1991.

[2] The Alliance for American Manufacturing website is www.americanmanufacturing.org.

[3] The Committee to Support U.S. Trade Laws website is www.supportustradelaws.com.

[4] Raymond J. Keating, "Trade, the Economy and Small Business," Small Business and Entrepreneurship Council, Analysis #31, May 2008.

[5] John Madigan, "Viewpoint -- More Than Just Earth-Friendly, Going 'Green' a Route To Jobs and Prosperity," *Industry Week*, July 2, 2008.

[6] "A Manufacturing Renaissance, Four Goals for Economic Growth", National Association of Manufacturers; nam.org/~/media/AF4039988F9241C09218152A709CD06D.ashx.

[7] The National Summit on Competitiveness, "Investing in U.S. Innovation," December 6, 2005; nist.gov/mep/upload/competitiveness-innovation-2.pdf.

[8] Letter to Deputy Secretary of Commerce David Sampson from The Manufacturing Council, March 22, 2006.

[9] Stephen Ezell and Robert D. Atkinson, "The Case for a National Manufacturing Strategy," Information Technology and Innovation Foundation, April 26, 2011.

[10] Joe Muckerman, "Without a Robust Industrial Base DOD will Lose Future Wars," *Manufacturing & Technology News,* Vol. 15, No. 7, April 17, 2008.

[11] "Approaches to Improve the Competitiveness of the U.S. Business Tax System for the 21st Century," Office of Tax Policy, Department of the Treasury, December 20, 2007.

[12] Josh Cable, "Regulations, Corporate Taxes 'Strangling' U.S. Manufacturing," *Industry Week*, November 13, 2011

[13] "Offshore Tax Havens, Secrecy, Financial Manipulation and the Offshore Economy: An Interview with William Brittain-Catlin," *Multinational Monitor*, Vol. 26 No. 7, July/August 2005.

[14] Robert S. McIntyre, "Putting Profits Over Patriotism," *The American Prospect*, March 7, 2002.

[15] James S. Henry, "Attack of the Global Pirate Bankers," *The Nation*, July 22, 2008.

[16] Kimberly A. Clausing, "The American Jobs Creation Act of 2004: Creating Jobs for Accountants and Lawyers," *Urban-Brookings Tax Policy Center*, December 2004.

[17] Ibid.

[18] Martin A. Sullivan, "Reported Corporate Effective Tax Rates Down since Late 1990s," *Tax Notes*, February 25, 2008.

[19] Alfred E. Eckes, Jr., *Opening America's Market: U.S. Foreign Trade Policy since 1776*, University of North Carolina Press, Chapel Hill, NC, 1995, p. 158.

[20] "General Agreement on Tariffs and Trade," *Wikipedia.*

[21] "Guest Editorial: Free Trade: Why Don't We Call a Spade a Spade?" *Manufacturing & Technology News*, Vol. 15 No. 7, Thursday, April 17, 2008.

[22] Joshua Aizenman and Jaewoo Lee, "Financial Versus Monetary Mercantilism-Long-Run View of Large International Reserves

Hoarding," National Bureau of Economic Research, NBER Working Paper 12718, December 2007.

[23] Raymond Richman, Howard Richman, and Jesse Richman, *Trading Away our Future: How to Fix our Government-Driven Trade Deficits and Faulty Tax System Before It's Too Late,*" Ideal Taxes Association, 1st Ed., March 15, 2008, p. 3.

[24] Id., atp. 5.

[25] Warren Buffet and Carol J. Loomis, "America's Growing Trade Deficit is Selling the Nation Out From Under Us," *Fortune*, November 10, 2003.

[26] *Trading Away our Future*, supra at 95-97.

[27] "Buy American Act," *Wikipedia*.

[28] Mike Ramsey and Jeff Green, "UAW to End GM Jobs Bank on Feb. 2, Following Chrysler (Update5)" *Bloomberg*, January 28, 2009.

Chapter 12

[1] Charles Pope, "FTC decides against altering definition of Made in USA," *Knight Ridder/Tribune News Service*, December 1, 1997.

[2] "More Americans Checking Product and Food Labels Sacred Heart University Poll Finds; Large Majority Call for Suspension of Chinese Imports," News Release, Sacred Heart University Polling Institute, PRNewswire-US Newswire, September 18, 2007.

[3] Roger Simmermaker, "*How Americans Can Buy American: The Power of Consumer Patriotism,*" Consumer Patriotism Corporation, 3rd ed., January 2, 2008.

[4] "Motor Trend Care of the Year," *Wikipedia*.

[5] "2006 State of the Business Incubation Industry," Linda Knopp, National Business Incubation Association, 2007.

[6] Lee Iacocca, *Where Have All the Leaders Gone*, Pocket Books, 2008.

Appendix A
Government Programs

Department of Commerce

Investigations and Compliance Unit – Recently established to take new and proactive measures to ensure that our trading partners honor their commitments; this office is staffed with experts in intellectual property rights, investigations, and intelligence. Works closely with United States Trade Representative and the Patent and Trademark Office to investigate and re-solve violations of trade agreements.

STOP! Initiative – The Commerce Department is a key member of the STOP! (Strategy Targeting Organized Piracy) Initiative announced in October 2004. This was created to coordinate government-wide activities to confront global piracy and counterfeiting. It seeks to keep global supply chains free of infringing goods and dismantle criminal enterprises that steal American intellectual property. It aims to stop fakes at U.S. borders and enforce intellectual property rights in international markets. It attempts to reach out to like-minded partners and build an international coalition to stop piracy and counterfeiting worldwide. For manufacturers or other parties who have observed violations or who have related concerns, there is a hotline, 866-999-HALT, and a Web site, stopfakes.gov.

Coordinator for International Intellectual Property Enforcement – Works with agencies across the government to develop policies to address international intellectual property violations and enforce intellectual property laws overseas. Heads the international work of the National Intellectual Property Law Enforcement Coordination Council, coordinating and supervising international intellectual-property protection plans with other agencies. Plays a significant role in the implementation of the STOP! Initiative.

Intellectual Property Rights Attaché in China – To deal specifically with intellectual property abuses in China, the Commerce Department arranged for the assignment of Mark Cohen through the U.S. Patent and Trademark Office. These two agencies have increased their intellectual property enforcement and compliance staff by 25 percent since 2001. Mr. Cohen is reachable at cohenma@state.gov.

Unfair Trade Practices Task Force – The Commerce Department established this in 2004 within its Import Administration to pursue the elimination of unfair foreign trade practices. The task force is available to advise U.S. manufacturers of their rights under U.S. trade law. Small companies may not have the resources to hire trade lawyers and the petition process may be difficult to understand; the task force can help. The mission of the Import Administration is to enforce laws and agreements to protect U.S. businesses from unfair competition within the United States resulting from unfair pricing by foreign companies and unfair subsidies to foreign companies by their governments.

Standards Initiative – In March 2003, the Department of Commerce launched the Standards Initiative, an eight-point plan that responds to industry concerns that divergent standards, redundant testing and compliance procedures, and regulatory red tape are becoming one of the greatest challenges to expanding exports. The report can be accessed through the International Trade Administration's Standards Home Page at ita.doc. gov/td/standards. The Assistant Secretary for Manufacturing and services has assumed responsibility for this initiative.

Services for Exporters

U.S. Commercial Service – The U.S. Commercial Service has a network of export and industry specialists in 108 U.S. offices and 150 international offices in 83 countries. The service helps SMMs grow their international sales by means of market research, trade events that promote products or services to qualified buyers, introductions to qualified buyers and distributors, and counseling through every step of the export process. The Service has a website, export.gov, which brings together resources from across the government to assist American businesses in planning their international sales strategies. From market research and trade leads from the Department of Commerce's Commercial Service to export finance information from the Export-Import Bank and the Small Business Administration to agricultural export assistance from the USDA, export.gov helps American exporters navigate the international sales process and avoid pitfalls like non-payment and stolen intellectual property. The ITA manages export.gov as a collaborative effort with the 19

Federal Agencies that offer export assistance programs and services. Reachable at 800-USA-TRADE or export.gov.

International Partner Search – For SMMs that want to find qualified international buyers, partners or agents without traveling overseas, U.S. Commercial Service specialists can deliver detailed company information on up to five prescreened international companies that have expressed an interest in the company's products and services. Reachable at 800-USA-TRADE or export.gov.

Customized Market Analysis– Custom-tailored research service that provides U.S. firms with specific information on marketing and foreign representation for individual products in particular markets. Interviews and surveys are conducted to determine the overall marketability of the pro-duct, key competitors, prices of comparable products, customary distrib-ution and promotion practices, trade barriers, possible business partners and applicable trade events. Reachable at 800-USA-TRADE or export.gov.

Gold Key Service – Custom-tailored business matching service offered by the Commercial Service in key export markets around the world. Includes orientation briefings, market research, appointments with potential partners, interpreter services, and assistance for development of follow-up strategies. Reachable at 800-USA-TRADE or export.gov.

International Company Profiles (ICPs) – Background reports on specific firms prepared by commercial officers overseas. Reachable at 800-USA-TRADE or export.gov.

Trade Event Programs – The Commercial Service in America's overseas embassies and local Export Assistance Centers in the United States can help exporters identify trade shows that may be appropriate for their products and take the necessary steps to participate in them. Reachable at 800-USA-TRADE.

Export Trading Company Affairs – This function, part of the Inter-national Trade Administration, can advise an SMM on forming a legally protected export joint venture, understanding the antitrust implications, finding export partners and trading partners, and finding an export trading company, export management company, or export intermediary. Reachable at 202-482-5131.

Office of Small and Disadvantaged Business Utilization – The Commerce Department, through its Prime Contractor Directory, can assist small businesses with their efforts to obtain suitable subcontracting opportunities and present their capabilities to prime contractors registered with the de-partment. Reachable at 202-482-1472.

Department of Labor Programs

Bureau of Apprenticeship and Training – Assists private industry in developing and improving apprenticeships and other training programs designed to provide the skilled workers needed to compete in today's global economy. Contact the Office of Apprenticeship Training, Employer and Labor Services, Department of Labor, at 202-693-3812 or doleta.gov.

National Association of Workforce Boards (NAWB) – represents the interests of the nation's Workforce Investment Boards. Across the country, more than 600 state and local WIBs are providing workforce development leadership in their communities. The business-led WIBs have the critical role of governance and oversight of the federal resources that support the national network of taxpayer-supported One-Stop Career Centers and federal training investments. Board membership consists of business and employer representatives working in concert with public sector representatives to design effective workforce development services for job seekers and employers alike. Reachable at 703-778-7900 or nawb.org.

Workforce Investment Act (WIA) – Provides federal support for employment and job training. In a February 2005 meeting with the Manufacturing Council Subcommittee on the U.S. Workforce, Assistant Secretary of Labor Emily DeRocco encouraged the subcommittee to develop a dialogue on how best to utilize these funds. (Available training resources often go unused because state and local workforce agencies to not know how to make use of them.) There is an opportunity for Workforce Investment Boards (WIBs) around the country to bring manufacturers into their membership and for manufacturers to inform WIBs of their workforce challenges.

High Growth Job Training Initiative – The purpose of this presidential initiative, implemented by the Labor Department, is to grow industries with advanced manufacturing occupations. It is a strategic effort to prepare workers to take advantage of new and increasing job opportunities in these high-growth, high-demand, and economically vital sectors and industries. The foundation of this initiative is partnerships that include the public workforce system, business and industry, education and training providers, and economic development authorities. The Initiative has awarded 31 grants for advanced manufacturing, for a total of $75 million. The grants ranged from lean manufacturing to training for dislocated workers. One grant of $1,956,700 went to a competency-based apprenticeship system for metalworking, which is at the heart of advanced manufacturing. The Initiative also gave 157 grants, worth $145 million, to 13 other sectors, ranging from hospitality to healthcare and information technology. Contact the Employment and Training Administration, Business Relations Group, at 877-US-2JOBSor visit doleta.gov.

Community-Based Job Training Initiative – This program aims to improve the capabilities of the U.S. workforce through community-based job training grants, in the form of a new employer-focused competitive grant program for training in community and technical colleges. Two rounds of $125 million grants were made available in 2005. Manufacturers can work regionally to define parameters for retraining to be implemented by com-munity colleges. Contact the Labor Department's Employment and Training Administration, Business Relations Group at 877-US-2JOBS or visit doleta.gov.

Advanced Manufacturing Initiative – In October 2004, Secretary of Labor Elaine Chao announced a series of investments of more than $43 million to address the workforce needs of the advanced manufacturing sector. The Department's Employment and Training Administration is sup-porting comprehensive partnerships that include employers, the public workforce system, and other entities that have developed innovative approaches helping workers find good jobs with good wages and promising career pathways in advanced manufacturing. This set of workforce solutions is based on manufacturing industry priorities such as training for innovation, pipeline development (too few young people consider manufacturing careers), image (manufacturing confronts a negative public image characterized by such phrases as "moving offshore," "declining," "dirty," "low pay," etc.), employability and soft skills, training program design, and matching training providers to business needs.

At a Greater Rome, Georgia Chamber of Commerce event on January 18, 2007, Elaine Chao mentioned the Workforce Innovation in Regional Economic Development (WIRED) initiative, which "integrates economic and workforce development activities and encourages regional governments, employers, education providers, foundations, venture capitalists, and others to come together and invest in the talent that promotes job creation." This program addresses the challenges associated with building a globally competitive and prepared workforce. The total appropriation is $195 million for 13 regional economies. First generation WIRED regions were awarded $15 million over three years to revitalize their local economies. The California Innovation Corridor, for example, is implementing a three-target approach for WIRED:

Innovation Support: Sustainable Entrepreneurship – Create an atmosphere in which the culture, environment and systems are characterized and driven by innovation and entrepreneurship.

Industrial Rejuvenation: Manufacturing Value Chain and Sup-pliers – Ensure common "smart supplier" competitiveness and enterprise-driven outcomes across supply chain provider/support networks.

Competitiveness Talent Development: Creation of 21st Century Innovation-Oriented Technical Talent – Integrate consideration of current and future industry enterprise needs into workforce and educational planning and policymaking.

San Diego County was included in the first generation grants in February 2006.

Department of Energy Programs

Industrial Technologies Program – Works with industry to improve industrial energy efficiency and environmental performance and invests in high-risk, high-value R&D to reduce industrial energy use. Also provides information to manufacturers on energy efficiency and renewable energy best practices through the EERE Information Center at 877-337-3463 or eere.energy.gov/industry.

Small Business Administration Programs

PRO-Net – The SBA's PRO-Net has recently been integrated with the Defense Department's Central Contractor Registration database. This database serves as an electronic gateway for procurement information for and about small businesses; a search engine for contracting officers; a marketing tool for small firms; and a database on more than 180,000 small, disadvantaged, and women-owned businesses. Reachable at pronet@sba.gov or ccr.gov.

Office of Advocacy – Represents the views of small business before federal agencies and Congress, receives criticisms of federal policies that affect small businesses, and makes proposals for minimizing the burden of regulations on small businesses. It monitors and reports to Congress on federal agencies' compliance with the Regulatory Flexibility Act, which requires an analysis of the impact of proposed rules on small entities. Reachable at 202-205-6533 or sba.gov/advo.

SBA Loan Programs – The SBA offers many loan programs to assist small businesses, primarily as a guarantor of loans made by private and other financial institutions.

Basic 7(a) Loan Guaranty – The SBA's primary business loan program to help qualified small businesses obtain financing when they might not be eligible for loans through normal lending channels. The program is delivered through commercial banks. See sba.gov/ financing.

504 Certified Development Company (CDC) Loan Program – Provides long-term, fixed-rate financing for small businesses to acquire real estate, machinery, or equipment for expansion or modernization. Typically, a 504 project includes a loan secured from a private-sector lender with a senior lien, a loan secured from a CDC (funded by a 100 percent SBA-guaranteed debenture), a junior lien covering up to 40 percent of the total cost, and a contribution of at least 10 percent equity from the borrower. CDCs are private, nonprofit corporations set up to contribute to the economic development of their regions. See sba.gov/ financing.

Export Express – Combines the SBA's lending assistance with technical assistance to help small businesses that have exporting potential but need funds to buy or produce goods services. See sba.gov/ financing.

Export Working Capital Program – Supports export financing for small businesses when that financing is not otherwise available on reasonable terms. The EWCP is a combined effort of the SBA and the Export-Import Bank. See sba.gov/financing.

Environmental Protection Agency Programs

Small Business Ombudsman – Provides an information clearinghouse and hotline to provide private citizens, small communities, small business enterprises and trade association information on environmental regulations. Reachable at 800-368-5888 or epa.gov/sbo.

Small Business Environmental Home Page – An EPA-sponsored Web site to help small businesses access environmental compliance and pollution prevention information. Visit smallbiz-enviroweb.org.

Suppliers Partnership for the Environment – A partnership of the EPA and the Manufacturing Extension Partnership that makes available environ-mental management tools, best practices and lessons learned based on the experience of OEMs and Tier I suppliers in the automotive supply chain. Visit suppliers-partnership.org.

Appendix B
Trade Associations

While there are 17,000 trade associations in the U.S., the following is a list of national manufacturing associations that have small and medium-sized manufacturers as members. Next is a list of professional societies whose members work in the manufacturing industry. Third is a list of sales representative associations in manufacturing. Many of these associations have annual meetings, newsletters, and regular conferences for their members.

Trade Associations

Aluminum Association
1525 Wilson Blvd., Ste. 600
Arlington, VA 22209
703-358-2960
aluminum.org

Aluminum Extruders Council
1000 N. Rand Rd., Ste. 214
Wauconda, IL 60084
312-526-2010
aec.org

American Gear Manufacturers Association
500 Montgomery St., Ste. 350
Alexandria, VA 22314
Joe Franklin, Jr., Pres.
703-684-0211

American Lighting Association
2050 Stemmons Fwy, Ste. 10046
Dallas, TX 75342

214-698-9898
americanlightingassoc.com

American Machine Tool Distributors Association
1445 Research Blvd, Ste. 450
Rockville, MD 20850
301-738-1200
amtda.org

American Mold Builders Association
701 E. Irving Park Rd., Ste. 207
Roselle, IL 60172
630-980-7667
info@amba.org

ASM International (formerly American Society for Materials)
9639 Kinsman Rd.
Materials Park, OH 414073
440-338-5151
asminernational.org

Association for Manufacturing Excellence
3115 N. Wilke Rd., Ste. G
Arlington Heights, IL 60004
224-232-5980
ame.org

Association for Manufacturing Technology
(formerly National Machine Tool Builders' Association)
7901 Westpark Dr.
McLean, VA 22102
703-893-2900
amtonline.org

Consumer Electronics Manufacturing Association
1919 S. Eads St.
Arlington, VA 22202

Appendix B

Jason Oxman, Sr. V.P., Industry Affairs
joxman@ce.org
703-907-7664

Fabricators and Manufacturers Association, International
833 Featherstone Rd.
Rockford, IL 61107
866-394-4363
fmanet.org

International Safety Equipment Association
1901 N. Moore St., Ste. 808
Arlington, VA 22209
David Shipp, Pres.
730-525-1695
safetyequipment.org

Investment Casting Institute
136 Summit Ave.
Montvale, NJ 07645
Michael Perry, Exec. Dir.
201-573-9770
mperry@investmentcasting.org

National Association of Manufacturers
7855 Walker Dr., Ste. 300
Greenbelt, MD 20770
Jay Timmons, Pres.
800-736-6627
nam.org

National Council for Advanced Manufacturing
2025 M St., NW, Ste. 800
Washington, DC 20036
Eric Mittelstadt, CEO
202-367-1178
nacfam.org

National Tooling and Machining Association
9300 Livingston Rd.
6363 Oak Tree Blvd.
Independence, OH 44131
800-248-6862
ntma.org

North American Die Casting Association
241 Holbrook Dr.
Wheeling, IL 60090
847-279-0001
diecasting.org

Photo Chemical Machining Institute
4113 Barberry Dr.
Lafayette Hill, PA 19444
Betty Berndt-Brown, Exec. Dir.
215-825-2506
pcmi.org

Precision Machined Products Association
6700 W. Snowville Rd.
Brecksville, OH 44141
Michael Duffin, Exec. Dir.
440-526-0300
mduffin@pmpa.org

Rubber Manufacturers Association
1400 K St., NW, Ste. 900
Washington, DC 20005
into@rma.org

Sporting Goods Manufacturers Association
1150 17th St., NW
Washington, DC 20036
Tom Cove, Pres.
202-775-1762
sgma.com

TechAmerica
601 Pennsylvania Ave., NW
North Bldg., Ste. 600
Washington, DC 20004
202-682-9110
techamerica.org

Society of the Plastics Industry
1667 K St., NW, Ste. 1000
Washington, DC 20006
202-974-5200
plasticsindustry.org

Tooling, Manufacturing & Technologies Association
28237 Orchard Lake Rd.
Farmington Hills, MI 48333
Robert Dumont, Pres.
800-969-9782
mtaonline.com

Engineering &Technical Societies

American Society of Quality
600 N. Plankinton Ave.
Milwaukee, WI 531023
800-248-1946
asq.org

American Society of Mechanical Engineers
3 Park Ave.
New York, NY 10016
800-843-2763
asme.org

Institute of Electrical and Electronics Engineers
3 Park Ave., 17th Fl.
New York, NY 10016
Jeffrey Raynes, Exec. Dir.

212-419-7900
ieee.org

Institute of Industrial Engineers
3577 Parkway Lane, Ste. 200
Norcross, GA 30092
800-494-0460
iienet2.org

Society of Manufacturing Engineers
One SME Dr.
Dearborn, MI 48121
Mark Tomlinson, Exec. Dir.
800-733-4763
leadership@sme.org

Representatives Organizations

Agricultural & Industrial Manufacturers Representatives Association
7500 Flying Cloud Dr., Ste. 900
Eden Prairie, MN 55344
Jim Manke, Exec. Dir.
952-835-4180
jrmanke@aol.com

AIMRA members sell agricultural, light industrial, environmental, lawn and garden equipment, plus parts and components. Their customers include dealers, agricultural and light industry, and OEM manufacturers.

American Lighting Association
P.O. Box 420288
Dallas, TX 75207
Eric Jacobson, VP of Membership
800-605-4448 or 214-698-9898
ejacobson@americanlightingassoc.com

ALA members sell residential lighting products, crystal chandeliers, light bulbs, lighting components, portable lighting, outdoor lighting, emergency lighting, and commercial lighting.

Association of Independent Manufacturers Representatives
1 Spectrum Pointe, Ste. 150
Lake Forest, CA 92630
Bryan Shirley, Exec. Dir.
866-729-0975 or 949-859-2884
info@aimr.net

AIM/R members sell plumbing, heating, cooling and piping products.

Automotive Aftermarket Industry Association (Manufacturers Rep Division)
7101 Wisconsin Ave., Ste. 1300
Bethesda, MD 20814
Kathleen Schmatz, Pres.
301-654-6664
aaia@aftermarket.org

AAIA members sell vehicle aftermarket products and parts.

BMC - A Foodservice Sales & Marketing Council
P.O. Box 150229
Arlington, TX 76015
Pam Bess, Exec. Dir.
682-518-6008
assnhqtrs@aol.com
bmcsales.com

BMC members are independent multiple-line sales and marketing companies primarily in the institutional foodservice industry. Broker members represent specific markets throughout the United States and Canada.

Communication Marketing Association
P.O. Box 36275
Denver, CO 80236
Mercy Contreras
303-988-3515
mercy@mktgconnection.com
CMA-CMC.org

CMA members sell electronic communication hardware.

Electronics Representatives Association
300 W. Adams St., #617
Chicago, IL 60606
Thomas Shanahan
312-527-3050
info@era.org

ERA members represent manufacturers of a varying spectrum of electronics products. There are eight product-marketing groups within ERA: communications, consumer electronics, components, computers, instrumentation and sensors, materials-assembly-production, RF/microwave, and sound-audio-visual-electronic-security.

The Foodservice Group
630 Village Trace NE
Bldg. 15, Ste. A
Marietta, GA 30067
Kenneth Reynolds, Exec. Dir.
770-989-0049
kreynolds@fsgroup.com

FSG members are independent food service brokers selling to restaurant, deli and food service distributors.

Foodservice Sales & Marketing Association
9192 Red Branch Rd., Ste. 200
Columbia, MD 21045

Rick Abraham, Pres.
410-715-6672
info@fsmaonline.com

The FSMA's self-described mission is to 1) promote sales and marketing agencies as the preferred method for suppliers to come to market, 2) be the national voice of the sales agency community, 3) advocate on behalf of sales agency interests, and 4) enhance relationships among suppliers, agencies, customers and other key stakeholders. Associate memberships for manufacturers and allied memberships for vendors are available.

Gift Home Trade Association
4380 Brockton Drive SE, Suite 1
Grand Rapids, MI 49512
Julie Dix, Pres.
877.600.4872
info@giftandhome.org
giftandhome.org

GHTA members sell a variety of products in the giftware industry. The Association was designed to help vendors, sales agencies, industry affiliates and retailers to work together, making business better by providing members with the opportunity to exchange ideas and network with industry leaders.

Health Industry Representatives Association
7315 E. 5th Ave.
Denver, CO 80230
Karen A. Hone, Exec. Dir.
303-756-8115
healthreps@comcast.net
hira.org

HIRA members sell all healthcare products except pharmaceuticals to these markets: hospitals, nursing homes, physicians/alternate care, home care, labs, x-ray, dental, veterinary, OEM, industrial, capital equipment, purchasing, sub-acute care, and rehab.

Independent Professional Representatives Organization
34157 W. 9 Mile Rd.
Farmington Hills, MI 48335
Raymond W. Wright
800-420-4268
ray@avreps.org

Members represent producers of A/V products which include audio, video, car stereo, lighting, and furniture.

Industrial Supply Association (ISA)
1300 Sumner Ave.
Cleveland, OH 44115
John Buckley, Exec. Dir.
718-423-2113
info@isapartners.org

ISA members sell industrial and construction products such as welding, specialty, and machine tools to industrial distributors, MRO (maintenance, repair, and overhaul) and OEM (original equipment manufacturer) markets.

International Association of Plastics Distribution
4707 College Blvd., Ste. 105
Leawood, KS 66211
Susan Avery
913-345-1005
iapd@iapd.org

IAPD representative members sell raw plastics, engineering materials, and semi-finished stock shapes such as sheet, rod, tube and pipe, valves and fittings. These materials are used in construction, marine, automotive, medical and industrial applications.

International Housewares Representatives Association
175 N. Harbor Dr., Ste. 3807
Chicago, IL 60601
William Weiner, Exec. Dir.
312-240-0774
info@ihra.org

IHRA members represent manufacturers in all product categories of the housewares industry.

International Sanitary Supply Association
7373 N. Lincoln Ave.
Lincolnwood, IL 60712
Anthony Trombetta, Dir. Mktg.
800-225-4772
anthony@issa.com

ISSA members sell all types of products in the cleaning and maintenance industry.

International Union of Commercial Agents and Brokers
General De Lairessestraat
131-135 1075 HJ Amsterdam,
The Netherlands
J.W.B. Baron van Till, Secretary
+31 (0) 20-470 01 77
info@iucab.nl
iucab.org

IUCAB is a consortium of 21 agent associations throughout Europe, North and South America. The members are geographically based; therefore they sell a wide variety of products in many industries.

Manufacturers' Agents Association for the Food Service Industry
2402 Mt. Vernon Rd. #110

Dunwoody, GA 30338
Alison Cody, Exec. Dir.
770-433-9844
acody@mafsi.org

MAFSI members sell food service equipment, supplies and furniture for the hospitality, school food service, military, restaurant, contract feeder, health care, and corrections industries.

Manufacturers Agents National Association
1 Spectrum Pointe, Ste. 150
Lake Forest, CA 92630
Bryan Shirley, Pres. and CEO
877-626-2776 or 949-859-4040
bryan@manaonline.org
manaonline.org

MANA is a horizontal association that has members in all industries and services covering and calling on end users, equipment manufacturers, distributors, governments, and retailers.

Manufacturers Representatives of America
P.O. Box 150229
Arlington, TX 76015
Pam Bess, Exec. Dir.
682-518-6008
assnhqtrs@aol.com
mra-reps.com

MRA members are independent multiple-line sales and marketing companies, primarily in the janitorial, paper, plastics, and packaging industries.

National Electrical Manufacturers Representatives Association
660 White Plains Rd., Ste. 600

Tarrytown, NY 10591
Henry P. Bergson, Pres.
914-524-8650
hank@nemra.org

NEMRA members sell to the electrical industry. This includes products used in commercial, industrial and residential construction, as well as the utility, datacom and lighting markets. They call on electrical distributors, contractors, specifiers, engineers, OEMs, and MROs.

National Kitchen and Bath Association
687 Willow Grove St.
Hackettstown, NJ 07840
Jennifer Fish
908-852-0033
jfish@nkba.org

NKBA members include manufacturers' representatives, manufacturers, designers and dealers in the kitchen and bath industry. Members provide the consumer with a complete range of products and services from design to installation.

Network of Ingredient Marketing Specialists
630 Village Trace NE
Bldg. 15, Ste. A
Marietta, GA 30067
Ken Reynolds, Exec. Dir.
770-989-0049
kreynolds@nimsgroup.com

NIMS members represent food ingredient producers selling all types of bulk foods to food manufacturers.

Business Solutions Association
(Formerly Office Products Representatives Association)
5024 Campbell Blvd., Suite R

Baltimore, MD 21236
Cal Clemons, Exec. VP
410-931-8100
cclemons@businesssolutionsassociation.com
opwa.org

OPWA members sell office products, furniture and supplies, school sup-plies, information processing supplies, creative industries, art/engineering/ drafting supplies, and equipment.

Power-Motion Technology Representatives Association
1 Spectrum Pointe, Ste. 150
Lake Forest, CA 92630
Jay Ownby, Exec. Dir.
888-817-7872
jay@ptra.org

PTRA serves the power transmission and motion control industries. PTRA strives to offer its members opportunities for education, information exchange, networking with other reps and manufacturers, plus an array of quality services designed to improve their career performance and professional stature.

Specialty Equipment Market Association
P.O. Box 4910
Diamond Bar, CA 91765
Jan Desma, Dir. of Council Relations
909-396-0289
jand@sema.org
sema.org/mrc

SEMA members are producers and marketers of specialty equipment pro-ducts and services for the automotive aftermarket. MRC members represent manufacturers and warehouse distributors in the automotive spec-ialty equipment market.

Specialty Tools and Fasteners Distributors Association
PO Box 44
Elm Grove, WI 53122
Georgia Foley, Exec. Dir.
800-352-2981
info@stafda.org

STAFDA consists of distributors, manufacturers, and representative agents serving the light construction and industrial markets, components, moldings, machining, meters, gauges, and more. The primary market is industrial products and services.

INDEX

About the Author

Michele Nash-Hoff has been in and out of San Diego's high-tech manufacturing industry since starting as an engineering secretary at age 18. Her career includes being part of the founding team of an electronic component manufacturer and working in the Marketing Department of Cubic Corporation's Military Systems Division. She took a hiatus from the high-tech industry to attend college and graduated from San Diego State University with a bachelor's degree in French and Spanish.

After returning to the manufacturing industry, she became Vice President of a sales agency covering 11 of the western states. After three years, Michele left the company to form her own sales agency, ElectroFab Sales, to work with companies to help them select the right manufacturing processes for their new and existing products.

In 1998, she also served as manager of the San Diego Enterprise Center, a new business incubator for start-up companies, while continuing to run ElectroFab. The National Business Incubation Association published Michele's first book, For Profit Business Incubators, that same year.

Michele has been president of the San Diego Electronics Network, the San Diego Chapter of the Electronics Representatives Association, and The High Technology Foundation, as well as several professional and non-profit organizations. She is an active member of the Soroptimist International of San Diego club. Michele is currently a director on the national board of the American Jobs Alliance and Chair of the California chapter of the Coalition for a Prosperous America.

She has a certificate in Total Quality Management and is a 1994 graduate of San Diego's leadership program (LEAD San Diego.) She has also taken classes in lean manufacturing and Six Sigma.

Michele is married to Michael Hoff and has raised two sons and two daughters. She enjoys spending time with her two grandsons and eight granddaughters. Her favorite leisure activities are hiking in the mountains, swimming, running, gardening, reading, and taking tap dance lessons.

Michele is available for speaking engagements. Please contact Michele through her website — www.savingusmanufacturing.com — to schedule speaking engagements and subscribe to her blog articles.

The Coalition for a Prosperous America is a nation-wide non-profit research and lobbying organization representing the interests of 2.7 million households through our agricultural, manufacturing and labor members.

Visit us at prosperousamerica.org and our blog at tradereform.org.

Also from CPA: *Free Trade Doesn't Work: What Should Replace it and Why*, by Ian Fletcher. Available from Amazon.com.

Made in the USA
Charleston, SC
13 April 2014